Exam Ref AZ-204
Developing Solutions for
Microsoft Azure

Santiago Fernández Muñoz

Exam Ref AZ-204 Developing Solutions for Microsoft Azure

Published with the authorization of Microsoft Corporation by:
Pearson Education, Inc.

ISBN-13: 978-0-13-679833-0
ISBN-10: 0-13-679833-0

Library of Congress Control Number: 2020942404

4 2023

TRADEMARKS

WARNING AND DISCLAIMER

SPECIAL SALES

For information about buying this title in bulk quantities, or for special sales opportunities (which may include electronic versions; custom cover designs; and content particular to your business, training goals, marketing focus, or branding interests), please contact our corporate sales department at corpsales@pearsoned.com or (800) 382-3419.

For government sales inquiries, please contact governmentsales@pearsoned.com.

For questions about sales outside the U.S., please contact intlcs@pearson.com.

CREDITS

EDITOR-IN-CHIEF
Brett Bartow

EXECUTIVE EDITOR
Loretta Yates

ASSOCIATE EDITOR
Charvi Arora

DEVELOPMENT EDITORS
Songlin Qiu, Charvi Arora

MANAGING EDITOR
Sandra Schroeder

SENIOR PROJECT EDITOR
Tracey Croom

COPY EDITOR
Charlotte Kughen

INDEXER
Cheryl Ann Lenser

PROOFREADER
Abigail Manheim

TECHNICAL EDITOR
Dave McCollough

EDITORIAL ASSISTANT
Cindy Teeters

COVER DESIGNER
Twist Creative, Seattle

COMPOSITOR
codeMantra

Contents at a glance

Contents

Acknowledgments

I want to say thank you to the people who gave me the opportunity to write this book and who also helped me during the entire process. Without their support, this book would not be a reality.

I also want to say thank you to my friend Rafa Hueso for his support and guidance during the last years of my professional career.

About the author

I started my career as a Linux and Windows instructor. At the same time, I also started to learn scripting programming languages such as bash and VBS that were useful for my work. During that period of my career, I realized scripting languages were helpful, but they were not enough to meet all my needs, so I started learning other languages like Java, PHP, and finally C#.

I've been working as a Microsoft technologies consultant for the last 14 years, and over the last 6 years, I've consulted on Azure-related technologies. I've participated in different types of projects, serving in a variety of capacities from .NET developer to solution architect. Now I'm focused on developing custom industrial IoT solutions for my company and clients.

Introduction

Most books take a very low-level approach, teaching you how to use individual classes and accomplish fine-grained tasks. Through this book, we review the main technologies that Microsoft offers for deploying different kinds of solutions into Azure. From the most classical and conservative approaches using Azure virtual machines to the latest technologies, implementing event-based or message-based patterns with Azure Event Grid or Azure Service Bus, this book reviews the basics for developing most types of solutions using Azure services. The book also provides code examples for illustrating how to implement most of the concepts covered through the different sections.

This book is intended for those professionals who are planning to pass the exam AZ-204. This book covers every major topic area found on the exam, but it does not cover every exam question. Only the Microsoft exam team has access to the exam questions, and Microsoft regularly adds new questions to the exam, making it impossible to cover specific questions. You should consider this book a supplement to your relevant real-world experience and other study materials. If you encounter a topic in this book that you do not feel completely comfortable with, use the "Need more review?" links in the text to find more information and take the time to research and study the topic. Great information is available on MSDN and TechNet and in blogs and forums.

Organization of this book

This book is organized by the "Skills measured" list published for the exam. The "Skills measured" list is available for each exam on the Microsoft Learn website: *http://aka.ms/examlist*. Each chapter in this book corresponds to a major topic area in the list, and the technical tasks in each topic area determine a chapter's organization. If an exam covers six major topic areas, for example, the book contains six chapters.

Microsoft certifications

Microsoft certifications distinguish you by proving your command of a broad set of skills and experience with current Microsoft products and technologies. The exams and corresponding certifications are developed to validate your mastery of critical competencies as you design and develop, or implement and support, solutions with Microsoft products and technologies both on premises and in the cloud. Certification brings a variety of benefits to the individual and to employers and organizations.

Check back often to see what is new!

Errata, updates, and book support

We've made every effort to ensure the accuracy of this book and its companion content. You can access updates to this book—in the form of a list of submitted errata and their related corrections—at

MicrosoftPressStore.com/ExamRefAZ204/errata.

If you discover an error that is not already listed, please submit it to us at the same page.

For additional book support and information, please visit

http://www.MicrosoftPressStore.com/Support.

Please note that product support for Microsoft software and hardware is not offered through the previous addresses. For help with Microsoft software or hardware, go to *http://support.microsoft.com*.

Stay in touch

Let's keep the conversation going! We're on Twitter:

http://twitter.com/MicrosoftPress

Important: How to use this book to study for the exam

Certification exams validate your on-the-job experience and product knowledge. To gauge your readiness to take an exam, use this Exam Ref to help you check your understanding of the skills tested by the exam. Determine the topics you know well and the areas in which you need more experience. To help you refresh your skills in specific areas, we have also provided "Need more review?" pointers, which direct you to more in-depth information outside the book.

The Exam Ref is not a substitute for hands-on experience. This book is *not* designed to teach you new skills.

We recommend that you round out your exam preparation by using a combination of available study materials and courses. Learn more about available classroom training and find free online courses and live events at *http://microsoft.com/learn*. Microsoft Official Practice Tests are available for many exams at *http://aka.ms/practicetests*.

This book is organized by the "Skills measured" list published for the exam. The "Skills measured" list for each exam is available on the Microsoft Learn website: *http://aka.ms/examlist.*

Note that this Exam Ref is based on this publicly available information and the author's experience. To safeguard the integrity of the exam, authors do not have access to the exam questions.

## CHAPTER 1

Develop Azure Infrastructure as a service compute solution

Today, cloud computing is a consolidated reality that any company or professional should consider when developing or maintaining new or existing products. When you are planning for developing or deploying an application, you can choose between two main models of cloud services, Infrastructure as a Service (IaaS) or Platform as a Service (PaaS), and each model has its pros and cons. If you decide to use the IaaS model, you have more granular control over the infrastructure that will support your application.

However, once the deployment in the production environment has finished, you need to maintain it. This maintenance means that you also need to allocate the budget for the support of the infrastructure, and you must have trained staff for conducting this maintenance.

Thanks to cloud technologies, you can drastically reduce these infrastructure planning and deployment requirements by deploying your software on a managed service known as Platform as a Service (PaaS). Doing so means you only need to worry about your code and how it interacts with other services in Azure. PaaS products such as Azure App Service or Azure Functions releases you from worrying about highly available or fault-tolerant configurations because the service provided by Azure already manages these things.

This chapter reviews how to work with the options that Azure makes available to you for developing your solutions based on the IaaS model. The chapter also covers the PaaS solutions that Azure provides, which allow you to focus on your code and forget about the underlying infrastructure.

> **IMPORTANT**
> **Have you read page xvii?**
> It contains valuable information regarding the skills you need to pass the exam.

Skills covered in this chapter:

- Skill 1.1: Implement solutions that use virtual machines (VM)
- Skill 1.2: Create Azure App Service web apps
- Skill 1.3: Implement Azure Functions

Skill 1.1: Implement solutions that use virtual machines (VM)

One of the main characteristics of the IaaS model is the higher level of control that it offers when deploying the infrastructure needed for your application. Typically, you need to work with this model because you need more control over the different elements of your application. Using IaaS, you deploy your virtual machines, where you will implement all the components required for your solution.

Azure provides you with all the underlying hardware and configuration needed for your virtual machine (VM) to run correctly. However, you still need to manage all administrative tasks related to the VM's operating system, such as installing operating system upgrades or security patches. Microsoft manages the configuration required for providing the fault tolerance for the physical hardware that supports your VM. But if you need your application or software solution to be highly available, you have to manage the configuration of the VMs that host your application.

This skill covers how to

- Provision VMs
- Configure VMs for remote access
- Create ARM templates
- Create container images for solutions by using Docker
- Publish an image to the Azure Container Registry
- Run containers by using Azure Container Instance

Provision VMs

Deploying a VM in Azure is a straightforward process, but you still need to think about some key points if you want to achieve the best balance between the costs and your requirements. Perhaps the most obvious decision is which operating system you should use. The good news is that Azure fully supports Windows, Windows Server, and the principal distributions of Linux.

> **NOTE SUPPORTED OPERATING SYSTEMS**
>
> You can review the full list of supported operating systems to be used in Azure VMs at the following URLs:
>
> - Windows: *https://support.microsoft.com/en-us/help/2721672/microsoft-server-software-support-for-microsoft-azure-virtual-machines*
>
> - Linux: *https://docs.microsoft.com/en-us/azure/virtual-machines/linux/endorsed-distros*

All these Windows and Linux OSes are preinstalled and available to you in the Azure Marketplace as VM Images. Apart from these default VM images, you will also find other images in the marketplace from other vendors containing preconfigured solutions that may better match your needs.

Once you have chosen your operating system, you need to decide other essential aspects of the VM:

- **Name** Enter the name of the VM. Names may be up to 15 characters long.
- **Location** Select the geographical region where you deploy your VM. Azure has several data centers distributed across the globe that are grouped in geographical regions. Choosing the wrong region or location may have adverse effects.
- **Size** Designate the number of resources that you will assign to your virtual machines. These resources include the amount of memory, processing power, number of virtual network interface cards (NICs) that you can attach to your VM, and total storage capacity that will be available for your VM.
- **Limits** Every subscription has default quota limits. These limits can affect you when deploying new virtual machines. By default, each subscription has a limit of 20 VMs per region. However, you can increase this limit by contacting Azure's support service.
- **Extensions** Extensions enable you to automate some tasks or configuration once the deployment of your VM completes successfully. Some of the most common extensions are
  - Run custom scripts
  - Deploy and manage configurations
  - Collect diagnostic data
- **Related resources** When you deploy a virtual machine, you need to think about the amount and type of storage, such as whether this VM will be connected to the internet and need a public IP or which kind of traffic is allowed to go to or from the VM. Some of these related resources, described in the following list, are mandatory for deploying a VM.
  - **Resource group** Every virtual machine needs to be contained in a resource group. You can create a new resource group or reuse an existing one.
  - **Storage account** The virtual disks needed by the VM are .vhd files stored as page blobs in a storage account. Depending on the performance requirements of your VM, you can use standard or premium Storage accounts. If you configure managed disks when deploying a VM, Azure handles the Storage account automatically and it won't appear in the VM configuration.
  - **Virtual network** To be able to communicate with the rest of the world, your new VM needs to be connected to a virtual network.
  - **Network interface** As in the physical world, your VM needs a network interface to connect to the virtual network for sending and receiving information.

Once you have gathered all the information that you need to deploy your VM, you are ready for deployment. You have several ways of doing this task:

- Using the Azure portal
- Using PowerShell
- Using Azure CLI
- Programmatically using REST API or C#

In general, when you want to deploy a new VM, you need to follow these steps:

1. Create a resource group for the VM. You can also use an existing resource group for this VM.

2. Create a virtual network. If you are using the Azure portal, you can do this while you are creating the VM. For PowerShell and Azure CLI, you need to specify the virtual network. However, if a virtual network doesn't already exist, one is created automatically.

3. Create a virtual NIC. If you are using Azure portal, PowerShell, or Azure CLI, you don't need to do this because the deployment process automatically creates the NIC for you.

4. Create the virtual machine.

The following example shows how to create a simple .NET Core console application for creating a VM:

1. Open Visual Studio Code. You need to have installed the Omnishare extension.

2. Create a folder for your project.

3. In the terminal window, change the working directory to the folder that you created in the previous step and type the following command.

   ```
   dotnet new console
   ```

4. Install the nuget package Microsoft.Azure.Management.Fluent.

   ```
   dotnet add package Microsoft.Azure.Management.Fluent
   ```

5. Create an empty file called **azureauth.properties**. Add the content shown in Listing 1-1 to the file. Replace the variables with the values from your Azure subscription.

6. Replace the content of Program.cs file with the content in Listing 1-2. Listing 1-2 shows how to create a virtual machine with managed disks in your Azure subscription.

LISTING 1-1   azureauth.properties

```
subscription=<subscription-id>
client=<client-id>
key=<client-secret>
tenant=<tenant-id>
managementURI=https://management.core.windows.net/
baseURL=https://management.azure.com/
authURL=https://login.windows.net/
graphURL=https://graph.windows.net/
```

LISTING 1-2 Program.cs

```
//dotnet core 2.2
using System;
using Microsoft.Azure.Management.Compute.Fluent;
using Microsoft.Azure.Management.Compute.Fluent.Models;
using Microsoft.Azure.Management.Fluent;
using Microsoft.Azure.Management.ResourceManager.Fluent;
using Microsoft.Azure.Management.ResourceManager.Fluent.Core;

namespace ch1_1_1
{
    class Program
    {
        static void Main(string[] args)
        {
            //Create the management client. This will be used for all the operations
            //that we will perform in Azure.
            var credentials = SdkContext.AzureCredentialsFactory
                                    .FromFile("./azureauth.properties");

            var azure = Azure.Configure()
                .WithLogLevel(HttpLoggingDelegatingHandler.Level.Basic)
                .Authenticate(credentials)
                .WithDefaultSubscription();

            //First of all, we need to create a resource group where we will add all
            //the resources
            // needed for the virtual machine
            var groupName = "az204-ResourceGroup";
            var vmName = "az204VMTesting";
            var location = Region.USWest2;
            var vNetName = "az204VNET";
            var vNetAddress = "172.16.0.0/16";
            var subnetName = "az204Subnet";
            var subnetAddress = "172.16.0.0/24";
            var nicName = "az204NIC";
            var adminUser = "azureadminuser";
            var adminPassword = "Pa$$w0rd!2019";

            Console.WriteLine($"Creating resource group {groupName} ...");
            var resourceGroup = azure.ResourceGroups.Define(groupName)
                .WithRegion(location)
                .Create();

            //Every virtual machine needs to be connected to a virtual network.
            Console.WriteLine($"Creating virtual network {vNetName} ...");
```

```csharp
var network = azure.Networks.Define(vNetName)
    .WithRegion(location)
    .WithExistingResourceGroup(groupName)
    .WithAddressSpace(vNetAddress)
    .WithSubnet(subnetName, subnetAddress)
    .Create();

//Any virtual machine need a network interface for connecting to the
//virtual network
Console.WriteLine($"Creating network interface {nicName} ...");
var nic = azure.NetworkInterfaces.Define(nicName)
    .WithRegion(location)
    .WithExistingResourceGroup(groupName)
    .WithExistingPrimaryNetwork(network)
    .WithSubnet(subnetName)
    .WithPrimaryPrivateIPAddressDynamic()
    .Create();

//Create the virtual machine
Console.WriteLine($"Creating virtual machine {vmName} ...");
azure.VirtualMachines.Define(vmName)
    .WithRegion(location)
    .WithExistingResourceGroup(groupName)
    .WithExistingPrimaryNetworkInterface(nic)
    .WithLatestWindowsImage("MicrosoftWindowsServer", "WindowsServer",
"2012-R2-Datacenter")
    .WithAdminUsername(adminUser)
    .WithAdminPassword(adminPassword)
    .WithComputerName(vmName)
    .WithSize(VirtualMachineSizeTypes.StandardDS2V2)
    .Create();
        {

        }
    }
  }
}
```

NOTE **APPLICATION REQUIREMENTS**

To run all the examples through this book, you need to have an Azure subscription. If you don't have an Azure subscription, you can create a free subscription for testing the code in this book.

As you can see in Listing 1-2, you need to create each of the related and required resources separately and then provide all the required dependencies to the Azure management client that creates the VM.

Before you proceed to deploy a new VM, you also need to take into account other considerations that would affect the deployment. For example, if your application or software solution must be highly available, you would typically use a load balancer. If your virtual machines use a load balancer, you need to put your VMs that host the application into an availability set. Using an availability set ensures that any virtual machine in the same availability set is not placed on the same hardware. Placing the virtual machines in different equipment ensures that the VMs are not restarted at the same time because of software upgrades on the servers running the VM. A virtual machine may only be added to an availability set during the creation of the VM. If you forget to add the VM to an availability set, you need to delete the VM and start from the beginning.

EXAM TIP

Creating a VM is a straightforward process, but you still need to plan the deployment. You need to consider whether you need to make the application highly available hosted in the virtual machine, or if you need to scale-up and down the number of VMs associated to a load balancer. In such cases, you need to remember to create the availability set before you create the VMs.

Configure VMs for remote access

The preceding section reviewed how to create a new VM programmatically. When you created the VM from the previous example, you were not able to access your new VM. The reason for this is that you didn't configure a public IP address that you can use for remotely accessing the VM.

As you can imagine, just adding a public IP to your VM may lead to excessive exposure to the internet. You could control that exposure by using the firewalls provided by the operating system. But maintaining all firewalls for a number VMs can be a time-consuming task. Azure provides you with Network Security Groups as a mechanism for filtering the traffic between your Azure resources and different networks, including the internet. If you need to configure the remote access for your VM, you need to add a security rule to a network security group associated with your VM.

By default, any VM that you deploy using an Azure virtual machine image has the corresponding remote access protocol enabled—that is, Remote Desktop Protocol or RDP for Windows VMs and Secure Shell or SSH for Linux VMs.

Following from the example in Listing 1-2, you need to add three additional items to the code to have remote access to your VM:

- **A public IP**   You can configure a static or dynamic IP. Static IP has costs associated, so this example uses a dynamic IP.

- **A network security group**   You need this for managing the security rules that allow or deny access to the VM.

- **A security rule**   You need to create a security rule for allowing access to the VM using the appropriate remote protocol. For this example, you need to allow the traffic to TCP/3389 port. This is the port for the Remote Desktop Protocol.

Listing 1-3 shows the modifications in bold that you need to make in your code for configuring the remote access to your VM during the deployment.

LISTING 1-3   Modified Program.cs

```
//dotnet core 2.2
using System;
using Microsoft.Azure.Management.Compute.Fluent;
using Microsoft.Azure.Management.Compute.Fluent.Models;
using Microsoft.Azure.Management.Network.Fluent;
using Microsoft.Azure.Management.Fluent;
using Microsoft.Azure.Management.ResourceManager.Fluent;
using Microsoft.Azure.Management.ResourceManager.Fluent.Core;
using Microsoft.Azure.Management.Network.Fluent.Models;

namespace ch1_1_2
{
    class Program
    {
        static void Main(string[] args)
        {
            //Create the management client. This will be used for all the operations
            //that we will perform in Azure.
            var credentials = SdkContext.AzureCredentialsFactory
                                    .FromFile("./azureauth.properties");
```

```
var azure = Azure.Configure()
    .WithLogLevel(HttpLoggingDelegatingHandler.Level.Basic)
    .Authenticate(credentials)
    .WithDefaultSubscription();

//First of all, we need to create a resource group where we will add all
//the resources
// needed for the virtual machine
var groupName = "az204-ResourceGroup";
var vmName = "az204VMTesting";
var location = Region.USWest2;
var vNetName = "az204VNET";
var vNetAddress = "172.16.0.0/16";
var subnetName = "az204Subnet";
var subnetAddress = "172.16.0.0/24";
var nicName = "az204NIC";
var adminUser = "azureadminuser";
var adminPassword = "Pa$$w0rd!2019";
var publicIPName = "az204publicIP";
var nsgName = "az204VNET-NSG";

Console.WriteLine($"Creating resource group {groupName} ...");
var resourceGroup = azure.ResourceGroups.Define(groupName)
    .WithRegion(location)
    .Create();

//Every virtual machine needs to be connected to a virtual network.
Console.WriteLine($"Creating virtual network {vNetName} ...");
var network = azure.Networks.Define(vNetName)
    .WithRegion(location)
    .WithExistingResourceGroup(groupName)
    .WithAddressSpace(vNetAddress)
    .WithSubnet(subnetName, subnetAddress)
    .Create();

//You need a public IP to be able to connect to the VM from the Internet
Console.WriteLine($"Creating public IP {publicIPName} ...");
var publicIP = azure.PublicIPAddresses.Define(publicIPName)
    .WithRegion(location)
    .WithExistingResourceGroup(groupName)
    .Create();

//You need a network security group for controlling the access to the VM
Console.WriteLine($"Creating Network Security Group {nsgName} ...");
var nsg = azure.NetworkSecurityGroups.Define(nsgName)
```

```
            .WithRegion(location)
            .WithExistingResourceGroup(groupName)
            .Create();

        //You need a security rule for allowing the access to the VM from the
        //Internet
        Console.WriteLine($"Creating a Security Rule for allowing the remote
access");
        nsg.Update()
            .DefineRule("Allow-RDP")
                .AllowInbound()
                .FromAnyAddress()
                .FromAnyPort()
                .ToAnyAddress()
                .ToPort(3389)
                .WithProtocol(SecurityRuleProtocol.Tcp)
                .WithPriority(100)
                .WithDescription("Allow-RDP")
                .Attach()
            .Apply();

        //Any virtual machine needs a network interface for connecting to the
        //virtual network
        Console.WriteLine($"Creating network interface {nicName} ...");
        var nic = azure.NetworkInterfaces.Define(nicName)
            .WithRegion(location)
            .WithExistingResourceGroup(groupName)
            .WithExistingPrimaryNetwork(network)
            .WithSubnet(subnetName)
            .WithPrimaryPrivateIPAddressDynamic()
            .WithExistingPrimaryPublicIPAddress(publicIP)
            .WithExistingNetworkSecurityGroup(nsg)
            .Create();

        //Create the virtual machine
        Console.WriteLine($"Creating virtual machine {vmName} ...");
        azure.VirtualMachines.Define(vmName)
            .WithRegion(location)
            .WithExistingResourceGroup(groupName)
            .WithExistingPrimaryNetworkInterface(nic)
            .WithLatestWindowsImage("MicrosoftWindowsServer", "WindowsServer",
"2012-R2-Datacenter")
            .WithAdminUsername(adminUser)
            .WithAdminPassword(adminPassword)
```

```
        .WithComputerName(vmName)
        .WithSize(VirtualMachineSizeTypes.StandardDS2V2)
        .Create();

    }
  }
}
```

The code that you used for creating and enabling the remote access to the VM is a good way to understand the relationship between the different components needed for deploying a VM. You need to understand these relationships if you need to deploy or reconfigure a VM using PowerShell or Azure CLI. After you have created the VM using the modified code in Listing 1-3, use the following procedure for verifying that everything is working correctly:

1. Open the Azure portal (*https://portal.azure.com*).

2. In the Search Resources text box on the middle-top side of the portal, type **az204VMTesting**.

3. In the result list, click the name of the virtual machine.

4. On the az204VMTesting virtual machine page, click Networking in the Settings section.

5. In the Network Security Group list of security rules, shown in Figure 1-1, ensure that there is a rule named Allow-RDP.

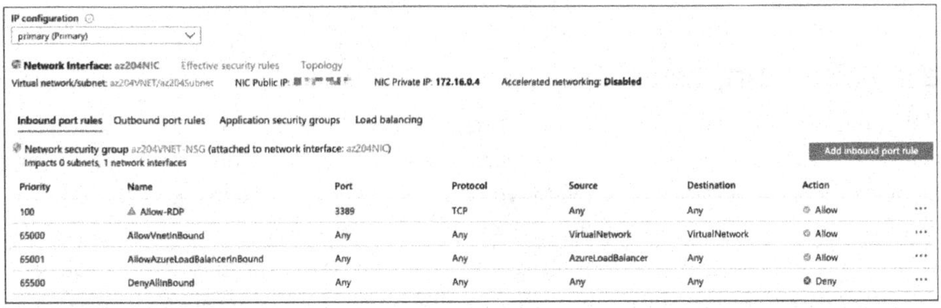

IP configuration ⓘ
primary (Primary) ▼

⬡ **Network Interface:** az204NIC   Effective security rules   Topology
Virtual network/subnet: az204VNET/az204Subnet   NIC Public IP: ▪ ▪ ▪ ▪ ▪   NIC Private IP: **172.16.0.4**   Accelerated networking: **Disabled**

Inbound port rules   Outbound port rules   Application security groups   Load balancing

⬡ Network security group az204VNET-NSG (attached to network interface: az204NIC)   **Add inbound port rule**
Impacts 0 subnets, 1 network interfaces

Priority	Name	Port	Protocol	Source	Destination	Action	
100	⚠ Allow-RDP	3389	TCP	Any	Any	⊘ Allow	···
65000	AllowVnetInBound	Any	Any	VirtualNetwork	VirtualNetwork	⊘ Allow	···
65001	AllowAzureLoadBalancerInBound	Any	Any	AzureLoadBalancer	Any	⊘ Allow	···
65500	DenyAllInBound	Any	Any	Any	Any	⊘ Deny	···

FIGURE 1-1 Virtual machine network security group

1. On the az204VMTesting page, click Connect in the Settings section in the navigation list on the left side of the page.

2. On the Connect page, ensure that the RDP tab is selected.

3. Ensure that the Public IP address option is selected in the IP Address drop-down menu.

4. Click the Download RDP File button.

5. Once the RDP file has been downloaded, double-click the RDP file for opening the remote session with your VM. You need to provide the password configured in the code in Listing 1-3.

When configuring remote access in a VM, you need to consider whether that VM needs to be accessible from the internet or if you can restrict the access. As a general rule of thumb, you should avoid configuring remote access from the internet for production VMs. For these VMs, you should consider deploying a virtual private network and remote access the VM using the private IP instead of a public IP. This way, you can use the public IP to publish only the service hosted in the VM , like an IIS service, while getting remote access to the VM using the private IP.

> **NEED MORE REVIEW?** **NETWORK SECURITY GROUPS**
>
> You can find more information about how to manage network security groups using the Azure portal, Azure PowerShell, or Azure CLI by reviewing the following articles:
>
> - *https://docs.microsoft.com/en-us/azure/virtual-network/security-overview*
>
> - *https://docs.microsoft.com/en-us/azure/virtual-network/tutorial-restrict-network-access-to-resources*

EXAM TIP

You need to carefully consider when to configure a VM for remote access from the internet. In general, you should not configure remote access over public IPs on production VMs. For those cases, you should deploy a virtual private network and connect to your VM using its private IP.

Create ARM templates

One of the most significant advantages of using Azure IaaS is the level of automation that you can achieve when deploying new services, resources, or infrastructure. One of the main reasons you can do this is because Microsoft provides you the Azure Resource Manager (ARM), which is the deployment and management service in Azure. The ARM service is in charge of creating, updating, and deleting the different services you can deploy in your subscription. You can interact with all actions offered by the ARM service using the same API. Because of this same API, no matter which mechanism you use—portal, PowerShell, Azure CLI, Rest API, or client SDKs— you get a consistent behavior and result when interacting with ARM.

When you work with the Azure Resource Manager, there are some concepts and terms that you need to understand clearly:

- **Resource**   These are the items you can manage in Azure.
- **Resource group**   This is a container that you use for holding resources. You can use any grouping criteria for your resources, but you need to remember that any single resource needs to be contained in a resource group. You can also use resource groups for managing different levels of management access to different groups of users.
- **Resource provider**   A resource provider is a service that offers different kinds of Azure resources, and they manage the resource's lifecycle. For example, the service in charge

of providing virtual machine resources is Microsoft.Compute provider. You can also use Microsoft.Storage provider for storage accounts or Microsoft.Network for all networking resources.

- **Resource Manager template** This is the file that you need to provide to the ARM API when you want to deploy one or more resources to a resource group or subscription. This file is written in JavaScript Object Notation (JSON).

The main advantage of using ARM templates is that you have the definition of all the resources that you want to deploy in a consistent structure. This allows you to reuse the same template for deploying the same group of resources in different subscriptions, resource groups, or regions. Some common scenarios in which you can take advantage of the ARM templates are disaster recovery plan implementations, high-availability configurations, or automatic provisioning scenarios (such as continuous deployment scenarios). In the following code snippet, you can see the most basic structure for an ARM template.

```
{

"$schema": "https://schema.management.azure.com/schemas/2015-01-01/deploymentTemplate.
json#",
    "contentVersion": "",
    "parameters": {  },
    "variables": {  },
    "functions": [  ],
    "resources": [  ],
    "outputs": {  }
}
```

Insofar as the ARM template structure is concerned, only the $schema, contentVersion, and resources sections are required to be present in a valid template. Following is a brief description of each section in a template:

- **$schema** This required section sets the JSON schema that describes the version of the template you will use in the file. You can choose between two different schemas depending on the deployment type:

  - **Resource group deployments** You should use *https://schema.management.azure. com/schemas/2015-01-01/deploymentTemplate.json#*.

  - **Subscription deployments** You should use *https://schema.management.azure. com/schemas/2018-05-01/subscriptionDeploymentTemplate.json#*.

- **contentVersion** In this required section, you set a value you can use for providing your internal version number to the template, such as 1.0.0. This version number is only meaningful for you; Azure does not use it. Typically, you change the version number when you make significant changes to the template.

- **parameters** This is an optional section that you can use to set the values provided to the Resource Manager when you perform a deployment. You can use customizable template parameters for different deployments without changing the content of the template.

- **variables** This optional section contains the values that you will reuse across the entire template. You use variables for improving the usability and readability of the template.

- **functions** You can use this optional section for defining your functions to be used in the template.

- **resources** This is a required section that contains all the resources that will be deployed or updated by the template.

- **outputs** This optional section defines the values that the Resource Manager should return once the deployment has finished.

Listing 1-4 shows the ARM template that you need to use for deploying new VMs with the same configuration. You may modify the values of the parameters according to your needs.

LISTING 1-4 ARM template for deploying a VM

```
{

"$schema": "https://schema.management.azure.com/schemas/2015-01-01/deploymentTemplate.
json#",
    "contentVersion": "1.0.0.0",
    "parameters": {
        "virtualNetworks_az204VNET_name": {
            "defaultValue": "az204demoVNET",
            "type": "string"
        },
        "networkInterfaces_az204NIC_name": {
            "defaultValue": "az204demoNIC",
            "type": "string"
        },
        "virtualMachines_az204VMTesting_name": {
            "defaultValue": "az204demoVM",
            "type": "string"
        },
        "subnets_az204Subnet_name": {
            "defaultValue": "az204demoSubnet",
            "type": "string"
        },
        "virtualMachines_az204VMTesting_id": {
            "defaultValue": "[concat(parameters('virtualMachines_az204VMTesting_name'),
                            '_OSDisk1_1')]",
            "type": "string"
        },
        "virtualMachines_adminUser": {
            "defaultValue": "azureadminuser",
            "type": "string"
        },
```

```json
        "virtualMachines_adminpassword": {
            "defaultValue": "Pa$$w0rd",
            "type": "securestring"
        }
    },
    "variables": {
        "osDiskName": "_OSDisk1_1_39c654d89d88405e968db84b722002d1"
    },
    "resources": [
        {
            "type": "Microsoft.Compute/virtualMachines",
            "name": "[parameters('virtualMachines_az204VMTesting_name')]",
            "apiVersion": "2018-06-01",
            "location": "westus2",
            "tags": {},
            "scale": null,
            "properties": {
                "hardwareProfile": {
                    "vmSize": "Standard_DS2_v2"
                },
                "storageProfile": {
                    "imageReference": {
                        "publisher": "MicrosoftWindowsServer",
                        "offer": "WindowsServer",
                        "sku": "2012-R2-Datacenter",
                        "version": "latest"
                    },
                    "osDisk": {
                        "osType": "Windows",
                        "name": "[concat(parameters('virtualMachines_az204VMTesting_
                                    name'), variables('osDiskName'))]",
                        "createOption": "FromImage",
                        "caching": "ReadWrite"
                    },
                    "dataDisks": []
                },
                "osProfile": {
                    "computerName": "[parameters(
                                        'virtualMachines_az204VMTesting_name')]",
                    "adminUsername": "azureadminuser",
                    "adminPassword": "Pa$$w0rd",
                    "windowsConfiguration": {
                        "provisionVMAgent": true,
                        "enableAutomaticUpdates": true
                    },
```

```
                    "secrets": [],
                    "allowExtensionOperations": true
                },
                "networkProfile": {
                    "networkInterfaces": [
                        {

"id": "[resourceId('Microsoft.Network/networkInterfaces', parameters
        ('networkInterfaces_az204NIC_name'))]",
                            "properties": {
                                "primary": true
                            }
                        }
                    ]
                }
            },
            "dependsOn": [

"[resourceId('Microsoft.Network/networkInterfaces', parameters(
  'networkInterfaces_az204NIC_name'))]"
            ]
        },
        {
            "type": "Microsoft.Network/networkInterfaces",
            "name": "[parameters('networkInterfaces_az204NIC_name')]",
            "apiVersion": "2018-10-01",
            "location": "westus2",
            "tags": {},
            "scale": null,
            "properties": {
                "ipConfigurations": [
                    {
                        "name": "primary",
                        "properties": {
                            "privateIPAllocationMethod": "Dynamic",
                            "subnet": {

"id": "[resourceId('Microsoft.Network/virtualNetworks/subnets',
        parameters('virtualNetworks_az204VNET_name'),
        parameters('subnets_az204Subnet_name'))]"
                            },
                            "primary": true,
                            "privateIPAddressVersion": "IPv4"
                        }
                    }
                ],
```

```
                    "dnsSettings": {
                        "dnsServers": [],
                        "appliedDnsServers": []
                    },
                    "enableAcceleratedNetworking": false,
                    "enableIPForwarding": false,
                    "primary": true,
                    "tapConfigurations": []
                },
                "dependsOn": [

"[resourceId('Microsoft.Network/virtualNetworks/subnets', parameters('virtualNetworks_
az204VNET_name'), parameters('subnets_az204Subnet_name'))]"
                ]
            },
            {
                "type": "Microsoft.Network/virtualNetworks",
                "name": "[parameters('virtualNetworks_az204VNET_name')]",
                "apiVersion": "2018-10-01",
                "location": "westus2",
                "tags": {},
                "scale": null,
                "properties": {
                    "resourceGuid": "145e7bfc-8b00-48cf-8fa1-082448a30bae",
                    "addressSpace": {
                        "addressPrefixes": [
                            "172.16.0.0/16"
                        ]
                    },
                    "dhcpOptions": {
                        "dnsServers": []
                    },
                    "subnets": [
                        {
                            "name": "[parameters('subnets_az204Subnet_name')]",
                            "properties": {
                                "addressPrefix": "172.16.0.0/24"
                            }
                        }
                    ],
                    "virtualNetworkPeerings": [],
                    "enableDdosProtection": false,
                    "enableVmProtection": false
                },
                "dependsOn": []
            },
```

```
        {
            "type": "Microsoft.Network/virtualNetworks/subnets",

"name": "[concat(parameters('virtualNetworks_az204VNET_name'), '/',
parameters('subnets_az204Subnet_name'))]",
            "apiVersion": "2018-10-01",
            "scale": null,
            "properties": {
                "addressPrefix": "172.16.0.0/24"
            },
            "dependsOn": [

"[resourceId('Microsoft.Network/virtualNetworks',
parameters('virtualNetworks_az204VNET_name'))]"
            ]
        }
    ]
}
```

This example has some interesting features. You have defined the parameters and variables that you will use throughout the template. If you look at any parameter definition, you can see that it has three elements—paramenterName, defaultValue, and type. The type element is almost self-explanatory; it sets the kind of value that this parameter will contain. The allowed types are string, securestring, int, bool, object, secureObject, and array. The parameterName is also quite straightforward and is any valid JavaScript identifier that represents the name of the parameter. However, why use a defaultValue element instead of a value element? You use defaultValue because when you define a parameter in the template file, the only required components are parameterName and type. The parameter's value is provided during the deployment process. If you don't provide a value for a parameter that you defined in the template, then the defaultValue will be used instead. You should bear in mind that this element is optional.

You can provide values to the parameters that you define for your template by using the command line or creating a file with the values that you want to provide to each parameter. The following example shows the content of a parameter file for the template shown previously in Listing 1-4:

```
{

"$schema": "https://schema.management.azure.com/schemas/2015-01-01/deploymentParameters.
json#",
    "contentVersion": "1.0.0.0",
    "parameters": {
        "virtualNetworks_az204VNET_name": {
            "value": "az204demoVNET"
        },
```

```
        "networkInterfaces_az204NIC_name": {
            "value": "az204demoNIC"
        },
        "virtualMachines_az204VMTesting_name": {
            "value": "az204demoVM"
        },
        "subnets_az204Subnet_name": {
            "value": "az204demoSubnet"
        },
        "virtualMachines_az204VMTesting_id": {
            "value": "[concat(parameters(
                       'virtualMachines_az204VMTesting_name'),
                       '_OSDisk1_1_39c654d89d88405e968db84b722002d1')]"
        },
        "virtualMachines_adminUser": {
            "value": "azureadminuser"
        },
        "virtualMachines_adminpassword": {
            "value": "Pa$$wOrd"
        }
    }
}
```

When you are defining the value for a parameter, you can also use functions to construct dynamic values. If you take a look at the virtualMachines_az204VMTesting_id parameter, you can see that its value is set to a function. In this case, the function returns a string that is the result of adding the string _OSDisk1_1_39c654d89d88405e968db84b722002d1 to the value of the parameter virtualMachines_az204VMTesting_name.

There are many predefined functions that you can use in your template. You can even define your custom functions for those complicated pieces of code that repeat in your template. When working with custom functions, beware of some limitations:

- Custom functions cannot access template variables, although you can pass them as a parameter of your function.
- Your custom function cannot access the template's parameters; instead, they have access only to the parameters that you define in your function.
- Parameters on your custom function cannot have default values.
- Your custom function cannot call other custom functions; you only can call predefined functions.
- You cannot use the reference() predefined function.

> **NOTE TEMPLATE REFERENCE**
>
> When you are working with ARM templates, it's useful to consult the template reference for each type of resource you are configuring. You can review the complete template reference at *https://docs.microsoft.com/en-us/azure/templates/*. You can also review the complete reference of predefined functions at *https://docs.microsoft.com/en-us/azure/azure-resource-manager/resource-group-template-functions*.

When I initially talked about the resources that you need for deploying a VM, I explained that there are some resources that you need for the VM to run correctly. For example, you need at least one virtual disk for storing the operating system. You also need a virtual network for connecting the VM with the world, and you need a virtual network interface card for connecting the VM to the virtual network. All those dependencies are defined in an ARM template by using the element dependsOn on each resource type. This element accepts a list of resource names, separated by commas, that define the resources that need to be deployed before the resource can be deployed. As a best practice to avoid ambiguity, you should reference any resource that you put on the dependsOn element by using its provider namespace and type. You can do this by using the resourceId() predefined function.

If you review the example, the virtual network virtualNetworks_az204VNET_name needs to be deployed before subnets_az204Subnet_name can be deployed (see Figure 1-2). The dependsOn element is required because the resources defined in the template are not deployed in the same order that appears in the template.

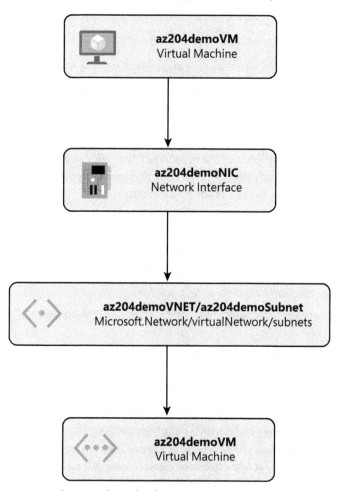

FIGURE 1-2 Resource dependencies

Once you are happy with your template, you can deploy it to your Azure subscription by using PowerShell, Azure CLI, Azure Cloud Shell, or REST API. Another exciting feature is that you can store your template JSON files in a remote location. This remote location needs to be publicly available. If your template contains information that shouldn't be public, you can provide that information as an inline parameter during the deployment. If you prefer your template not to be open to the world, you can also store your template in a Storage account and protect it by using a SAS token.

The following command shows how to deploy the example template using the template file az204-template.json and the properties file az204-parameters.json.

```
#!/bin/bash
#Azure CLI template deployment
az group create --name AZ204-ResourceGroup --location "West US"
az group deployment create \
  --name AZ204DemoDeployment \
  --resource-group AZ204-ResourceGroup \
  --template-file az204-template.json \
  --parameters @az204-parameters.json
```

The previous command creates the resource group called AZ204-ResoureGroup in the West US region. Then it creates a new deployment called AZ204DemoDeployment that will generate the resources defined in the az204-template.json template using the values provided in the parameters file named az204-parameters.json. Note the use of the @ symbol in front of the parameters file. This @ symbol is required by the az group deployment create command.

EXAM TIP

ARM templates are powerful tools that enable you to create custom functions for automating some repeating actions. When you create your custom function, remember the limitations when calling predefined or other custom functions. You should also bear in mind the visibility of the template variables and parameters when working with custom functions.

Create container images for solutions by using Docker

With the evolution of technology and the emergence of the cloud, you need to meet other challenges presented by this technical evolution. One of these requirements is the ability to deploy pieces of software in a reliable and quick manner. Virtualization technologies were one of the keys for making this kind of reliable and quick deployment possible.

However, in the context of operating system virtualization using virtual machines, one of the main drawbacks is the fact that you have a complete set of binaries, libraries, and resources that are duplicated between virtual machines. This is where containerization provides a different approach to deploying pieces of software across multiple servers reliably and quickly.

A container is a piece of software that packages your code and all its dependencies in a single package that can be run directly by the computer environment. When a container is executed, it uses a read-only copy of the shared libraries of the operating system that your code needs to run. This reduces the required amount of resources that a container needs to run your code when compared to running the same code on a virtual machine. Container technology was initially born on Linux environments, but it also has been ported to the Microsoft Windows environment. There are several implementations of container technology in the Linux ecosystem, but Docker Containers are the most widely used.

When you move the container technology to an enterprise environment, scaling dynamically and automatically is a problem, just as it is with virtual machines. There are several available solutions in the market, such as Docker Swarm, DC/OS, or Kubernetes. All these solutions are orchestration solutions that automatically scale and deploy your containers in the available resources.

Azure provides several services that allow you to deploy your application in a container. It doesn't matter if you decide to use Azure Kubernetes Services, Service Fabric, Azure Web Apps for Containers, Azure Container Registry, or Azure Container Instances; all these services use the same container technology implementation, Docker.

Before you can deploy your application to any of these services, you need to put your application into a container by creating an image of your container. A container image is a package that contains everything you need—code, libraries, environment variables, and configuration files—to run your application. Once you have your container images, you can create instances of the image for running the code, each of which is a container. If you need to make modifications to one of your containers, you need to modify the image definition and redeploy the container. In general, any change that you make to a container is not persisted across reboots. If you need to ensure that some information in your container is not deleted when a container reboots, you need to use external mount points, known as volumes.

When you create your container image, you must define your application's requirements, which are placed in a file called Dockerfile. This Dockerfile contains the definition and requirements needed for creating your container image. Use the following high-level procedure for creating an image:

1. **Create a directory for the new image.** This directory contains your Docker file, your code, and any other dependency that you need to include in the image, and that is not available in a separate image.

2. **Create the Dockerfile.** This file contains the definition of your image. Listing 1-5 shows an example of a functional Dockerfile.

3. **Open a command line.** You use this command line to run the Docker commands.

4. **Create the container image.** Use the command docker build to create the image. When you create an image, you should add a tag to identify the image and the version.

If you don't set a version number, docker automatically assigns the default value *latest*. You need to provide the path of the folder that contains the Dockerfile. This command has the following structure:

```
docker build --tag=<tag_name>[:<version>] <dockerfile_dir>
```

5. **List the newly created image.** Once Docker finishes downloading all the dependencies for your image, you can ensure that your image has been created by executing this command:

```
docker image ls
```

LISTING 1-5 Dockerfile example

```
# Use an official Python runtime as a parent image
FROM python:2.7-slim

# Set the working directory to /app
WORKDIR /app

# Copy the current directory contents into the container at /app
COPY . /app

# Install any needed packages specified in requirements.txt
RUN pip install --trusted-host pypi.python.org -r requirements.txt

# Make port 80 available to the world outside this container
EXPOSE 80

# Define an environment variable
ENV NAME World

# Run app.py when the container launches
CMD ["python", "app.py"]
```

NEED MORE REVIEW? **BEST PRACTICES FOR WRITING DOCKERFILES**

When you are writing your Dockerfile, you should bear in mind some best practices detailed at *https://docs.docker.com/develop/develop-images/dockerfile_best-practices/*.

For complex applications, creating an image for each component of the application can become a complicated task. For scenarios in which you need to define and run multiple containers, you can use Docker Compose. You can also think of Docker Compose as the definition of your images for a production environment. If your application is comprised of several images, you can define the relationship between those images and how they are exposed to the external world. Using Docker Compose you can also set the limits of the resources assigned to each container when it executes and define what happens if one container associated with a service fails.

A service in the Docker world is each of the pieces that are part of your application. A service has a one-to-one relationship with an image. It's important to remember that a service can have multiple instances of the same image, which means you can have various containers. The docker-composer.yaml file contains the definitions of the relationships and requirements needed for running your application.

> **NEED MORE REVIEW?**   **FULLY FUNCTIONAL EXAMPLE**
>
> You can run a fully functional example in your local environment by reviewing the instructions published by Microsoft *at https://docs.microsoft.com/en-us/azure/aks/tutorial-kubernetes-prepare-app.*

EXAM TIP

The modifications that you make to a container while it's running do not persist if you reboot the container. If you need to make changes to the content of a container, you need to modify the image container and then redeploy the container. If you need your container to save information that needs to be persisted across reboots, you need to use volumes.

Publish an image to the Azure Container Registry

The main purpose of creating an image is to make your code highly portable and independent from the server that executes your code. To achieve this objective, your image needs to be accessible by all the servers that can execute your image. Therefore, you need to store your image in a centralized storage service.

Azure Container Registry (ACR) is Microsoft's implementation of a Docker registry service, based on the Docker Registry 2.0 definition. Using this managed Docker registry service, you can privately store your images for later distribution to container services, such as Azure Managed Kubernetes Service. You can also use ACR for building your images on the fly and automating the building of the image based on the commits of your source code.

Before you can upload an image to your private container registry, you need to tag the image. To do this, you need to include the name of your private container registry in the tag. You will use the name structure <acr_name>.azurecr.io/[repository_name][:version]. The following list breaks down each part of the tag:

- **acr_name**   This is the name that you gave to your registry.
- **repository_name**   This is an optional name for a repository in your registry. ACR allows you to create multilevel repositories inside the registry. If you want to use a custom repository, just put its name in the tag.
- **version**   This is the version that you use for the image.

Use the following procedure for pushing your image to your ACR registry. These steps assume that you already created an Azure Container Registry and installed the latest Azure CLI:

1. Log in to your Azure subscription.

   ```
   az login
   ```

2. Log in to your registry using this command:

   ```
   az acr login ---name <acr_name>
   ```

3. Tag the image that you want to upload to the registry using this command:

   ```
   docker tag foobar <acr_name>.azurecr.io/<repository_name>/<image_name>
   ```

4. Push the image to the registry using this command:

   ```
   docker push <acr_name>.azurecr.io/<repository_name>/<image_name>
   ```

When Docker finishes pushing your image to the registry, you can browse the repositories in your registry, as shown in Figure 1-3, to verify that it has been successfully uploaded.

FIGURE 1-3 Browse container repository

The next section reviews how to run the container from the image you have already pushed to the registry.

EXAM TIP

A container registry is useful not only for storing your container images but also for automating the deployment of containers into the Azure Container services. Any continuous delivery service, like Azure Pipelines, would need a container registry for deploying the container images.

Run containers by using Azure Container Instance

Once you have created your image and made it available to Azure services by pushing it to your container registry, it is time to run the container in any of the services that Azure offers to you. Follow this high-level procedure:

1. Create as many images as your application needs to run correctly.

2. Upload or push your application images to a container registry.

3. Deploy the application.

When you want to create an image in the Azure Container Instance (ACI) service from your Azure Container Registry (ACR), you need to authenticate before you can pull the image from your ACR. For the purpose of demonstration, the following procedure uses **Admin** account authentication to show how to create and run a container in ACI:

1. Sign in to the Azure cloud shell (*https://shell.azure.com*).

2. In the Shell Selector, select Bash.

3. Open the online editor by clicking the curly brace icon to the right of the Shell Selector.

4. Use the script in Listing 1-6 to create a service principal password and to create a container from your images in the registry.

LISTING 1-6   Creating a service principal password

```
#!/bin/bash

#Some variable definition useful for the script
ACR_NAME=az204demo
SP_NAME=az204demo_sp
IMAGE_TAG=az204demo.azurecr.io/develop/foobar:latest
RESOURCE_GROUP=AKSdemo-RG
APP_NAME=foobar
APP_DNS_NAME=prueba



#Get the registry ID. You will need this ID for creating the authorization to the
#service principal
ACR_ID=$(az acr show --name $ACR_NAME --query id --output tsv)

#Get the ACR login server
ACR_SERVER=$(az acr show --name $ACR_NAME --query loginServer --output tsv)

#Get the service principal password. We will grant pull only privileges to the service
#principal
echo "Generating Service Principal password"
SP_PASS=$(az ad sp create-for-rbac --name http://$SP_NAME --scopes $ACR_ID
--role acrpull --query password --output tsv)
```

```
#Get the App ID associated to the service principal
SP_ID=$(az ad sp show --id http://$SP_NAME --query appId --output tsv)

echo "Service principal ID: $SP_ID"
echo "Service principal password: $SP_PASS"

#Create the container in the Container Instance service
az container create --resource-group $RESOURCE_GROUP --name $APP_NAME --image
$IMAGE_TAG --cpu 1 --memory 1 --registry-login-server $ACR_SERVER --registry-username
$SP_ID --registry-password $SP_PASS --dns-name-label $APP_DNS_NAME --ports 80
```

5. In the top-right corner of the online editor, below the user information, click the ellipsis icon, and then click Save. Provide a name for the script.

6. In the Azure Cloud Shell, execute the script by typing the following command in the bash shell:

```
sh <your_script_name>
```

Once you have executed this procedure, you can access your container by looking for your container's name in the Azure portal. You can also access the application that you put in this container by entering the URL of the container into a browser. The URL for this container will be in the form of <APP_DNS_NAME>.<region>.azurecontainer.io, based on the value of the variable APP_DNS_NAME that you provided in the previous script.

EXAM TIP

You can use several authentication mechanisms, such as an individual login with Azure AD, an admin account, or a service principal. Authentication with Azure AD is a good approach for your development and testing environment. Using the admin account is disabled by default and is discouraged for production environments because you need to put the admin account password in your code. For production environments, the recommended way to pull images is using service principals for authentication with the ACR.

Skill 1.2: Create Azure App Service web apps

Azure App Service is a Platform as a Service (PaaS) solution that Microsoft offers to assist with developing your applications, mobile app back end, or REST APIs without worrying about the underlying infrastructure.

You use most of the more popular programming languages—.NET, .NET Core, Java, Ruby, Node.js, PHP, or Python—on top of your preferred platform (Linux or Windows). Azure App Service provides you with enterprise-level infrastructure capabilities, such as load balancing, security, autoscaling, and automated management. You can also include Azure App Service in your continuous deployment lifecycle thanks to the integration with GitHub, Docker Hub, and Azure DevOps.

Create an Azure App Service web app

Azure App Service is a PaaS service based on HTTP that allows you to deploy your web or mobile back-end applications or REST APIs to the cloud. Using Azure App Services enables you to develop your application in any of the most popular languages of the moment, like .NET, .NET Core, Java, Ruby, Node.js, PHP, or Python. Azure App Services also offers you the flexibility of working with any of your favorite platforms: Windows, Linux, or Linux-based containers. The advantage of using Azure App Services is not limited only to the different options for developing. It also integrates quite well with different continuous integration and deployment platforms.

When you plan to create an Azure App Service, there are some concepts about how your application performs that you need to understand. Every App Service needs resources to execute your code. Virtual machines are the base of these resources. Although Azure automatically provides the low-level configuration for running these virtual machines, you still need to provide some high-level information. An App Service plan manages the group of virtual machines that host your web application.

You can think of an App Service plan like a server farm that runs in a cloud environment. This also means that you are not limited to running a single App Service in an App Service plan. You can share the same computing resources between several App Services that you deploy on the same App Service plan.

When you create a new App Service plan, you need to provide the following information:

- **Region**   This is the region where you deploy the App Service plan. Any App Service in this App Service plan is placed in the same region as the App Service plan.
- **Number of instances**   This is the number of VMs added to your App Service plan. Bear in mind that the maximum number of instances that you can configure for your App Service plan depends on the pricing tier that you select. You can scale the number of instances manually or automatically.
- **Size of the instances**   You configure the size of the VM used in the App Service plan.
- **Operating system platform**   This controls whether your web application runs on Linux or Windows VMs. Depending on the operating system, you have access to different pricing tiers. Beware that once you have selected the operating system platform, you cannot change the OS for the App Service without re-creating the App Service.

- **Pricing tier** This sets the features and capabilities available for your App Service plan and how much you pay for the plan. For Windows VMs, two basic pricing tiers use shared VMs—F1 and D1. This shared tier is not available for Linux VMs. When you use the basic pricing tiers, your code runs alongside other Azure customers' code.

When you run an App Service in an App Service plan, all instances configured in the plan execute the code corresponding to your app. This means that if you have five virtual machines, any app you deploy into the App Service runs on each of the five VMs. Other operations related to the App Service, such as additional deployment slots, diagnostic logs, backups, or WebJobs, also are executed using the resources of each virtual machine in the App Service plan.

Azure App Service also provides you with the ability to integrate the authentication and authorization of your web application, REST API, a mobile app back end, or even Azure Functions. You can use different well-known authentication providers, like Azure, Microsoft, Google, Facebook, and Twitter, for authenticating users in your application. You can also use other authentication and authorization mechanisms on your apps. However, by using this security module, you can provide a reasonable level of security to your application with minimal or even no required code changes.

There are situations when your application may require access to resources on your on-premises infrastructure, and App Service provides you with two different approaches:

- **VNet integration** This option is available only for Standard, Premium, or PremiumV2 pricing tiers. This integration allows your web app to access resources in your virtual network. If you create a site-to-site VPN with your on-premises infrastructure, you can access your private resources from your web app.

- **Hybrid connections** This option depends on the Azure Service Bus Relay and creates a network connection between the App Service and an application endpoint. This means that hybrid connections enable the traffic between specific TCP host and port combinations.

The following procedure shows how to create an App Service plan and upload a simple web application based on .NET Core using Visual Studio 2019. Ensure that you have installed the ASP.NET and web development workload, and you have installed the latest updates.

1. Open Visual Studio 2019 on your computer.
2. In the Visual Studio 2019 Home window, in the column named Get Started, click the Continue Without Code link at the bottom of the column.
3. Click the Tools menu and choose Get Tools And Features. Verify that the ASP.NET And Web Development In The Web & Cloud section is checked.
4. In the Visual Studio 2019 window, click File > New > Project to open the New Project window.
5. In the Create a New Project window, select C# in the drop-down menu below the Search For Templates text box at the top right of the window.
6. In the All Project Types drop-down menu, select Web.

7. In the list of templates on the right side of the window, select ASP.NET Core Web Application.

8. In the Configure Your New Project window, complete the following steps:

   - Select a name for the project.
   - Enter a path for the location of the solution.
   - In the Solution drop-down menu, select Create A New Solution.
   - Enter a name for the solution.

9. Click the Create button in the bottom-right corner of the Configure Your New Project window. This opens the Create A New ASP.NET Core Web Application window.

10. In the Create A New ASP.NET Core Web Application window, ensure that the following values are selected in the two drop-down menus at the top of the window:

   - .NET Core
   - ASP.NET Core 3.1

11. Select Web Application from the Project Templates area in the center of the window.

12. Uncheck the option Configure For HTTPS on the bottom-right side of the window.

13. Click the Create button in the bottom-right corner of the Create A New ASP.NET Core Web Application window.

At this point, you have created a simple ASP.NET Core web application. You can run this application in your local environment to ensure that the application is running correctly before you publish the application to Azure.

Now you need to create the Resource Group and App Service plan that hosts the App Service in Azure:

1. In your Visual Studio 2019 window, ensure that you have opened the solution of the web application that you want to publish to Azure.

2. On the right side of the Visual Studio window, in the Solution Explorer window, right-click the project's name.

3. In the contextual menu, click Publish. This opens the Pick A Publish Target window.

4. In the Pick A Publish Target window, make sure that App Service is selected from the list of Available Targets on the left side of the window.

5. In the Azure App Service section, in the right side of the window, ensure that Create New Option is selected.

6. In the bottom-right corner of the window, click the Create Profile button, which opens the Create App Service window.

7. In the Create App Service window, add a new Azure account. This account needs to have enough privileges in the subscription for creating new resource groups, app services, and an App Service plan.

8. Once you have added a valid account, you can configure the settings for publishing your web application, as shown in Figure 1-4.

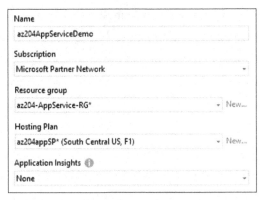

FIGURE 1-4 Creating an app service

9. In the App Name text box, enter a name for the App Service. By default, this name matches the name that you gave to your project.

10. In the Subscription drop-down menu, select the subscription in which you want to create the App Service.

11. In the Resource Group drop-down menu, select the resource group in which you want to create the App Service and the App Service plan. If you need to create a new resource group, you can do so by clicking the New link on the right side of the drop-down menu.

12. To the right of the Hosting Plan drop-down menu, click the New link to open the Configure Hosting Plan window.

13. In the Configure Hosting Plan window, type a name for the App Service plan in the App Service Plan text box.

14. Select a region from the Location drop-down menu.

15. Select a virtual machine size from the Size drop-down menu.

16. Click the OK button in the bottom-right corner of the window. This closes the Configure Hosting Plan window.

17. At the bottom-right corner of the Create App Service window, click the Create button. This starts the creation of the needed resources and the upload of the code to the App Service.

18. Once the publishing process has finished, Visual Studio opens your default web browser with the URL of the newly deployed App Service. This URL will have the structure https://<*your_app_service_name*>.azurewebsites.net.

Depending on the pricing tier that you selected, some features are enabled, such as configuring custom domains or configuring SSL connections for your web applications. For production deployment, you should use Standard or Premium pricing tiers. As your feature needs change, you can choose different pricing tiers. You can start by using the free tier, F1, in the early stages of your deployment and then increase to an S1 or P1 tier if you need to make backups of your web application or need to use deployment slots.

Even if the premium pricing tiers do not fit your computer requirements, you can still deploy a dedicated and isolated environment, called Isolated pricing tier. This tier provides you with dedicated VMs running on top of dedicated virtual networks where you can achieve the maximum level of scale-out capabilities. Bear in mind that you cannot use the shared tier D1 to deploy a Linux App Service plan.

EXAM TIP

Because Azure App Service does not support the same features for Linux and Windows, you cannot mix Windows and Linux apps in the same resource group in the same region. For more information about the limitations of Linux App Services, review the following article: *https://docs.microsoft.com/en-us/azure/app-service/containers/app-service-linux-intro.*

Enable diagnostics logging

Troubleshooting and diagnosing the behavior of an application is a fundamental operation in the lifecycle of every application. This is especially true if you are developing your application. Azure App Service provides you with some mechanisms for enabling diagnostics logging at different levels that can affect your application:

- **Web server diagnostics** These are message logs generated from the web server itself. You can enable three different types of logs:

  - **Detailed error logging** This log contains detailed information for any request that results in an HTTP status code 400 or greater. When an error 400 happens, a new HTML file is generated, containing all the information about the error. A separate HTML file is generated for each error. These files are stored in the file system of the instance in which the web app is running. A maximum of 50 error files can be stored. When this limit is reached, the oldest 26 files are automatically deleted from the file system.

  - **Failed request tracing** This log contains detailed information about failed requests to the server. This information contains a trace of the IIS components that were involved in processing the request. It also contains the time taken by each IIS component. These logs are stored in the file system. The system creates a new folder for each new error, applying the same retention policies as for detailed error logging.

  - **Web server logging** This log registers the HTTP transaction information for the requests made to the web server. The information is stored using the W3C extended log file format. You can configure custom retention policies to these log files. By default, these diagnostic logs are never deleted, but they are restricted by the space they can use in the file system. The default space quota is 35 MB.

- **Application diagnostics** You can send a log message directly from your code to the log system. You use the standard logging system of the language that you use in your app for sending messages to the application diagnostics logs. This is different from Application Insights because application diagnostics are just logged information that you register from your application. If you want your application to send logs to Application Insights, you need to add the Application Insights SDK to your application.

- **Deployment diagnostics**   This log is automatically enabled for you, and it gathers all information related to the deployment of your application. Typically, you use this log for troubleshooting failures during the deployment process, especially if you are using custom deployment scripts.

You can enable the different diagnostics logs, shown in Figure 1-5, using the Azure portal. When you enable application logging, you can select the level of error log that will be registered on the files. These error levels are

- **Disabled**   No errors are registered.
- **Error**   Critical and Error categories are registered.
- **Warning**   Registers Warning, Error, and Critical categories.
- **Information**   Registers Info, Warning, Error, and Critical log categories.
- **Verbose**   Registers all log categories (Trace, Debug, Info, Warning, Error, and Critical).

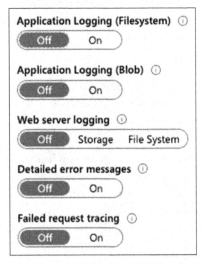

FIGURE 1-5 Enabling diagnostics logging

When you configure application logging, you can set the location for storing the log files. You can choose between saving the logs in the file system or using Blob Storage. Storing application logs in the file system is intended for debugging purposes. If you enable this option, it will be automatically disabled after 12 hours. If you need to enable the application logging for a longer period, you need to save the log files in Blob Storage. When you configure application logging for storing the log files in Blob Storage, you can also provide a retention period in days. When log files become older than the value that you configure for the retention period, the files are automatically deleted. By default, there is no retention period set. You can configure the web server logging in the same way that you configure the storage for your application logging.

If you configure application or web server logging for storing the log files in the file system, the system creates the following structure for the log files:

- **/LogFiles/Application/**   This folder contains the logs files from the application logging.

- **/LogFiles/W3SVC########/**   This folder contains the files from the failed request traces. The folder contains an XSL file and several XML files. The XML files contain the actual tracing information, whereas the XSL file provides the formatting and filtering functionality for the content stored in the XML files.

- **/LogFiles/DetailedErrors/**   This folder contains the *.htm files related to the detailed error logs.

- **/LogFiles/http/RawLogs/**   This folder contains the web server logs in W3C extended log format.

- **/LogFiles/Git**   This folder contains the log generated during the deployment of the application. You can also find deployment files in the folder D:\home\site\deployments.

You need this folder structure when you want to download the log files. You can use two different mechanisms for downloading the log files: FTP/S or Azure CLI. The following command shows how to download log files to the current working directory:

```
az webapp log download --resource-group <Resource group name> --name <App name>
```

The logs for the application *<App name>* are automatically compressed into a file named webapp_logs.zip. Then, this file is downloaded in the same directory where you executed the command. You can use the optional parameter --log-file for downloading the log files to a different path in a different zip file.

There are situations in which you may need to view the logs for your application in near real time. For these situations, App Service provides you with log streams. Using streaming, you can see the log messages as they are being saved to the log files. Any text file stored in the D:\home\LogFiles\ folder is also displayed on the log stream. You can view log streams by using the embedded viewer in the Azure portal, on the Log Stream item under the monitoring section in your App Service. You can also use the following Azure CLI command for viewing your application or web server logs in streaming:

```
az webapp log tail --resource-group <Resouce group name> --name <App name>
```

> **NEED MORE REVIEW?**   **INTEGRATE LOGS WITH AZURE MONITOR**
>
> You can also send the diagnostics information from your Windows or Linux App Services to Azure Monitor. At the time of this writing, this feature is in preview. You can get more information about how to integrate your Azure App Service logs with Azure Monitor by reviewing the following article: *https://azure.github.io/AppService/2019/11/01/App-Service-Integration-with-Azure-Monitor.html.*

Deploy code to a web app

As part of the typical development lifecycle of your application, there is a point where you need to deploy your code to an Azure App Service. The "Create an Azure App Service web app" section earlier in this chapter reviews how to deploy the code directly from Visual Studio 2019. This section explains how to deploy your code using other alternatives more suitable to continuous deployment or continuous integration workflows.

When you are developing your web application, you need to test your code on both your local environment and in development or testing environments that are similar to the production environment. Starting with the Standard pricing tier, Azure App Service provides you with the deployment slots. These slots are deployments of your web application that reside in the same App Service of your web application. A deployment slot has its configuration and host name. You can use these additional deployment slots for testing your code before moving to the production slot. The main benefit of using these deployment slots is that you can swap these slots without any downtime. You can even configure an automated swap of the slots by using Auto Swap.

When you plan for deploying your web application into an App Service, Azure offers you several options:

- **ZIP or WAR files** When you want to deploy your application, you can package all your files into a ZIP or WAR package. Using the Kudu service, you can deploy your code to the App Service.

- **FTP** You can copy your application files directly to the App Service using the FTP/S endpoint configured by default in the App Service.

- **Cloud synchronization** Powered by the Kudu deployment engine, this method allows you to have your code in a OneDrive or Dropbox folder, and it syncs that folder with the App Service.

- **Continuous deployment** Azure can integrate with GitHub, BitBucket, or Azure Repos repositories for deploying the most recent updates of your application to the App Service. Depending on the service, you can use the Kudu build server, or Azure Pipelines for implementing a continuous delivery process. You can also configure the integration manually with other cloud repositories like GitLab.

- **Your local Git repository** You can configure your App Service as a remote repository for your local Git repository and push your code to Azure. Then the Kudu build server automatically compiles your code for you and deploys to the App Service.

- **ARM template** You can use Visual Studio and an ARM template for deploying your code into an App Service.

The following example shows how to deploy your code to a web app using Azure Pipelines. For this example, you need to have your code deployed in an Azure Repos repository. If you don't already have your code in an Azure Repos repository, you can use the following article for creating a new repo: *https://docs.microsoft.com/en-us/azure/devops/repos/git/creatingrepo.*

1. Open the Azure portal (*https://portal.azure.com*).

2. In the search text box at the top of the Azure portal, type the name of your App Service.

3. In the result list below the search text box, click your App Service.

4. On your App Service blade, on the menu on the left side of the page, under the Deployment section, click Deployment Center.

5. On the Deployment Center, shown in Figure 1-6, in the source control step, click Azure Repos.

6. At the bottom of the page, click Continue.

7. In the Build Provider step, click Azure Pipelines (Preview) and click Continue at the bottom of the page.

8. In the Configure step, on the Code section, select your organization in the Azure DevOps Organization drop-down menu.

9. In the Project drop-down menu, select the project with the repository that contains the code that you want to deploy to the Azure App Service.

10. In the Repository drop-down menu, select the repository that contains your code.

11. In the Branch drop-down menu, select the branch that you want to deploy.

12. In the Build section, in the Web Application Framework drop-down menu, select the appropriate framework for your code.

13. Click the Continue button at the bottom of the page.

14. In the Summary step, review the details for the configuration.

15. At the bottom of the page, click Finish.

At this point, you have configured an Azure Pipeline in your Azure Repo that automatically deploys your code to the Azure App Service. When you make a commit to the branch that you selected in the previous example, the Azure Pipeline automatically uses the code in the last commit. Once you have configured the continuous deployment for your Azure App Service, you can review the status of the different deployments in the Deployment Center of your Azure App Service.

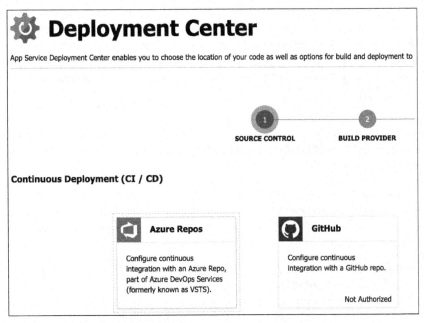

FIGURE 1-6 Enabling diagnostics logging

NEED MORE REVIEW? APP SERVICE DEPLOYMENT EXAMPLES

You can review samples of the different types of deployments by following the cases published in the following articles:

- Deploy ZIP or WAR files: *https://docs.microsoft.com/en-us/azure/app-service/deploy-zip*

- Deploy via cloud sync: *https://docs.microsoft.com/en-us/azure/app-service/deploy-content-sync*

- Deploy from local Git: *https://docs.microsoft.com/en-us/azure/app-service/deploy-local-git*

When you deploy your code to an Azure App Service, you can do it in different deployment slots. A deployment slot is a live app that is different from the main app. Each deployment slot has its own host name and group of settings. You usually use the various slots as a staging environment for testing purposes. You can switch between the different slots without losing requests. Deployment slots are available only to Standard, Premium, and Isolated App Services tiers.

NEED MORE REVIEW? DEPLOYMENT SLOTS

You can learn more about how to work with deployment slots by reviewing the following article: *https://docs.microsoft.com/en-us/azure/app-service/deploy-staging-slots*.

Configure web app settings including SSL, API, and connection strings

After you have created your App Service application, you can manage the various parameters that may affect your application. You can access these settings in the Configuration menu on the Settings section in the App Service blade. The available parameters are grouped by the following four main categories of settings:

- **Application Settings** You can configure the environment variables that are passed to your code. Using these settings is equivalent to setting the same variables in the <appSettings> section in the Web.config or appsettings.json files in an ASP.NET or ASP.NET Core project. If you set a variable in this section that matches a variable in Web. config or appsettings.json files, the value of the variables in the configuration files will be replaced with the value in your Azure Web App settings. These settings are always encrypted at rest, that is, when they are stored.

- **Connection Strings** You use this section for configuring the connection strings for the database that your code needs to use. This is similar to using the <connectionString> section in the Web.config or appsettings.json files in ASP.NET or ASP.NET Core projects.

- **General Settings** These settings are related to the environment and platform in which your app runs. You can control the following items:

  - **Stack Settings** You configure the stack and the version used for running your application.

    - **Stack** You can choose between .NET Core, .NET, Java, PHP, and Python.

    - **Version** This is the version for the stack that you chose in the previous setting.

  - **Platform Settings** This section controls the different settings related to the platform that runs your code:

    - **Platform** This setting controls whether your application runs on a 32- or 64-bit platform.

    - **Managed Pipeline Version** Configures the IIS pipeline mode. You should set this to *classic* if you need to run a legacy application that requires an older version of IIS.

    - **FTP State** Configures the possibility of using FTP or FTPS to deploy your web app to the Azure App Service. By default, both FTP and FTPS protocols are enabled.

    - **HTTP Version** This enables the HTTPS/2 protocol.

- **Web Sockets**   If your application uses SignalR or socket.io, you need to enable web sockets.

- **Always On**   Enabling this setting means your app is always loaded. By default, the application is unloaded if it is idle for some amount of time. You can configure this idle timeout in the host.json project file. The default value for App Service is 30 minutes.

- **ARR Affinity**   Enabling this setting ensures that client requests are routed to the same instance for the life of the session. This setting is useful for stateful applications but can negatively affect stateless applications.

- **Debugging**   Enable remote debugging options so you can directly connect from your IDE to the Azure App Service for debugging your ASP.NET, ASP.NET Core, or Node.js apps. This option automatically turns off after 48 hours.

- **Incoming Client Certificates**   If you require mutual SSL authentication for your application, you need to enable this option.

- **Default Documents**   This setting configures which web page is displayed at the root URL of your app. You can set a list of different default documents, where the first valid match is shown at the root URL of your website.

- **Path Mappings**   The settings in this section depend on the type of operating system that you choose for your Azure App Service:

  - **Windows Apps (Uncontainerized)**   These settings are similar to the ones that you can find in IIS:

    - **Handler Mappings**   You can configure custom script processors for different file extensions.

    - **Virtual Applications And Directories**   This setting allows you to add additional virtual directories or applications to your App Service.

  - **Containerized Apps**   You can configure the mount points that are attached to the containers during the execution. You can attach up to five Azure files or blob mount points per app. Figure 1-7 shows the dialog box for configuring an Azure File mount point.

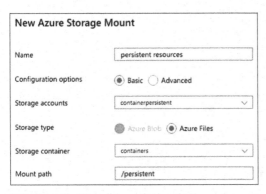

FIGURE 1-7 Enabling diagnostics logging

Once you have created an app setting or connection string variable, you can access these values from your code by using environment variables. The following code snippet shows how to access an app setting named testing-var1 and connection string named testing-connsql1 from a PHP page:

```php
<?php
    $testing_var1 = getenv('APPSETTING_testing-var1')
    $connection_string = getenv('SQLAZURECONNSTR_testing-connsql1')
?>
```

As you can see in the previous code snippet, you need to prepend the string APPSETTING_ to your app setting variable's name. In the case of connection strings, the string that you need to prepend to your connection string's name depends on the type that you configure in the connection string in the Azure portal:

- **SQL Databases**   SQLAZURECONNSTR_
- **SQL Server**   SQLCONNSTR_
- **MySQL**   MYSQLCONNSTR_
- **PostgreSQL**   POSTGRESQLCONNSTR_
- **Custom**   CUSTOMCONNSTR_

For ASP.NET applications, you can also access app settings and connection strings by using the traditional ConfigurationManager. If you decide to use the ConfigurationManager, you don't need to prepend any string to the name of your app setting or connection string. The following code snippet shows how to access your app settings or connection string from ASP.NET code:

```
System.Configuration.ConfigurationManager.AppSettings["testing-var1"]
System.Configuration.ConfigurationManager.ConnectionStrings["testing-connsql1"]
```

When you are configuring an Azure web app for a production environment, you usually need to secure the connections with the web app. You also need to make your Azure web app available through your own domain instead of the default azurewebsites.net domain. You can do it by configuring the Custom Domain and SSL settings.

Use the following procedure for configuring SSL settings for an existing web app. Remember that SSL settings are available only for B1 or higher pricing tiers:

1. Open the Azure portal (*https://portal.azure.com*).
2. In the Search Resources text box, type the name of your Azure web app.
3. In the result list, click the name of your Azure web app.
4. On your Azure web app page, on the navigation list on the left side of the page, click Custom Domain in the Settings section.
5. Click the Add Custom Domain button in the middle of the Custom Domains page.
6. On the Add Custom Domain blade on the right side of the page, in the Custom Domain text box, type a name for your domain.
7. Click the validate button and follow the instructions for validating your domain.

8. Once you have validated your custom domain, click the Add Custom Domain button in the Add Custom Domain blade.

9. Click TLS/SSL Settings in the Settings section on the left side of your Azure Web App page.

10. In the TLS/SSL Settings page, in the TLS/SSL Bindings sections, click Add TLS/SSL Binding. Note that you need the appropriate pfx certificate for configuring this binding. You can import an existing certificate or buy a new one.

11. In the TLS/SSL Binding blade, in the Custom Domain drop-down menu, select the custom domain that you added in step 8.

12. In the Private Certificate Thumbprint drop-down menu, select a valid certificate for your custom domain.

13. In the TLS/SSL Type drop-down menu, select SNI SSL.

14. At the bottom of the TLS/SSL Binding blade, click the Add Binding button.

NOTE **AZURE STORAGE IN APP SERVICE**

At the time of this writing, using Azure Storage in App Services is a feature that is in preview and should not be used in production environments.

NEED MORE REVIEW? **CONFIGURE APP SETTINGS**

You can review more details about how to configure the different settings in your Azure web app by reviewing the article at *https://docs.microsoft.com/en-us/azure/app-service/configure-common*.

EXAM TIP

Remember that the settings that you configure in the Application Settings section overwrite the values that you configure in the <appSettings> or <connectionStrings> in your Web.config or appsettings.json files.

Implement autoscaling rules, including scheduled autoscaling, and scaling by operational or system metrics

One of the biggest challenges that you face when you deploy your application in a production environment is to ensure that you provide enough resources, so your application has the expected performance. Determining the number of resources you should allocate is the big question when it comes to configuring the resources for your app. If you allocate too many resources, your application will perform well during usage peaks, but you are potentially wasting resources. If you allocate fewer resources, you are saving resources, but your app may not perform well during usage peaks. Another issue with the application performance is that it's challenging to anticipate when a heavy usage peak may happen. This statement is especially true for applications that have unpredictable usage patterns.

Fortunately, Azure provides a mechanism for addressing this issue. You can dynamically assign more resources to your application when you need them. Autoscaling is the action of automatically adding or removing resources to an Azure service and providing needed computing power for your application in each situation. An application can scale in two different ways:

- **Vertically**   You add more computing power by adding more memory, CPU resources, and IOPS to the application. At the end of the day, your application runs on a virtual machine. It doesn't matter if you use an IaaS virtual machine, Azure App Service, or Azure Service Fabric, you are using virtual machines under the hood. Vertically scaling an application means moving from a smaller VM to a larger VM and adding more memory, CPU, and IOPS. Vertically scaling requires stopping the system while the VM is resizing. This type of scaling is also known as "scaling up and down."

- **Horizontally**   You can also scale your application by creating or removing instances of your application. Each instance of your application is executed in a virtual machine that is part of a virtual machine scale set. The corresponding Azure service automatically manages for you the virtual machines in the scale set. All these instances of your application work together to provide the same service. The advantage of scaling horizontally is that the availability of your application is not affected because there is no need for rebooting all the instances of your application that provide the service. This type of scaling is also known as "scaling out and in."

When you work with autoscaling, we refer to horizontal scaling because vertical scaling requires the service interruption while the Azure Resource Manager is changing the size of the virtual machine. For that reason, vertical scaling is not suitable for autoscaling.

You configure autoscaling based on some criteria that your application should meet for providing the right performance level. You configure these criteria in Azure by using autoscaling rules. A rule defines which metric should use Azure Monitor for performing the autoscaling. When that metric reaches the configured condition, Azure automatically performs the action configured for that rule. The typical action that you may think the rule should do is adding or removing a VM to the scale set, but it also can perform other actions like sending an email or making an HTTP request to a webhook. You can configure three different types of rules when working the autoscaling rules:

- **Time-based**   The Azure Monitor executes the autoscaling rule based on a schedule. For example, if your application requires more resources during the first week of the month, you can add more instances and reduce the number of resources for the rest of the month.

- **Metric-based**   You configure the threshold for standard metrics, such as the usage of the CPU, the length of the HTTP queue, or the percentage of memory usage, as shown in Figure 1-8.

- **Custom-based** You can create your metrics in your application, expose them using Application Insight, and use them for autoscaling rules.

FIGURE 1-8 Configuring a metric-based autoscale rule

You can only use the built-in autoscaling mechanism with a limited group of Azure resource types:

- **Azure virtual machines** You can apply autoscaling by using virtual machine scale sets. All the VMs in a scale set are treated as a group. By using autoscaling, you can add virtual machines to the scale set or remove virtual machines from it.
- **Azure Service Fabric** When you create an Azure Service Fabric cluster, you define different node types. A different virtual machine scale set supports each node type that you define in an Azure Service Fabric cluster. You can apply the same type of autoscaling rules that you use in a standard virtual machine scale set.
- **Azure App Service** This service has built-in autoscaling capabilities that you can use for adding or removing instances to the Azure App Service. The autoscale rules apply to all apps inside the Azure App Service.
- **Azure Cloud Services** This service has built-in autoscaling capabilities that you can use for adding or removing resources to the roles in the Azure Cloud Service.

When you work with the autoscale feature in one of the supported Azure Service, you define a profile condition. A profile condition defines the rule that you configure for adding or removing resources. You can also define the default, minimum, and maximum allowed instances for this profile. When you define a minimum and maximum, your service cannot decrease or grow beyond the limits you define in the profile. You can also configure the profile for scaling based on a schedule or based on the values of built-in or custom metrics. You can use the following procedure for adding a metric-based autoscale rule to an Azure App Service. This rule adds an instance to the Azure App Service plan when the average percentage of CPU usage is over 80 percent more than 10 minutes:

1. Open the Azure portal (*https://portal.azure.com*).

2. In the search text box at the top of the Azure portal, type the name of your Azure App Service.

3. Click the name of your Azure App Service in the results list.

4. On your Azure App Service blade, on the navigation menu on the left side of the blade, click the Scale-Out (App Service Plan) option in the Settings section.

5. On the Scale-Out (App Service Plan) blade, on the Configure tab, click the Custom Autoscale button. Autoscale rules are available only for the App Service plans that are Standard size or bigger.

6. On the Scale-Out (App Service Plan) blade, on the Configure tab, in the Default Auto Created Scale Condition window shown in Figure 1-9, click the Add A Rule link.

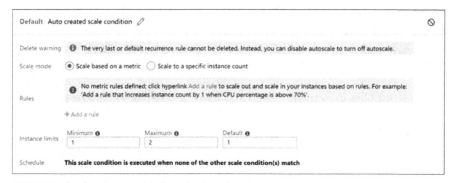

FIGURE 1-9 Configuring a metric-based autoscale rule

7. On the Scale rule panel, in the Criteria section, ensure that the CPU Percentage value is selected in the Metric Name drop-down menu.

8. Ensure that the Greater Than value is selected from the Operator drop-down menu.

9. Type the value **80** in the Metric Threshold To Trigger Scale Action text box.

10. In the Action section, ensure that the Instance count value is set to **1**.

11. Click the Add button at the bottom of the panel.

12. On the Scale-Out (App Service Plan) blade, in the Default Profile condition, set the Maximum Instance Limit to **3**.

13. Click the Save button in the top-left corner of the blade.

You can use different common autoscale patterns, based on the settings that I have reviewed so far:

- **Scale based on CPU** You scale your service (Azure App Service, VM Scale Set, or Cloud Service) based on CPU. You need to configure Scale-Out and Scale-In rules for adding and removing instances to the service. In this pattern, you also set a minimum and a maximum number of instances.

- **Scale differently on weekdays versus weekends** You use this pattern when you expect to have the primary usage of your application occur on weekdays. You configure the default profile condition with a fixed number of instances. Then you configure another profile condition for reducing the number for instances during weekends.

- **Scale differently during holidays** You use the Scale based on CPU pattern. Still, you add a profile condition for adding additional instances during holidays or days that are important to your business.

- **Scale based on custom metrics** You use this pattern with a web application comprised of three layers: front end, back end, and API tiers. The front end of an API tier communicates with the back-end tier. You define your custom metrics in the web application and expose them to the Azure Monitor by using Application Insights. You can then use these custom metrics for adding more resources to any of the three layers.

Skill 1.3: Implement Azure Functions

Based on Azure App Service, Azure Functions allow you to run pieces of code that solve particular problems inside the whole application. You use these functions in the same way that you may use a class or a function inside your code. That is, your function gets some input, executes the piece of code, and provides an output.

The big difference between Azure Functions and other app services models is that with Azure Functions (using the Consumption pricing tier), you are charged per second only when your code is running. If you use App Service, you are charged hourly when the App Service Plan is running—even if there is no code executing. Because Azure Functions is based on App Service, you can also decide to run your Azure Function in your App Service Plan if you already have other app services executing.

> **This skill covers how to**
> - Implement input and output bindings for a function
> - Implement function triggers by using data operations, timers, and webhooks
> - Implement Azure Durable Functions

Implement input and output bindings for a function

When you are writing a function in your code, that function may require data as input information for doing the job that you are writing. The function can also produce some output information as the result of the operations performed inside the function. When you work with Azure Functions, you may also need these input and output flows of data.

Binding uses Azure Functions for connecting your function with the external world without hard-coding the connection to the external resources. An Azure Function can have a mix of input and output bindings, or it can have no binding at all. Bindings pass data to the function as parameters.

Although triggers and bindings are closely related, you should not confuse them. Triggers are the events that cause the function to start its execution; bindings are like the connection to the data needed for the function. You can see the difference in this example:

One publisher service sends an event (to an Event Grid that reads a new image that has been uploaded to Blob Storage) to an Azure Storage account. Your function needs to read this image, process it, and place some information in a Cosmos DB document. When the image has been processed, your function also sends a notification to the user interface using SignalR.

In this example, you can find one trigger, one input binding, and two output bindings:

- **Trigger**   The Event Grid should be configured as the trigger for the Azure Function.
- **Input binding**   Your function needs to read the image that has been uploaded to the Blob Storage. In this case, you need to use Blob Storage as an input binding.
- **Output bindings**   Your function needs to write a Cosmos DB document with the results of processing the image. You need to use the Cosmos DB output binding. Your function also needs to send a notification to the user interface using the SignalR output binding.

Depending on the language that you use for programming your Azure Function, the way you declare a binding changes:

- **C#**   You declare bindings and triggers by decorating methods and parameters.
- **Other**   Update the function.json configuration file.

When defining a binding for non-C# language functions, you need to define your binding using the following minimum required attributes:

- **type**   This string represents the binding type. For example, you would use eventHub when using an output binding for Event Hub.
- **direction**   The only allowed values are in for input bindings and out for output bindings. Some bindings also support the special direction inout.
- **name**   The function uses this attribute for binding the data in the function. For example, in JavaScript, the key in a key-value list is an attribute.

Depending on the specific binding that you are configuring, there could be some additional attributes that should be defined.

> **NOTE   SUPPORTED BINDINGS**
>
> **For a complete list of supported bindings, please refer to the article at *https://docs.microsoft.com/en-us/azure/azure-functions/functions-triggers-bindings#supported-bindings*.**

Before you can use a binding in your code, you need to register it. If you are using C# for your functions, you can do this by installing the appropriate NuGet package. For other languages, you need to install the package with the extension code using the func command-line utility. The following example installs the Service Bus extension in your local environment for non-C# projects:

```
func extensions install –package Microsoft.Azure.WebJobs.ServiceBus
```

If you are developing your Azure Function using the Azure portal, you can add the bindings in the Integrate section of your function. When you add a binding that is not installed in your environment, you will see the warning message shown in Figure 1-10. You can install the extension by clicking the Install link.

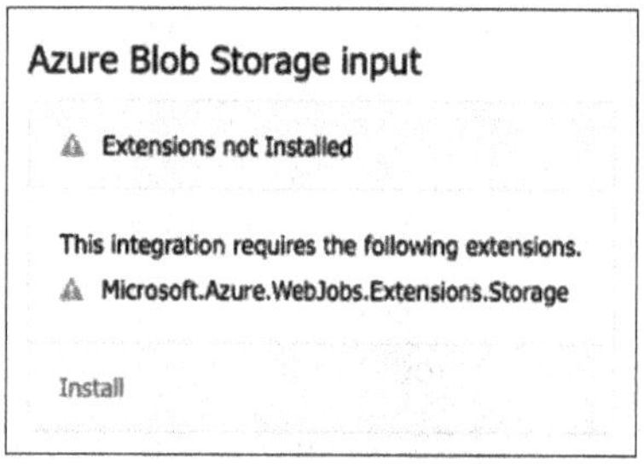

FIGURE 1-10 Installing a binding extension

> **NEED MORE REVIEW?** **MANUALLY INSTALL BINDING EXTENSIONS FROM THE AZURE PORTAL**
>
> When you develop your Azure Function using the Azure portal, you can use the standard editor or the advanced editor. When you use the advanced editor, you can directly edit the function.json configuration file. If you add new bindings using the advanced editor, you need to manually install any new binding extensions that you added to the function.json. You can review the following article for manually installing binding extensions from the Azure portal at *https://docs.microsoft.com/en-us/azure/azure-functions/install-update-binding-extensions-manual*.

If you decide to program your Azure Function using C#, you make the configuration of the bindings by using decorators for function and parameters. The function.json file is automatically constructed based on the information that you provide in your code. Listing 1-7 shows how to configure input and output bindings using parameter decorators.

LISTING 1-7 Configuring input and output bindings

```
// C# ASP.NET Core
using System;
using System.IO;
using Microsoft.Azure.WebJobs;
using Microsoft.Extensions.Logging;
using Microsoft.Azure.WebJobs.Extensions.SignalRService;
using Microsoft.Azure.WebJobs.Extensions.EventGrid;
using Microsoft.Azure.EventGrid.Models;
using System.Threading.Tasks;

namespace  Company.Functions
{
    public static class BlobTriggerCSharp
    {
        [FunctionName("BlobTriggerCSharp")]
```

```
    public static Task Run(
        [EventGridTrigger]EventGridEvent eventGridEvent,

[Blob("{data.url}", FileAccess.Read, Connection = "ImagesBlobStorage")] Stream
imageBlob,
        [CosmosDB(
            databaseName: "GIS",
            collectionName: "Processed_images",
            ConnectionStringSetting = "CosmosDBConnection")] out dynamic document,

[SignalR(HubName = "notifications")]IAsyncCollector<SignalRMessage> signalRMessages,
        ILogger log)
    {
        document = new { Description = eventGridEvent.Topic,
id = Guid.NewGuid() };

log.LogInformation($"C# Blob trigger function Processed event\n Topic: {eventGridEvent.
Topic} \n Subject: {eventGridEvent.Subject} ");
        return signalRMessages.AddAsync(
        new SignalRMessage
            {
                Target = "newMessage",
                Arguments = new [] { eventGridEvent.Subject }
            });
    }
  }
}
```

Let's review the portions of Listing 1-7 that are related to the binding configuration. In this example, you configured one input binding and two output bindings. The parameter image-Blob is configured as an input binding. You have decorated the parameter with the attribute Blob, which takes the following parameters:

- **Path** The value {data.url} configures the path of the blobs that are passed to the function. In this case, you are using a binding expression that resolves to the full path of the blob in the Blob Storage.

- **Blob access mode** In this example, you access the blob in read-only mode.

- **Connection** This sets the connection string to the storage account where the blobs are stored. This parameter sets the app setting name that contains the actual connection string.

You have also configured two output bindings, though you have configured them differently. The first output binding is configured using the keyword out in the parameter definition. Just as you did with the input parameter, you configured the output parameter document by using a parameter attribute. In this case, you used the CosmosDB attribute. You use the following parameters for configuring this output binding:

- **databaseName**   Sets the database in which you save the document that you create during the execution of the function.
- **collectionName**   Sets the collection in which you save the generated document.
- **ConnectionStringSetting**   Sets the name of the app setting variable that contains the actual connection string for the database. You should not put the actual connection string here.

Setting a value for this output binding is as simple as assigning a value to the parameter document. You can also configure output bindings by using the return statement of the function. In the example, you configure the second output binding this way.

The function parameter signalRMessages is your second output binding. As you can see in Listing 1-7, you didn't add the out keyword to this parameter because you can return multiple output values. When you need to return multiple output values, you need to use ICollector or IAsyncCollector types with the output binding parameter, as you did with signalRMessages. Inside the function, you add needed values to the signalRMessages collection and use this collection as the return value of the function. You used the SignalR parameter attribute for configuring this output binding. In this case, you only used one parameter for configuring the output binding.

- **HubName**   This is the name of the SignalR hub where you send your messages.
- **ConnectionStringSetting**   In this case, you didn't use this parameter, so it uses its default value AzureSignalRConnectionString. As you saw in the other bindings, this parameter sets the name of the app setting variable that contains the actual connection string SignalR.

When you are configuring bindings or triggers, there are situations when you need to map the trigger or binding to a dynamically generated path or element. In these situations, you can use binding expressions. You define a binding expression by wrapping your expression in curly braces. You can see an example of a binding expression shown previously in Listing 1-7. The path that you configure for the input binding contains the binding expression {data.url}, which resolves to the full path of the blob in the Blob Storage. In this case, EventGridTrigger sends a JSON payload to the input binding that contains the data.url attribute.

> **NEED MORE REVIEW?**   **BINDING EXPRESSION PATTERNS**
>
> You can learn about more binding expression patterns by reviewing this article about Azure Functions binding expression patterns in Microsoft Docs at *https://docs.microsoft.com/en-us/azure/azure-functions/functions-bindings-expressions-patterns*.

The way you configure the bindings for your code depends on the language that you used for your Azure Function. In the previous example, you review how to configure input and output bindings using C# and parameter decorations. If you use any of the other supported languages in your Azure Function, the way you configure input and output bindings changes.

The first step when configuring bindings in non-C# languages is to modify the function.json configuration file. Listing 1-8 shows the equivalent function.json for the binding configuration made in Listing 1-7. Once you have configured your bindings, you can write your code to access the bindings that you configured. Listing 1-9 shows an example written in JavaScript for using bindings in your code.

LISTING 1-8 Configuring input and output bindings in function.json

```json
{
  "disabled": false,
  "bindings": [
    {
      "name": "eventGridEvent",
      "type": "eventGridTrigger",
      "direction": "in"
    },
    {
      "name": "imageBlob",
      "type": "blob",
      "connection": "ImagesBlobStorage",
      "direction": "in",
      "path": "{data.url}"
    },
    {
      "name": "document",
      "type": "cosmosDB",
      "direction": "out",
      "databaseName": "GIS",
      "collectionName": "Processed_images",
      "connectionStringSetting": "CosmosDBConnection",
      "createIfNotExists": true
    },
    {
      "name": "signalRMessages",
      "type": "signalR",
      "direction": "out",
      "hubName": "notifications"
    }
  ]
}
```

LISTING 1-9   Using bindings in JavaScript

```
// NodeJS. Index.js
const uuid = require('uuid/v4');
module.exports = async function (context, eventGridEvent) {
    context.log('JavaScript Event Grid trigger function processed a request.');
    context.log("Subject: " + eventGridEvent.subject);
    context.log("Time: " + eventGridEvent.eventTime);
    context.log("Data: " + JSON.stringify(eventGridEvent.data));

    context.bindings.document = JSON.stringify({
        id: uuid(),
        Description: eventGridEvent.topic
    });

    context.bindings.signalRMessages = [{
        "target": "newMessage",
        "arguments": [ eventGridEvent.subject ]
    }];

    context.done();
};
```

Listings 1-8 and 1-9 represent the equivalent code in JavaScript to the code in the C# code shown in Listing 1-7. Most important is that name attributes in the binding definitions shown in Listing 1-8 correspond to the properties of the context object shown in Listing 1-9. For example, you created a Cosmos DB output binding and assigned the value document to the name attribute in the binding definition in Listing 1-8. In your JavaScript code, you access this output binding by using context.bindings.document.

EXAM TIP

Remember that you need to install the extensions on your local environment before you can use bindings or triggers. You can use the func command-line command from the Azure Function CLI tools.

Implement function triggers by using data operations, timers, and webhooks

When you create an Azure Function, that function is executed based on events that happen in the external world. Some examples include

- Executing a function periodically
- Executing a function when some other process uploads a file to Blob Storage or sends a message to a queue storage
- Executing a function when an email arrives in Outlook

Triggers programmatically manage all these events.

You can configure function triggers in the same way that you configure input or output bindings, but you need to pay attention to some additional details when dealing with triggers. You configure a trigger for listening to specific events. When an event happens, the trigger object can send data and information to the function.

You can configure three different types of triggers:

- **data operation** The trigger is started based on new data that is created, updated, or added to the system. Supported systems are Cosmos DB, Event Grid, Event Hub, Blob Storage, Queue Storage, and Service Bus.

- **timers** You use this kind of trigger when you need to run your function based on a schedule.

- **webhooks** You use HTTP or webhooks triggers when you need to run your function based on an HTTP Request.

Triggers send data to the function with information about the event that caused the trigger to start. This information depends on the type of trigger. Listing 1-10 shows how to configure a data operation trigger for Cosmos DB.

LISTING 1-10 Configuring a Cosmos DB trigger

```
// C# ASP.NET Core
using System.Collections.Generic;
using Microsoft.Azure.Documents;
using Microsoft.Azure.WebJobs;
using Microsoft.Azure.WebJobs.Host;
using Microsoft.Extensions.Logging;
namespace Company.Function
{
    public static class CosmosDBTriggerCSharp
    {
        [FunctionName("CosmosDBTriggerCSharp")]
        public static void Run([CosmosDBTrigger(
            databaseName: "databaseName",
            collectionName: "collectionName",
            ConnectionStringSetting = "AzureWebJobsStorage",
            LeaseCollectionName = "leases",

CreateLeaseCollectionIfNotExists = true)]IReadOnlyList<Document> input, ILogger log)
        {
            if (input != null && input.Count > 0)
            {
                log.LogInformation("Documents modified " + input.Count);
                log.LogInformation("First document Id " + input[0].Id);
                log.LogInformation("Modified document: " + input[0]);
            }
        }
    }
}
```

Just as with bindings, you need to install the corresponding NuGet package with the appropriate extension for working with triggers. In this case, you need to install the package Microsoft.Azure.WebJobs.Extensions.CosmosDB. You used the CosmosDBTrigger parameter attribute for configuring the trigger with the following parameters:

- **databaseName**   This is the name of the database that contains the collection this trigger should monitor.

- **collectionName**   This is the name of the collection that this trigger should monitor. This collection needs to exist before your function runs.

- **ConnectionStringSetting**   This is the name of the app setting variable that contains the connection string to the Cosmos DB database. If you want to debug your function in your local environment, you should configure this variable in the file local.settings.json file and assign the value of the connection string to your development CosmosDB database. This local.settings.json file is used by Azure Functions Core Tools to store app settings, connection strings, and settings locally and won't be automatically uploaded to Azure when you publish your Azure Function.

- **LeaseCollectionName**   This is the name of the collection used for storing leases over partitions. By default, this collection is stored in the same database as the collection-Name. If you need to store this collection in a separate database, use the parameter leaseDatabaseName or leaseConnectionStringSetting if you need to store the database in a separate Cosmos DB account.

- **CreateLeaseCollectionIfNotExists**   This creates the lease collection set by the LeaseCollectionName parameter if it does not exist in the database. Lease collection should be a nonpartitioned collection and needs to exist before your function runs.

The Cosmos DB trigger monitors for new or updated documents in the database that you configure in the parameters of the trigger. Once the trigger detects a change, it passes detected changes to the function using an IReadOnlyList<Document>. Once you have the information provided by the trigger in the input list, you can process the information inside your function. If you have enabled Application Insight integration, you should be able to see the log messages from your function, as shown in Figure 1-11.

FIGURE 1-11 View Azure Function logs in Application Insight

> **NOTE**   **VERSION 1.0 VERSUS VERSION 2.0 VERSUS VERSION 3.0**
>
> When you work with Azure Functions, you can choose between versions 1.0, 2.0, and 3.0. The main difference between the versions 1.0 and the other versions is that you can only develop and host Azure Functions 1.0 on Azure portal or Windows computers. Functions 2.0 and 3.0 can be developed and hosted on all platforms supported by .NET Core. The Azure Function you use affects the extension packages that you need to install when configuring triggers and bindings. Review the overview of Azure Functions runtime versions at *https://docs.microsoft. com/en-us/azure/azure-functions/functions-versions*.

When you work with timer and webhooks triggers, the main difference between them and a data operations trigger is that you do not need to install the extension package that supports the trigger explicitly.

Timer triggers execute your function based on a schedule. This schedule is configured using a CRON expression that is interpreted by the NCronTab library. A CRON expression is a string compound of six different fields with this structure:

```
{second} {minute} {hour} {day} {month} {day-of-week}
```

Each field can have numeric values that are meaningful for the field:

- **second**   Represents the seconds in a minute. You can assign values from 0 to 59.
- **minute**   Represents the minutes in an hour. You can assign values from 0 to 59.
- **hour**   Represents the hours in a day. You can assign values from 0 to 23.
- **day**   Represents the days in a month. You can assign values from 1 to 31.
- **month**   Represents the months in a year. You can assign values from 1 to 12. You can also use names in English, such as January, or you can use abbreviations of the name in English, such as Jan. Names are case-insensitive.
- **day-of-week**   Represents the days of the week. You can assign values from 0 to 6, where 0 is Sunday. You can also use names in English, such as Monday, or you can use abbreviations of the name in English, such as Mon. Names are case-insensitive.

All fields need to be present in a CRON expression. If you don't want to provide a value to a field, you can use the asterisk character *. This means that the expression uses all available values for that field. For example, the CRON expression * * * * * * means that the trigger is executed every second, in every minute, in every hour, in every day, and every month of the year. You can also use some operators with the allowed values in fields:

- **Range of values**   Use the dash operator (–) for representing all the values available between two limits. For example, the expression 0 10–12 * * * * means that the function is executed at hh:10:00, hh:11:00, and hh:12:00 where hh means every hour. That is, it is executed three times every hour.

- **Set of values**   Use the comma operator (,) for representing a set of values. For example, the expression 0 0 11,12,13 * * * means that the function will be executed three times a day, every day, once at 11:00:00, a second time at 12:00:00, and finally at 13:00:00.

- **Interval of values**   Use the forward slash operator (/) for representing an interval of values. The function is executed when the value of the field is divisible by the value that you put on the right side of the operator. For example, the expression */5 * * * * * will execute the function every five seconds.

Listings 1-11 and 1-12 show how to configure a timer trigger and how to use the trigger with JavaScript code.

LISTING 1-11   Configuring a timer trigger in function.json

```
{
  "disabled": false,
  "bindings": [
    {
      "name": "myTimer",
      "type": "timerTrigger",
      "direction": "in",
      "schedule": "0 */5 * * * *",
      "useMonitor": true,
      "runOnStartup": true
    }
  ]
}
```

LISTING 1-12   Using a timer trigger with JavaScript

```
//NodeJS. Index.js file
module.exports = async function (context, myTimer) {
    var timeStamp = new Date().toISOString();

    if(myTimer.isPastDue)
    {
        context.log('JavaScript is running late!');
    }
```

```
    context.log('JavaScript timer trigger Last execution: ', myTimer.ScheduleStatus.
Last);
    context.log('JavaScript timer trigger Next execution: ', myTimer.ScheduleStatus.
Next);
};
```

Just as you did when you configured bindings in the previous section, when you configure a trigger for non-C# languages, you need to add them to the function.json configuration file. You configure your triggers in the bindings section. Listing 1-11 shows the appropriate properties for configuring a timer trigger:

- **name**   This is the name of the variable that you use on your JavaScript code for accessing the information from the trigger.

- **type**   This is the type of trigger that you are configuring. In this example, the value for the timer trigger is timerTrigger.

- **direction**   This is always included in a trigger.

- **schedule**   This is the CRON expression used for configuring the execution scheduling of your function. You can also use a TimeSpan expression.

- **useMonitor**   This property monitors the schedule even if the function app instance is restarted. The default value for this property is true for every schedule with a recurrence greater than one minute. Monitoring the schedule occurrences will ensure that the schedule is maintained correctly.

- **runOnStartup**   This indicates that the function should be invoked as soon as the runtime starts. The function will be executed after the function app wakes up after going idle because of inactivity or if the function app restarts because of changes in the function. Setting this parameter to true is not recommended on production environments because it can lead to unpredictable execution times of your function.

> **NOTE   TROUBLESHOOTING FUNCTIONS ON YOUR LOCAL ENVIRONMENT**
>
> While you are developing your Azure Functions, you need to troubleshoot your code in your local environment. If you are using non-HTML triggers, you need to provide a valid value for the AzureWebJobsStorage attribute in the local.settings.json file.

You use TimeSpan expressions to specify the time interval between the invocations of the function. If the function execution takes longer than the specified interval, then the function is invoked immediately after the previous invocation finishes. TimeSpan expressions are strings with the format hh:mm:ss where hh represents hours, mm represents minutes, and ss represents seconds. Hours in a TimeSpan expression need to be less than 24. The TimeSpan expression 24:00:00 means the function is going to be executed every day. 02:00:00 means the function will be invoked every two hours. You can use TimeSpan expressions only on Azure Functions that are executed on App Service Plans. That is, you cannot use TimeSpan expressions when you are using the Consumption pricing tier.

You use HTTP triggers for running your Azure Function when an external process makes an HTTP request. This HTTP request can be a regular request using any of the available HTTP methods or a webhook. A web callback or webhook is an HTTP request made by third-party systems, or external web applications, or as a result of an event generated in the external system. For example, if you are using GitHub as your code repository, GitHub can send a webhook to your Azure Function each time a new pull request is opened.

When you create an Azure Function using HTTP triggers, the runtime automatically publishes an endpoint with the following structure:

```
http://<your_function_app>.azurewebsites.net/api/<your_function_name>
```

This is the URL or endpoint that you need to use when calling to your function using a regular HTTP request or when you configure an external webhook for invoking your function. You can customize the route of this endpoint by using the appropriate configuration properties. This means that you can also implement serverless APIs using HTTP triggers. You can even protect the access to your function's endpoints by requesting authorization for any request made to your API using the App Service Authentication/Authorization. Listing 1-13 shows how to configure an HTTP trigger with a custom endpoint.

LISTING 1-13 Configuring an HTTP trigger

```csharp
// C# ASP.NET Core
using System.Security.Claims;
using System;
using System.IO;
using System.Threading.Tasks;
using Microsoft.AspNetCore.Mvc;
using Microsoft.Azure.WebJobs;
using Microsoft.Azure.WebJobs.Extensions.Http;
using Microsoft.AspNetCore.Http;
using Microsoft.Extensions.Logging;
using Newtonsoft.Json;

namespace Company.Function
{
    public static class HttpTriggerCSharp
    {
        [FunctionName("HttpTriggerCSharp")]
        public static async Task<IActionResult> Run(
            [HttpTrigger(AuthorizationLevel.Anonymous, "get", "post", Route = "devices/
            {id:int?}")] HttpRequest req,
             int? id,
             ILogger log)
        {
            log.LogInformation("C# HTTP trigger function processed a request.");
```

```
//We access to the parameter in the address by adding a function parameter
//with the same name
log.LogInformation($"Requesting information for device {id}");


//If you enable Authentication / Authorization at Function App level,
//information
//about the authenticated user is automatically provided in the
//HttpContext
ClaimsPrincipal identities = req.HttpContext.User;
string username = identities.Identity?.Name;

log.LogInformation($"Request made by user {username}");

string name = req.Query["name"];

string requestBody = await new StreamReader(req.Body).ReadToEndAsync();
dynamic data = JsonConvert.DeserializeObject(requestBody);
name = name ?? data?.name;

//We customize the output binding
return name != null

        ? (ActionResult)new JsonResult(new { message = $"Hello, {name}",
username = username, device = id})

        : new BadRequestObjectResult("Please pass a name on the query string or
in the request body");
    }
  }
}
```

The example in Listing 1-13 shows the following points when working with HTTP triggers:

- How to work with authentication.
- How to work with the authorization level.
- How to customize the function endpoint, using route parameters.
- How to customize the output binding.

HTTP triggers are automatically provided to you out-of-the-box with the function runtime. There is no need to install a specific NuGet package for working with this extension. You use the HTTPTrigger parameter attribute for configuring the HTTP trigger. This trigger accepts the following parameters:

- **AuthLevel** This parameter configures the authorization key that you should use for accessing the function. Allowed values are

- **anonymous** No key is required.
- **function** This is the default value. You need to provide a function-specific key.
- **admin** You need to provide the master key.

- **Methods** You can configure the HTTP methods that your function accepts. By default, the function runtime accepts all HTTP methods. Listing 1-13 reduces these accepted HTTP methods to GET and POST. Don't use this parameter if you set the WebHookType parameter.

- **Route** You can customize the route of the endpoint used for the function to listen to a new request. The default route is https://<your_function_app>.azurewebsites.net/api/<your_function_name>.

- **WebHookType** This parameter is available only for version 1.x runtime functions. You should not use the Methods and WebHookType parameters together. This parameter sets the webhook type for a specific provider. Allowed values are
    - **genericJson** This parameter is used for nonspecific providers.
    - **github** This parameter is used for interacting with GitHub webhooks.
    - **slack** This parameter is used for interacting with Slack webhooks.

When you declare the variable type that your function uses as the input from the trigger, you can use HttpRequest or a custom type. If you use a custom type, the runtime tries to parse the request body as a JSON object for getting needed information for setting your custom type properties. If you decide to use HttpRequest for the type of the trigger input parameter, you get full access to the request object.

Every Azure Function App that you deploy automatically exposes a group of admin endpoints that you can use for accessing programmatically some aspects of your app, such as the status of the host. These endpoints look like

```
https://<your_function_app_name>.azurewebsites.net/admin/host/status
```

By default, these endpoints are protected by an access code or authentication key that you can manage from your Function App in the Azure portal, as shown in Figure 1-12.

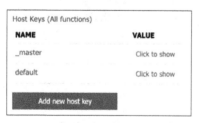

FIGURE 1-12 Managing host keys for a Function App

When you use the HTTP trigger, any endpoint that you publish is also protected by the same mechanism, although the keys that you use for protecting those endpoints are different. You can configure two types of authorization keys:

- **host**   These keys are shared by all functions deployed in the Function App. This type of key allows access to any function in the host.
- **function**   These keys only protect the function where they are defined.

When you define a new key, you assign a name to the key. If you have two keys of a different type—host and function—with the same name, the function key takes precedence. There are also two default keys—one per type of key—that you can also use for accessing your endpoints. These default keys take precedence over any other key that you created. If you need access to the admin endpoints that I mentioned earlier, you need to use a particular host key called _master. You also need to use this administrative key when you set the admin value to the AuthLevel trigger configuration parameter. You can provide the appropriate key when you make a request to your API by using the code parameter or using the x-function-key HTTP header.

Protecting your endpoints using the authorization keys is not a recommended practice for production environments. You should only use authorization keys on testing or development environments for controlling the access to your API. For a production environment, you should use one of the following approaches:

- **Enable Function App Authorization/Authentication**   This integrates your API with Azure Active Directory or other third-party identity providers to authenticate clients.
- **Use Azure API Management (APIM)**   This secures the incoming request to your API, such as filtering by IP address or using authentication based on certificates.
- **Deploy your function in an App Service Environment (ASE)**   ASEs provides dedicated hosting environments that allow you to configure a single front-end gateway that can authenticate all incoming requests.

If you decide to use any of the previous security methods, you need to ensure that you configure the AuthLevel as anonymous. You can see this configuration in Listing 1-13 in this line:

```
HttpTrigger(AuthorizationLevel.Anonymous…
```

When you enable the App Service Authentication/Authorization, you can access the information about the authentication users by reading special HTTP headers set by the App Service. These special headers cannot be set by external resources; they can be set only by the App Service. For ASP.NET projects, the framework automatically fills a ClaimsPrincipal object with the authentication information. You can use ClaimsPrincipal as an additional parameter of your function signature or from the code—using the request context—as shown previously in Listing 1-13.

```
ClaimsPrincipal identities = req.HttpContext.User;
string username = identities.Identity?.Name;
```

As described in this section, Azure Functions runtime exposes your function by default using the following URL schema:

```
https://<your_function_app_name>.azurewebsites.net/api/<your_function_name>
```

You can customize the endpoint by using the route HTTPTrigger parameter. In Listing 1-13, you set the route parameter to devices/{id:int?}. This means that your endpoint looks like this:

```
https://<your_function_app_name>.azurewebsites.net/api/devices/{id:int?}
```

When you customize the route for your function, you can also add parameters to the route, which are accessible to your code by adding them as parameters of your function's signature. You can use any Web API Route Constraint (see *https://www.asp.net/web-api/overview/web-api-routing-and-actions/attribute-routing-in-web-api-2#constraints*) that you may use when defining a route using Web API 2.

By default, when you make a request to a function that uses an HTTP trigger, the response is an empty body with these status codes:

```
HTTP 200 OK in case of Function 1.x runtime
HTTP 204 No Content in case of Function 2.x runtime
```

If you need to customize the response of your function, you need to configure an output binding. You can use any of the two types of output bindings, using the return statement or a function parameter. Listing 1-13 shows how to configure the output binding for returning a JSON object with some information.

It is important to remember the limits associated with the function when you plan to deploy your function in a production environment. These limits are

- **Maximum request length**   The HTTP request should not be larger than 100 MB.
- **Maximum URL length**   Your custom URL is limited to 4096 bytes.
- **Execution timeout**   Your function should return a value in less than 230 seconds. Your function can take more time to execute, but if it doesn't return anything before that time, the gateway will time out with an HTTP 502 error. If your function needs to take more time to execute, you should use an async pattern and return a ping endpoint to allow the caller to ask for the status of the execution of your function.

NEED MORE REVIEW?   **HOST PROPERTIES**

You can also make some adjustments to the host where your function is running by using the host.json file. Visit the following article for reviewing all the properties available in the host.json file at *https://docs.microsoft.com/en-us/azure/azure-functions/functions-bindings-http-webhook#trigger---hostjson-properties*.

You can also review which are the limits associated with the different framework versions and hosting plans by reviewing the article at *https://docs.microsoft.com/en-us/azure/azure-functions/functions-scale*.

Implement Azure Durable Functions

One crucial characteristic of Azure functions is that they are stateless. This characteristic means that function runtime does not maintain the state of the objects that you create during the execution of the function if the host process or the VM where the function is running is recycled or rebooted.

Azure Durable Functions are an extension of the Azure Functions that provide stateful workflow capabilities in a serverless environment. These stateful workflow capabilities allow you to

- **Chain function calls together** This chaining means that a function can call other functions, which maintains the status between calls. These calls can be synchronous or asynchronous.

- **Define workflow by code** You don't need to create JSON workflow definitions or use external tools.

- **Ensure that the status of the workflow is always consistent** When a function or activity on a workflow needs to wait for other functions or activities, the workflow engine automatically creates checkpoints for saving the status of the activity.

The main advantage of using Azure Durable Functions is that it eases the implementation of complex stateful coordination requirements in serverless scenarios. Although Durable Azure Functions is an extension of Azure Functions, at the time of this writing, it doesn't support all languages supported by Azure Functions. The following languages are supported:

- **C#** Both precompiled class libraries and C# script are supported.

- **F#** Precompiled class libraries and F# script are supported. F# script is available only for Azure Functions runtime 1.x.

- **JavaScript** Supported only for Azure Functions runtime version 2.x runtime. Version 1.7.0 or later or Azure Durable Functions is required.

Durable Functions are billed using the same rules that apply to Azure Functions. That is, you are charged only for the time that your functions are running.

Working with Durable Functions means that you need to deal with different kinds of functions. Each type of function plays a different role in the execution of the workflow. These roles are

- **Activity** These are the functions that do the real work. An activity is a job that you need your workflow to do. For example, you may need your code to send a document to a content reviewer before other activity can publish the document, or you need to create a shipment order to send products to a client.

- **Orchestrator** Any workflow executes activity functions in a particular order. Orchestrator functions define the actions that a workflow executes. These actions can be activity functions, timers, or waiting for external events or suborchestrations. Each instance of an orchestrator function has an instance identifier. You can generate this identifier manually or leave the Durable Function framework to generate it dynamically.

- **Client** This is the entry point of a workflow. Triggers such as HTTP, queue, or event triggers create instances of a client function. Client functions create instances of orchestrator functions by sending an orchestrator trigger.

In the same way that Azure Functions uses triggers and bindings for sending and receiving information from functions, you need to use triggers and bindings for setting the communication between the different types of durable functions. Durable functions add two new triggers to control the execution of orchestration and activity functions:

- **Orchestration trigger** These allow you to work with orchestration functions by creating new instances of the function or resuming instances that are waiting for a task. The most important characteristic of these triggers is that they are single-threaded. When you use orchestration triggers, you need to ensure that your code does not perform async calls—other than waiting for durable function tasks—or I/O operations. This ensures that the orchestration function is focused on calling activity functions in the correct order and waiting for the correct events or functions.

- **Activity trigger** This is the type of trigger that you need to use when writing your activity functions. These triggers allow communications between orchestration functions and activity functions. They are multithreaded and don't have any restrictions related to threading or I/O operations.

The following example shows how the different types of functions and triggers work together for processing and saving a hypothetical order generated from an external application and saved to a Cosmos DB database. Although the example is quite simple, it shows how the different functions interact. Figure 1-13 shows a diagram of the workflow implemented on the functions shown in Listings 1-14 to 1-21. For running this example, you need to meet the following requirements:

- An Azure subscription.

- An Azure Storage Account. The orchestration function needs an Azure Storage Account for saving the status of each durable function instance during the execution of the workflow.

- An Azure Cosmos DB database.

- Install the following dependencies using this command:

  ```
  func extensions install -p <package_name> -v <package_version>
  ```

- Cosmos DB:

  - Package name: Microsoft.Azure.WebJobs.Extensions.CosmosDB
  - Version: 3.0.3

- Durable Functions extension:
  - Package name: Microsoft.Azure.WebJobs.Extensions.DurableTask
  - Version: 1.8.0

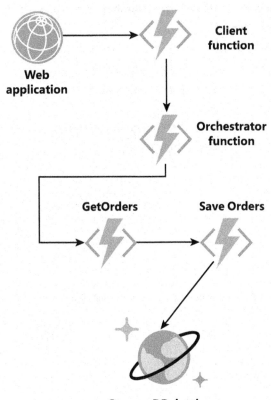

FIGURE 1-13 Durable function workflow

You can run this example using your favorite Integrated Development Environment (IDE). Visual Studio and Visual Studio Code offer several tools that make working with Azure projects more comfortable. Use the following steps for configuring your Visual Studio Code and creating the durable functions:

1. Open your Visual Studio Code.

2. Click the Extensions icon on the left side of the window.

3. On the Extensions panel, on the Search Extensions In Marketplace text box, type **Azure Functions**.

4. In the result list, on the Azure Functions extension, click the Install button. Depending on your Visual Studio Code version, you may need to restart Visual Studio Code.

5. Click the Azure icon on the left side of the Visual Studio Code window.

6. In the Functions section, click Sign In To Azure For Log Into Azure.

7. In the Functions section, click the lightning bolt icon, which creates a new Azure Function.

8. In the Create New Project dialog box, select JavaScript.

9. In the Select A Template For Your Project's First Function dialog box, select HTTP Trigger.

10. For the Provide A Function Name option, type **HTTPTriggerDurable**. This creates the first function that you need for this example.

11. Select Anonymous for the Authorization Level.

12. Select Open In Current Window to open the project that you just created.

Repeat steps 5 to 12 for all the Durable Functions that you need for this example. It is important to save all the functions you need in the same folder.

Listings 1-14 and 1-15 show the JavaScript code and the JSON configuration file that you need to create the client function that calls the orchestration function.

LISTING 1-14 Azure Durable Functions client function code

```
// NodeJS. HTTPTriggerDurable/index.js
const df = require("durable-functions");

module.exports = async function (context, req) {
    context.log('JavaScript Durable Functions example');
    const client = df.getClient(context);
    const instanceId = await client.startNew(req.params.functionName, undefined,
req.body);

    context.log('Started orchestration with ID = '${instanceId}'.');

    return client.createCheckStatusResponse(context.bindingData.req, instanceId);
};
```

LISTING 1-15 Durable Functions—Client function JSON configuration file

```
{
  "disabled": false,
  "bindings": [
    {
      "authLevel": "anonymous",
      "type": "httpTrigger",
      "direction": "in",
      "name": "req",
      "route": "orchestrators/{functionName}",
      "methods": [
        "get",
        "post"
      ]
    },
```

```
  {
    "type": "http",
    "direction": "out",
    "name": "$return"
  },
  {
    "name": "context",
    "type": "orchestrationClient",
    "direction": "in"
  }
  ]
}
```

Listings 1-16 and 1-17 show the JavaScript code and the JSON configuration file that you need to create the Orchestration function that invokes, in the correct order, all the other activity functions. This function also returns to the client's function the results of the execution of the different activity functions.

LISTING 1-16   Azure Durable Functions Orchestrator function code

```
// NodeJS. OrchestratorFunction/index.js
const df = require("durable-functions");

module.exports = df.orchestrator(function*(context) {
    context.log("Starting workflow: chain example");

    const order = yield context.df.callActivity("GetOrder");
    const savedOrder = yield context.df.callActivity("SaveOrder", order);

    return savedOrder;
});
```

LISTING 1-17   Durable Functions—Orchestrator function JSON configuration file

```
{
  "disabled": false,
  "bindings": [
    {
      "type": "orchestrationTrigger",
      "direction": "in",
      "name": "context"
    }
  ]
}
```

Listings 1-18 and 1-19 show the JavaScript code and the JSON configuration file that you need to create the activity function Get Order. In this example, this function is in charge of constructing the information that is used in the Save Order function. In a more complex scenario, this function could get information from the user's shopping cart from an e-commerce system or any other potential source.

LISTING 1-18 Azure Durable Functions activity function code

```
// NodeJS. GetOrder/index.js
module.exports = async function (context) {
    //Create a mock order for testing
    var order = {
        "id" : Math.floor(Math.random() * 1000),
        "name" : "Customer",
        "date" : new Date().toJSON()
    }
    context.log(order);
    return order;

};
```

LISTING 1-19 Azure Durable Functions activity function JSON configuration file

```
{
  "disabled": false,
  "bindings": [
    {
      "type": "activityTrigger",
      "direction": "in",
      "name": "name"
    }
  ]
}
```

Listings 1-20 and 1-21 show the JavaScript code and the JSON configuration file that you need to create the activity function that saves the order in a Cosmos DB database. In a much more complex scenario, you could use this function to insert the order into your ERP system or send it to another activity function that could do further analysis or processing.

LISTING 1-20 Azure Durable Functions activity function code

```
// NodeJS. SaveOrder/index.js
module.exports = async function (context) {

    //Saves the order object received from other activities to a CosmosDB document
    context.bindings.orderDocument = JSON.stringify({
```

```
        "id": '${context.bindings.order.id}',
        "customerName": context.bindings.order.name,
        "orderDate": context.bindings.order.date,
        "cosmosDate": new Date().toJSON()
    });
    context.done();
};
```

LISTING 1-21 Azure Durable Functions activity function JSON configuration file

```
{
  "disabled": false,
  "bindings": [
    {
      "type": "activityTrigger",
      "direction": "in",
      "name": "order"
    }
    ,
    {
      "name": "orderDocument",
      "type": "cosmosDB",
      "databaseName": "ERP_Database",
      "collectionName": "Orders",
      "createIfNotExists": true,
      "connectionStringSetting": "CosmosDBStorage",
      "direction": "out"
    }
  ]
}
```

The entry point in any workflow implemented using Durable Functions is always a client function. This function uses the orchestration client for calling the orchestrator function. Listing 1-15 shows how to configure the output binding.

```
{
  "name": "context",
  "type": "orchestrationClient",
  "direction": "in"
}
```

When you are using JavaScript for programming your client function, the orchestrator client output binding is not directly exposed using the value of the name attribute set in the function. json configuration file. In this case, you need to extract the actual client from the context variable using the getClient() function declared in the durable-functions package, as shown in Listing 1-14.

```
const client = df.getClient(context);
```

Once you have the correct reference to the orchestrator client output binding, you can use the method startNew() for creating a new instance of the orchestrator function. The parameters for this method are

- **Name of the orchestrator function**   In the example, you get this name from the HTTP request, using the URL parameter functionName, as previously shown in Listings 1-14 and 1-15.

- **InstanceId**   Sets the Id assigned to the new instance of the orchestration function. If you don't provide a value to this parameter, then the method creates a random Id. In general, you should use the autogenerated random Id.

- **Input**   This is where you place any data that your orchestration function may need. You need to use JSON-serializable data for this parameter.

Once you have created the instance of the orchestration function and saved the *Id* associated with the instance, the client function returns a data structure with several useful HTTP endpoints. You can use these endpoints to review the status of the execution of the workflow, or terminate the workflow, or send external events to the workflow during the execution. Following is an example of the workflow management endpoints for the execution of the example in a local computer environment:

> **NOTE   CONSOLE OUTPUT**
>
> For the shake of the space, some lines have been trimmed. Your output should show longer lines, including the instance id and other codes.
>
> ```
> {
>     "id": "789e7eb945a04ab78e74e9216870af28",
>     "statusQueryGetUri": "http://localhost:7071/runtime/webhooks/durabletask/
> instances…",
>     "sendEventPostUri": "http://localhost:7071/runtime/webhooks/durabletask/
> instances…",
>     "terminatePostUri": "http://localhost:7071/runtime/webhooks/durabletask/
> instances…",
>     "rewindPostUri": "http://localhost:7071/runtime/webhooks/durabletask/
> instances…",
> "purgeHistoryDeleteUri": "http://localhost:7071/runtime/webhooks/durabletask/
> instances."
> }
> ```

This example uses an Azure Function based on an HTTP trigger, but your client function is not limited to use this trigger. You can use any of the triggers available in the Azure Function framework.

Once you have created the instance of the orchestrator function, this function calls the activity functions by the order defined in the code, as previously shown in Listing 1-16.

```
const order = yield context.df.callActivity("GetOrder");
const savedOrder = yield context.df.callActivity("SaveOrder", order);
```

The orchestrator function uses an orchestration trigger for getting the information that the client function sends when it creates the instance. The orchestration trigger creates the instances of the different activity functions by using the callActivity() method of the durable-functions package. This method takes two parameters:

- **Name of the activity function**
- **Input**   You put here any JSON-serializable data that you want to send to the activity function.

In the example, you execute the activity function GetOrder, previously shown in Listing 1-18, for getting the order object that you use as the input parameter for the next activity function SaveOrder, previously shown in Listing 1-20, for saving the information in the Cosmos DB database configured in Listing 1-21.

You can test this example on your local computer by running the functions that reviewed in this section, in the same way that you test any other Azure Function. Once you have your function running, you can test it by using curl or postman. You should make a GET or POST HTTP request to this URL: *http://localhost:7071/api/orchestrators/OrchestratorFunction*.

Notice that the parameter functionName of the URL matches with the name of the orchestrator function. Your client function allows you to call different orchestration functions just by providing the correct orchestration function name.

You can use different patterns when you are programming the orchestration function. These patterns show how the orchestration and activity functions interact with each other:

- **Chaining**   The activity functions are executed in a specific order, where the output of one activity function is the input of the next one. This is the pattern that you used in your example.
- **Fan out/fan in**   Your orchestration function executes multiple activity functions in parallel. The result of these parallel activity functions is processed and aggregated by a final aggregation activity function.
- **Async HTTP APIs**   This pattern coordinates the state of long-running operations with external clients.
- **Monitor**   This pattern allows you to create recurrent tasks using flexible time intervals.
- **Human Interaction**   Use this pattern when you need to run activity functions based on events that a person can trigger. An example of this type of pattern is the document approval workflow, where publishing a document depends on the approval of a person.

> **NEED MORE REVIEW?**   **DURABLE FUNCTION PATTERNS**
>
> You can get more information about Durable Function patterns by reviewing the article Patterns and Concepts in Microsoft Docs at *https://docs.microsoft.com/en-us/azure/azure-functions/durable/durable-functions-concepts*.

EXAM TIP

When working with Azure Durable Functions, remember that you can pass information between the different functions in the workflow by using the binding mechanism.

Chapter summary

- Azure provides computing services for deploying your own virtualized infrastructure directly in the cloud. You can also deploy hybrid architectures to connect your on-premises infrastructure with your IaaS resources.

- Azure Resource Manager is the service in Azure that manages the different resources that you can deploy in the cloud. You can define the resources and their dependencies by using a JSON-based file called an ARM template.

- A container image is a package of software in which you store your code and any library or dependencies for running your application in a highly portable environment.

- When you create a new instance of a container image, each of these instances is named a "container."

- You can store your container images in a centralized store called a registry.

- Azure Container Registry is a managed registry, which is based on the open-source specification of Docker Registry 2.0.

- You can run your containers in several Azure services, such as Azure Managed Kubernetes Service, Azure Container Instance, Azure Batch, Azure App Service, or Azure Container Service.

- Azure provides you with needed services for deploying serverless solutions, allowing you to center on the code and forget about the infrastructure.

- Azure App Services is the base of the serverless offering. On top of App Services, you can deploy web apps, mobile back-end apps, REST APIs, or Azure Functions and Azure Durable Functions.

- When you work with App Services, you are charged only by the time that your code is running.

- App Services runs on top of App Services Plans.

- An App Service Plan provides the resources and virtual machines needed for running your App Services code.

- You can run more than one App Service on top of a single App Service Plan.

- When troubleshooting your App Service application, you can use several types for diagnostics logging: webserver logging and diagnostics, detailed error, failed requests, application diagnostics, and deployment diagnostics.

- Diagnostics logging is stored locally on the VM, where the instance of your application is running.

- Horizontal scaling or in-out scaling is the process of adding or removing instances of an application.

- Vertical scaling or up-down scaling is the process of adding or removing resources to the same virtual machine that hosts your application.

- Scale In/Out doesn't have an effect on the availability of the application.

- Vertical scaling affects the availability of the application because the application needs to be deployed in a virtual machine with the new resources assignment.

- You can add and remove resources to your applications by using autoscale rules.

- You can apply autoscale only to some Azure Resource types.

- Autoscale depends on Azure virtual machine scale sets.

- Your application needs to be aware of the changes in the resources assignment.

- Azure Functions is the evolution of WebJobs.

- Azure Functions use triggers and bindings for creating instances of Azure functions and sending or receiving data to or from external services, like Queue storage or Event Hub.

- There are three versions of Azure Functions. Version 1.0 only supports .NET Framework and Windows environments. Version 2.0 and later support .NET Core and Windows and Linux environments.

- When you work with triggers and bindings, you need to install the appropriate NuGet package for function extension that contains that trigger or binding.

- Azure Function runtime already includes extensions for Timers and HTTP triggers. You don't need to install specific packages for using these trigger bindings.

- Triggers that create function instances can be based on data operations, timers, or webhooks.

- Azure Durable Functions is the evolution of Azure Functions that allow you to create workflows where the state of the instances is preserved in case of VM restart or function host process respawn.

- Orchestration functions define the activity and the order of execution of the functions that do the job.

- Activity functions contain the code that makes the action that you need for a step in the workflow, like sending an email, saving a document, or inserting information in a database.

- Client functions create the instance of the orchestration function using an orchestration client.

- Azure Function Apps provides the resources needed for running Azure Functions and Durable Functions.

Thought experiment

In this Thought Experiment, you can demonstrate your skills and knowledge about the topics covered in this chapter. You can find the answers to this Thought Experiment in the next section.

You are developing an application for making the integration between several systems. One of the systems is a legacy application that generates some reports in a specific file format. Those file reports are uploaded to an Azure Storage account. Your application reads the information from these file reports and inserts the information in different destination systems. Answer the following questions related to the described scenario:

1. Before your application can insert information on the destination, the information needs to be approved. This approval workflow needs to start when a new report file is added to the Azure Storage Account. Which Azure service best fits your needs?

2. Your application is suffering from performance issues. The performance issues only happen during some days in the month. You need to ensure that your application doesn't suffer performance issues during the usage peaks. How can you achieve this?

Thought experiment answers

This section contains the solutions to the Thought Experiment.

1. As the information needs to be approved before it can be inserted in the target systems, you should use Azure Durable Functions. By implementing a Human Interaction pattern, you can wait for the information to be validated before inserting it into the correct destination system. You can also use Azure Blob Storage triggers for starting the workflow. Because you need to wait for human confirmation, you should use Azure Durable Function instead of Azure Functions.

2. You can deploy Azure Durable Functions to Azure App Service Plans. Starting with the Standard pricing tier, you can configure Autoscale rules for your Azure App Service Plan. Using autoscale rules, you can add or remove resources to the App Service Plan based on your needs. In this scenario, you can add more resources based on CPU consumption or during specific days. Because no specific pattern has been described in the scenario, you should first study the usage pattern before configure the appropriate autoscale rules.

CHAPTER 2

Develop for Azure storage

All applications work with information or data. Applications create, transform, model, or operate with that information. Regardless of the type or volume of the data that your application uses, sooner or later, you need to save it persistently so that it can be used later.

Storing data is not a simple task, and designing storage systems for that purpose is even more complicated. Perhaps your application needs to deal with terabytes of information, or you may work with an application that needs to be accessed from different countries, and you need to minimize the time required to access it. Also, cost efficiency is a requirement in any project. In general, many requirements make designing and maintaining storage systems difficult.

Microsoft Azure offers different storage solutions in the cloud to satisfy your application storage requirements. Azure offers solutions for making your storage cost-effective and minimizing latency.

Skills covered in this chapter:

- Skill 2.1: Develop solutions that use Cosmos DB storage
- Skill 2.2: Develop solutions that use Blob Storage

Skill 2.1: Develop solutions that use Cosmos DB storage

Cosmos DB is a premium storage service that Azure provides for satisfying your need for a globally distributed, low-latency, highly responsive, and always-online database service. Cosmos DB has been designed with scalability and throughput in mind. One of the most significant differences between Cosmos DB and other storage services offered by Azure is how easily you can scale your Cosmos DB solution across the globe by merely clicking a button and adding a new region to your database.

Another essential feature that you should consider when evaluating this type of storage service is how you can access this service from your code and how hard it would be to migrate your existing code to a Cosmos DB–based storage solution. The good news is that Cosmos DB offers different APIs for accessing the service. The best API for you depends on the type of data that you want to store in your Cosmos DB database. You store your data using Key-Value, Column-Family, Documents, or Graph approaches. Each of the different APIs that Cosmos DB offers allows you to store your data with different schemas. Currently, you can access Cosmos DB using SQL, Cassandra, Table, Gremlin, and MongoDB APIs.

Select the appropriate API for your solution

When you are planning how to store the information that your application needs to work, you need to consider the structure that you need to use for storing that information. You may find that some parts of your application need to store information using a Key-Value structure. In contrast, others may need a more flexible, schemaless structure in which you need to save the information into documents. Maybe one fundamental characteristic of your application is that you need to store the relationship between entities, and you need to use a graph structure for storing your data.

Cosmos DB offers a variety of APIs for storing and accessing your data, depending on the requirements that your application has:

- **SQL** This is the core and default API for accessing your data in your Cosmos DB account. This core API allows you to query JSON objects using SQL syntax, which means you don't need to learn another query language. Under the hood, the SQL API uses the JavaScript programming model for expression evaluation, function invocations, and typing system. You use this API when you need to use a data structure based on documents.

- **Table** You can think of the Table API as the evolution of the Azure Table Storage service. This API benefits from the high-performance, low-latency, and high-scalability features of Cosmos DB. You can migrate from your current Azure Table Storage service with no code modification in your application. Another critical difference between Table API for Cosmos DB and Azure Table Storage is that you can define your own indexes in your tables. In the same way that you can do with the Table Storage service, Table API allows you to store information in your Cosmos DB account using a data structure based on documents.

- **Cassandra** Cosmos DB implements the wire protocol for the Apache Cassandra database into the options for storing and accessing data in the Cosmos DB database. This allows you to forget about operations and performance-management tasks related to managing Cassandra databases. In most situations, you can migrate your application from your current Cassandra database to Cosmos DB using the Cassandra API by merely changing the connection string. Azure Cosmos DB Cassandra API is compatible with the CQLv4 wire protocol. Cassandra is a column-based database that stores information using a key-value approach.

- **MongoDB**   You can access your Cosmos DB account by using the MongoDB API. This NoSQL database allows you to store the information for your application in a document-based structure. Cosmos DB implements the wire protocol compatible with MongoDB 3.2. This means that any MongoDB 3.2 client driver that implements and understands this protocol definition can connect seamlessly with your Cosmos DB database using the MongoDB API.

- **Gremlin**   Based on the Apache TinkerPop graph transversal language or Gremlin, this API allows you to store information in Cosmos DB using a graph structure. This means that instead of storing only entities, you store

  - **Vertices**   You can think of a vertex as an entity in other information structures. In a typical graph structure, a vertex could be a person, a device, or an event.

  - **Edges**   These are the relationships between vertices. A person can know another person, a person might own a type of device, or a person may attend an event.

  - **Properties**   These are each of the attributes that you can assign to a vertex or an edge.

Beware that you cannot mix these APIs in a single Cosmos DB account. You need to define the API that you want to use for accessing your Cosmos DB account when you are creating the account. Once you have created the account, you won't be able to change the API for accessing it.

Azure offers SDKs for working with the different APIs that you can use for connecting to Cosmos DB. Supported languages are .NET, Java, Node.js, and Python. Depending on the API that you want to use for working with Cosmos DB, you can also use other languages like Xamarin, Golang, or PHP. In this section, you can review an example of each API and learn how to create, read, update, and delete data using the different APIs.

Before starting with the examples, you need to create a Cosmos DB account for storing your data. The following procedure shows how to create a Cosmos DB free account with the SQL API. You can use this same procedure for creating accounts with the other APIs we have reviewed in this skill:

1. Sign in to the Azure portal (*http://portal.azure.com*).

2. In the top-left corner in the Azure portal, click the menu icon represented by three horizontal bars, and then click Create A Resource.

3. On the New panel, under the Azure Marketplace column, click Databases. On the Featured column, click Azure Cosmos DB.

4. On the Create Azure Cosmos DB Account blade, in the Resource Group drop-down menu, click the Create New link below the drop-down menu. In the pop-up dialog box, type a name for the new Resource Group. Alternatively, you can select an existing Resource Group from the drop-down menu.

5. In the Instance Details section, type an Account Name.

6. In the API drop-down menu, ensure that you have selected the option Core (SQL), as shown in Figure 2-1.

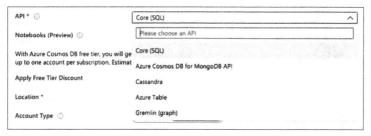

FIGURE 2-1 Selecting a Cosmos DB API

7. Ensure that the Notebooks switch is set to Off.

8. Ensure that the Apply Free Tier Discount switch is set to Apply.

9. On the Location drop-down menu, select the region most appropriate for you. If you are using App Services or virtual machines, you should select the same region in which you deployed those services.

10. In the Account Type, set the value Non-Production.

11. Leave Geo-Redundancy and Multi-Region Write disabled.

12. In the bottom-left corner of the Create Azure Cosmos DB Account blade, click the Review + Create button.

13. In the bottom-left corner of the Review + Create tab, click the Create button to start the deployment of your Cosmos DB account.

> **NOTE** **AZURE COSMOS DB EMULATOR**
> You can use the Azure Cosmos DB emulator during the development stage of your application. You should bear in mind that there are some limitations when working with the emulator instead of a real Cosmos DB account. The emulator is only supported on Windows platforms or Docker for Windows. You can review all characteristics of the Cosmos DB emulator at *https://docs.microsoft.com/en-us/azure/cosmos-db/local-emulator.*

> **EXAM TIP**
> You can use different APIs for accessing your Cosmos DB database. Each API offers different feature depending on the way you need to represent your data. Remember that you cannot change the API once you have created your Cosmos DB database.

Implement partitioning schemes

When you save data to your Cosmos DB account—independently of the API that you decide to use for accessing your data—Azure places the data in different servers to accommodate the performance and throughput that you require from a premium storage service like Cosmos DB. The storage services use partitions to distribute the data. Cosmos DB slices your data into smaller pieces called partitions that are placed on the storage server. There are two different types of partitions when working with Cosmos DB:

- **Logical** You can divide a Cosmos DB container into smaller pieces based on your criteria. Each of these smaller pieces is a logical partition. All items stored in a logical partition share the same partition key.
- **Physical** These partitions are a group of replicas of your data that is physically stored on the servers. Azure automatically manages this group of replicas or replica sets. A physical partition can contain one or more logical partitions.

> **NEED MORE REVIEW?** **PHYSICAL PARTITION**
>
> The only control that you have on how the data is distributed across physical partitions is setting the partition keys. If you want to review how the logical partitions and physical partitions are related to each other, consult the following article: *https://docs.microsoft.com/en-us/ azure/cosmos-db/partition-data#physical-partitions*.

By default, any logical partition has a limit of 20 GB for storing data. When you are configuring a new collection, you need to decide whether you want your collection to be stored in a single logical partition and keep it under the limit of 20 GB or allow it to grow over that limit and span across different logical partitions. If you need your container to split over several partitions, Cosmos DB needs some way to know how to distribute your data across the different logical partitions. This is where the partition key comes into play. Bear in mind that this partition key is immutable, which means you cannot change the property that you want to use as the partition key once you have selected it.

Choosing the correct partition key is critical for achieving the best performance. The reason choosing the proper partition key is so important is because Azure creates a logical partition for each distinct value of your partition key. Listing 2-1 shows an example of a JSON document.

LISTING 2-1 Example JSON document

```
{
    "id": "1",
    "firstName": "Santiago",
    "lastName": "Fernández",
    "city": "Sevilla",
    "country": "Spain"
}
```

Depending on your data, city or country properties would be the right choice for the partition key. You can find in your data that some documents have the same value for the country property, so they are stored together in the same logical partition. Using the id property as the partition key means that you end with a logical partition with a single document on each partition. This configuration can be beneficial when your application usually performs read workloads and uses parallelization techniques for getting the data.

On the other hand, if you select a partition key with just a few possible values, you can end with "hot" partitions. A "hot" partition is a partition that receives most of the requests when working with your data. The main implication for these "hot" partitions is that they usually reach the throughput limit for the partition, which means you need to provision more throughput. Another potential drawback is that you can reach the limit of 20 GB for a single logical partition. Because a logical partition is the scope for efficient multidocument transactions, selecting a partition key with a few possible values allows you to execute transactions on many documents inside the same partition.

Use the following guidelines when selecting your partition key:

- The storage limit for a single logical partition is 20 GB. If you foresee that your data would require more space for each value of the partition, you should select another partition key.

- The requests to a single logical partition cannot exceed the throughput limit for that partition. If your requests reach that limit, they are throttled to avoid exceeding the limit. If you reach this limit frequently, you should select another partition key because there is a good chance that you have a "hot" partition. The minimum throughput limit is different from databases to containers. The minimum throughput for databases is 100 request units per second (RU/s). The minimum throughput for containers is 400 RU/s.

- Choose partition keys with a wide range of values and access patterns that can evenly distribute requests across logical partitions. This allows you to achieve the right balance between being able to execute cross-document transactions and scalability. Using timestamp-based partition keys is usually a lousy choice for a partition key.

- Review your workload requirements. The partition key that you choose should allow your application to perform well on reading and writing workloads.

- The parameters that you usually use on your requests and filtering queries are good candidates for a partition key.

> **NEED MORE REVIEW? PARTITIONING**
>
> You can review more information about how partitioning works reviewing the following article: *https://docs.microsoft.com/en-us/azure/cosmos-db/partitioning-overview*

There could be situations where none of the properties of your items are appropriate for the partition keys. In those situations, you can create synthetic partition keys. A synthetic partition key is a key compound of two concatenated properties. In our previous document example shown in Listing 2-1, you created a new property named partitionKey containing a string that concatenates the values of city and country. For the example document, the value of the partitionKey should be *Sevilla-Spain*.

EXAM TIP

Remember that your data is distributed across the different logic partitions by using the partition key. For this reason, once you have chosen a partition key, you cannot change it.

Interact with data using the appropriate SDK

Cosmos DB allows you to access data using different types of APIs. Once you have your Cosmos DB account ready, you can start creating your databases and containers for working with data. Remember that once you choose the API for your Cosmos DB account, you cannot change it.

The following example shows how to create a console application using .NET Core. The first example uses Cosmos DB SQL API for creating, updating, and deleting some elements in the Cosmos DB account:

1. Open Visual Studio Code and create a directory for storing the example project.

2. Open the Terminal, switch to the project's directory, and type the following command:

   `dotnet new console`

3. Install the NuGet package for interacting with your Cosmos DB account using the SQL API. Type the following command in the Terminal:

   `dotnet add package Microsoft.Azure.Cosmos`

4. Change the content of the Program.cs file using the content provided in Listing 2-2. You need to change the namespace according to your project's name.

5. Sign in to the Azure portal (*http://portal.azure.com*).

6. In the Search box at the top of the Azure portal, type the name of your Cosmos DB account and click the name of the account.

7. On your Cosmos DB Account blade, in the Settings section, click Keys.

8. On the Keys panel, copy the URI and Primary Keys values from the Read-Write Keys tab. You need to provide these values to the EndpointUri and Key Constants in the code shown in Listing 2-2. (The most important parts of the code are shown with bold format.)

LISTING 2-2 Cosmos DB SQL API example

```
//C# .NET Core. Program.cs
using System.Collections.Immutable;
using System.Xml.Linq;
using System.Diagnostics;
using System.Runtime.CompilerServices;
```

```csharp
using System;

using System.Linq;
using Microsoft.Azure.Cosmos;
using System.Threading.Tasks;
using ch2_1_3_SQL.Model;
using System.Net;

namespace ch2_1_3_SQL
{
    class Program
    {
        private const string EndpointUri = "<PUT YOUR ENDPOINT URL HERE>";
        private const string Key = "<PUT YOUR COSMOS DB KEY HERE>";
        private CosmosClient client;
        private Database database;
        private Container container;

        static void Main(string[] args)
        {

            try
            {
                Program demo = new Program();
                demo.StartDemo().Wait();
            }
            catch (CosmosException ce)
            {
                Exception baseException = ce.GetBaseException();
                System.Console.WriteLine($"{ce.StatusCode} error ocurred:
                {ce.Message}, Message: {baseException.Message}");
            }
            catch (Exception ex)
            {
                Exception baseException = ex.GetBaseException();
                System.Console.WriteLine($"Error ocurred: {ex.Message}, Message:
                {baseException.Message}");
            }

        }

        private async Task StartDemo()
        {
            Console.WriteLine("Starting Cosmos DB SQL API Demo!");

            //Create a new demo database
```

```
        string databaseName = "demoDB_" + Guid.NewGuid().ToString().
Substring(0, 5);

        this.SendMessageToConsoleAndWait($"Creating database {databaseName}...");

        this.client = new CosmosClient(EndpointUri, Key);
        this.database = await this.client.CreateDatabaseIfNotExistsAsync
(databaseName);

        //Create a new demo collection inside the demo database.
        //This creates a collection with a reserved throughput. You can customize
the options using a ContainerProperties object
        //This operation has pricing implications.
        string containerName = "collection_" + Guid.NewGuid().ToString().
Substring(0, 5);


        this.SendMessageToConsoleAndWait($"Creating collection demo
{containerName}...");

        this.container = await this.database.CreateContainerIfNotExistsAsync
(containerName, "/LastName");

        //Create some documents in the collection
        Person person1 = new Person
        {
            Id = "Person.1",
            FirstName = "Santiago",
            LastName = "Fernandez",
            Devices = new Device[]
            {

                new Device { OperatingSystem = "iOS", CameraMegaPixels = 7,
                Ram = 16, Usage = "Personal"},
                new Device { OperatingSystem = "Android", CameraMegaPixels = 12,
                Ram = 64, Usage = "Work"}
            },
            Gender = "Male",
            Address = new Address
            {
                City = "Seville",
                Country = "Spain",
                PostalCode = "28973",
                Street = "Diagonal",
                State = "Andalucia"
            },
```

```
                IsRegistered = true
        };


        await this.CreateDocumentIfNotExistsAsync(databaseName, containerName,
person1);

        Person person2 = new Person
        {
            Id = "Person.2",
            FirstName = "Agatha",
            LastName = "Smith",
            Devices = new Device[]
            {

                new Device { OperatingSystem = "iOS", CameraMegaPixels = 12,
                Ram = 32, Usage = "Work"},
                new Device { OperatingSystem = "Windows", CameraMegaPixels = 12,
                Ram = 64, Usage = "Personal"}
            },
            Gender = "Female",
            Address = new Address
            {
                City = "Laguna Beach",
                Country = "United States",
                PostalCode = "12345",
                Street = "Main",
                State = "CA"
            },
            IsRegistered = true
        };


        await this.CreateDocumentIfNotExistsAsync(databaseName, containerName,
person2);

        //Make some queries to the collection
        this.SendMessageToConsoleAndWait($"Getting documents from the collection
{containerName}...");

        //Find documents using LINQ

        IQueryable<Person> queryablePeople = this.container.GetItemLinqQueryable
<Person>(true)
            .Where(p => p.Gender == "Male");

        System.Console.WriteLine("Running LINQ query for finding men...");
```

```
                foreach (Person foundPerson in  queryablePeople)
                {
                    System.Console.WriteLine($"\tPerson: {foundPerson}");
                }


                //Find documents using SQL

                var sqlQuery = "SELECT * FROM Person WHERE Person.Gender = 'Female'";

                QueryDefinition queryDefinition = new QueryDefinition(sqlQuery);
                FeedIterator<Person> peopleResultSetIterator = this.container.GetItemQuery
Iterator<Person>(queryDefinition);

                System.Console.WriteLine("Running SQL query for finding women...");
                while (peopleResultSetIterator.HasMoreResults)
                {
                    FeedResponse<Person> currentResultSet = await peopleResultSetIterator.
ReadNextAsync();
                    foreach (Person foundPerson in currentResultSet)
                    {
                        System.Console.WriteLine($"\tPerson: {foundPerson}");
                    }
                }

                Console.WriteLine("Press any key to continue...");
                Console.ReadKey();

                //Update documents in a collection
                this.SendMessageToConsoleAndWait($"Updating documents in the collection
{containerName}...");
                person2.FirstName = "Mathew";
                person2.Gender = "Male";

                await this.container.UpsertItemAsync(person2);
                this.SendMessageToConsoleAndWait($"Document modified {person2}");

                //Delete a single document from the collection
                this.SendMessageToConsoleAndWait($"Deleting documents from the collection
{containerName}...");

                PartitionKey partitionKey = new PartitionKey(person1.LastName);
                await this.container.DeleteItemAsync<Person>(person1.Id, partitionKey);
                this.SendMessageToConsoleAndWait($"Document deleted {person1}");

                //Delete created demo database and all its children elements
                this.SendMessageToConsoleAndWait("Cleaning-up your Cosmos DB account...");
```

```
            await this.database.DeleteAsync();
        }
        private void SendMessageToConsoleAndWait(string message)
        {
            Console.WriteLine(message);
            Console.WriteLine("Press any key to continue...");
            Console.ReadKey();
        }


        private async Task CreateDocumentIfNotExistsAsync(string database,
string collection, Person person)
        {
            try
            {

                await this?.container.ReadItemAsync<Person>(person.Id,
new PartitionKey(person.LastName));

                this.SendMessageToConsoleAndWait($"Document {person.Id} already exists
in collection {collection}");
            }
            catch (CosmosException dce)
            {
                if (dce.StatusCode == HttpStatusCode.NotFound)
                {

                    await this?.container.CreateItemAsync<Person>(person,
new PartitionKey(person.LastName));

                    this.SendMessageToConsoleAndWait($"Created new document
{person.Id} in collection {collection}");
                }
            }
        }
    }
}
```

When you work with the SQL API, the Azure Cosmos DB SDK provides you with the appro-priate classes for working with the different elements of the account. In the example shown in Listing 2-2, you need to create a CosmosClient object before you can access your Azure Cosmos DB account. The Azure Cosmos DB SDK also provides you with the classes Database and Container for working with these elements. When you need to create a Database or a Container, you can use CreateDatabaseIfNotExistsAsync or CreateContainerIfNotExistsAsync, respectively. These IfNotExists methods automatically check to determine whether the

Container or Database exists in your Cosmos DB account; if they don't exist, the method automatically creates the Container or the Database. When you create a new container in your database, notice that in this example, you have provided the PartitionKey using the appropriate constructor overload.

However, when you need to create a new document in the database, you don't have available this type of IfNotExists method. In this situation, you have two options:

1. Use the method UpsertItemAsync, which creates a new document if the document doesn't exist or updates an existing document.

2. Implement your own version of the IfNotExists method, so you need to check whether the document already exists in the container. If the document doesn't exist, then you create the actual document, as shown in the following fragment from Listing 2-2. (The code in bold shows the methods that you need to use for creating a document.)

```
try
{

    await this?.container.ReadItemAsync<Person>(person.Id, new PartitionKey
(person.LastName));

    this.SendMessageToConsoleAndWait($"Document {person.Id} already exists in
collection {collection}");
}
catch (CosmosException dce)
{
    if (dce.StatusCode == HttpStatusCode.NotFound)
    {

        await this?.container.CreateItemAsync<Person>(person,
new PartitionKey(person.LastName));

        this.SendMessageToConsoleAndWait($"Created new document {person.Id} in
collection {collection}");
    }
}
```

When you create the document using the CreateItemAsync method, notice that you can provide the value for the partition key by using the following code snippet new PartitionKey(person.LastName). If you don't provide the value for the partition key, the correct value is inferred from the document that you are trying to insert into the database.

You need to do this verification because you get a CosmosException with StatusCode 409 (Conflict) if you try to create a document with the same Id of an already existing document in the collection. Similarly, you get a CosmosException with StatusCode 404 (Not Found) if you try to delete a document that doesn't exist in the container using the DeleteItemAsync method or if you try to replace a document that doesn't exist in the container using the ReplaceItemAsync method. Notice that these two methods also accept a partition key parameter.

When you create a document, you need to provide an Id property of type string to your document. This property needs to identify your document inside the collection uniquely. If you don't provide this property, Cosmos DB automatically adds it to the document for you, using a GUID string.

As you can see in the example code in Listing 2-2, you can query your documents using LINQ or SQL sentences. In this example, I have used a pretty simple SQL query for getting documents that represent a person with the male gender. However, you can construct more complex sentences like a query that returns all people who live in a specific country, using the WHERE Address.Country = 'Spain' expression, or people that have an Android device using the WHERE ARRAY_CONTAINS(Person.Devices, { 'OperatingSystem': 'Android'}, true) expression.

> **NEED MORE REVIEW?** **SQL QUERIES WITH COSMOS DB**
>
> You can review all the capabilities and features of the SQL language that Cosmos DB implements by reviewing this article:
>
> - **SQL Language Reference for Azure Cosmos DB** *https://docs.microsoft.com/en-us/ azure/cosmos-db/sql-api-query-reference*

Once you have modified the Program.cs file, you need to create some additional classes that you use in the main program for managing documents. You can find these new classes in Listings 2-3 to 2-5.

1. In the Visual Studio Code window, create a new folder named **Model** in the project folder.

2. Create a new C# class file in the Model folder and name it **Person.cs**.

3. Replace the content of the Person.cs file with the content of Listing 2-3. Change the namespace as needed for your project.

4. Create a new C# class file in the Model folder and name it **Device.cs**.

5. Replace the content of the Device.cs file with the content of Listing 2-4. Change the namespace as needed for your project.

6. Create a new C# class file in the Model folder and name it **Address.cs**.

7. Replace the content of the Address.cs file with the content of Listing 2-5. Change the namespace as needed for your project.

8. At this point, you can run the project by pressing F5 in the Visual Studio Code window. Check to see how your code is creating and modifying the different databases, document collections, and documents in your Cosmos DB account. You can review the changes in your Cosmos DB account using the Data Explorer tool in your Cosmos DB account in the Azure portal.

LISTING 2-3 Cosmos DB SQL API example: Person.cs

```
//C# .NET Core.
using Newtonsoft.Json;

namespace ch2_1_3_SQL.Model
{
```

```csharp
    public class Person
    {
        [JsonProperty(PropertyName="id")]
        public string Id { get; set; }
        public string FirstName { get; set; }
        public string LastName { get; set; }
        public Device[] Devices { get; set; }
        public Address Address { get; set; }
        public string Gender { get; set; }
        public bool IsRegistered { get; set; }
        public override string ToString()
        {
            return JsonConvert.SerializeObject(this);
        }
    }
}
```

LISTING 2-4 Cosmos DB SQL API example: Device.cs

```csharp
//C# .NET Core.
namespace ch2_1_3_SQL.Model
{
    public class Device
    {
        public int Ram { get; set; }
        public string OperatingSystem { get; set; }
        public int CameraMegaPixels { get; set; }
        public string Usage { get; set; }
    }
}
```

LISTING 2-5 Cosmos DB SQL API example: Address.cs

```csharp
//C# .NET Core.
namespace ch2_1_3_SQL.Model
{
    public class Address
    {
        public string City { get; set; }
        public string State { get; set; }
        public string PostalCode { get; set; }
        public string Country { get; set; }
        public string Street { get; set; }
    }
}
```

At this point, you can press F5 in your Visual Studio Code window to execute the code. The code stops on each step for you to be able to view the result of the operation directly on the Azure portal. Use the following steps for viewing the modifications in your Cosmos DB account:

1. Sign in to the Azure portal (*http://portal.azure.com*).

2. In the Search box at the top of the Azure portal, type the name of your Cosmos DB account and click the name of the account.

3. On your Cosmos DB Account blade, click Data Explorer.

4. On the Data Explorer blade, on the left side of the panel, under the label SQL API, you should be able to see the list of databases created in your Cosmos DB account.

Working with the MongoDB API for Cosmos DB is as easy as working with any other Mongo DB library. You only need to use the connection string that you can find in the Connection String panel under the Settings section in your Azure Cosmos DB account.

The following example shows how to use Cosmos DB in your MongoDB project. For this example, you are going to use MERN (MongoDB, Express, React, and Node), which is a full-stack framework for working with MongoDB and NodeJS. Also, you need to meet the following requirements:

- You must have the latest version of NodeJS installed on your computer.

- You must have an Azure Cosmos DB account configured for using MongoDB API. Remember that you can use the same procedure used earlier for creating a Cosmos DB with the SQL API to create an Azure Cosmos DB account with the MongoDB API. You only need to select the correct API when you are creating your Cosmos DB account.

- You need one of the connection strings that you can find in the Connection String panel in your Azure Cosmos DB account in the Azure portal. You need to copy one of these connection strings because you need to use it later in the code.

Use the following steps to connect a MERN project with Cosmos DB using the MongoDB API:

1. Create a new folder for your project.

2. Open the terminal and run the following commands:

```
git clone https://github.com/Hashnode/mern-starter.git
cd mern-starter
npm install
```

3. Open your preferred editor and open the mern-starter folder. Don't close the terminal window that you opened before.

4. In the mern-starter folder, in the server subfolder, open the config.js file and replace the content of the file with the following code:

```
const config = {
  mongoURL: process.env.MONGO_URL || '<YOUR_COSMOSDB_CONNECTION_STRING>',
  port: process.env.PORT || 8000,
};
export default config;
```

5. On the terminal window, run the command npm start. This command starts the NodeJS project and creates a Node server listening on port 8000.

6. Open a web browser and navigate to *http://localhost:8000*. This opens the MERN web project.

7. Open a new browser window, navigate to the Azure portal, and open the Data Explorer browser in your Azure Cosmos DB account.

8. In the MERN project, create, modify, or delete some posts. Review how the document is created, modified, and deleted from your Cosmos DB account.

> ***NEED MORE REVIEW?*** **GREMLIN AND CASSANDRA EXAMPLES**
>
> As you can see in the previous examples, integrating your existing code with Cosmos DB doesn't require too much effort or many changes to your code. For the sake of brevity, we decided to omit the examples of how to connect your Cassandra or Gremlin applications with Cosmos DB. You can learn how to do these integrations by reviewing the following articles:
>
> - **Quickstart: Build a .NET Framework or Core application Using the Azure Cosmos DB Gremlin API account** *https://docs.microsoft.com/en-us/azure/cosmos-db/create-graph-dotnet*
>
> - **Quickstart: Build a Cassandra App with .NET SDK and Azure Cosmos DB** *https://docs.microsoft.com/en-us/azure/cosmos-db/create-cassandra-dotnet*

Set the appropriate consistency level for operations

One of the main benefits offered by Cosmos DB is the ability to have your data distributed across the globe with low latency when accessing the data. This means that you can configure Cosmos DB for replicating your data between any of the available Azure regions while achieving minimal latency when your application accesses the data from the nearest region. If you need to replicate your data to an additional region, you only need to add to the list of regions in which your data should be available.

This replication across the different regions has a drawback—the consistency of your data. To avoid corruption, your data needs to be consistent between all copies of your database. Fortunately, the Cosmos DB protocol offers five levels of consistency replication. Going from consistency to performance, you can select how the replication protocol behaves when copying your data between all the replicas that are configured across the globe. These consistency levels are region agnostic, which means the region that started the read or write operation or the number of regions associated with your Cosmos DB account doesn't matter, even if you configured a single region for your account. You configure this consistency level at the Cosmos DB level, and it applies to all databases, collections, and documents stored inside the same account. You can choose among the consistency levels shown in Figure 2-2. Use the following procedure to select the consistency level:

1. Sign in to the Azure portal (*http://portal.azure.com*).

2. In the Search box at the top of the Azure portal, type the name of your Cosmos DB account and click the name of the account.

3. On your Cosmos DB account blade, click Default Consistency in the Settings section.

4. On the Default Consistency blade, select the desired consistency level. Your choices are Strong, Bounded Staleness, Session, Consistent Prefix, and Eventual.

5. Click the Save icon in the top-left corner of the Default Consistency blade.

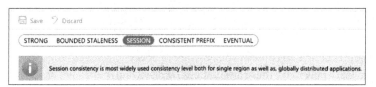

FIGURE 2-2 Selecting the consistency level

- **Strong** The read operations are guaranteed to return the most recently committed version of an element; that is, the user always reads the latest committed write. This consistency level is the only one that offers a linearizability guarantee. This guarantee comes at a price. It has higher latency because of the time needed to write operation confirmations, and the availability can be affected during failures.

- **Bounded Staleness** The reads are guaranteed to be consistent within a precon-figured lag. This lag can consist of a number of the most recent (K) versions or a time interval (T). This means that if you make write operations, the read of these operations happens in the same order but with a maximum delay of K versions of the written data or T seconds since you wrote the data in the database. For reading operations that hap-pen within a region that accepts writes, the consistency level is identical to the Strong consistency level. This level is also known as "time-delayed linearizability guarantee."

- **Session** Scoped to a client session, this consistency level offers the best balance between a strong consistency level and the performance provided by the eventual consistency level. It best fits applications in which write operations occur in the context of a user session.

- **Consistent Prefix** This level guarantees that you always read data in the same order that you wrote the data, but there's no guarantee that you can read all the data. This means that if you write "A, B, C" you can read "A", "A, B" or "A, B, C" but never "A, C" or "B, A, C."

- **Eventual** There is no guarantee for the order in which you read the data. In the absence of a write operation, the replicas eventually converge. This consistency level offers better performance at the cost of the complexity of the programming. Use this consistency level if the order of the data is not essential for your application.

The best consistency level choice depends on your application and the API that you want to use to store data. As you can see in the different consistency levels, your application's requirements regarding data read consistency versus availability, latency, and throughput are critical factors that you need to consider when making your selection.

You should consider the following points when you use SQL or Table API for your Cosmos DB account:

- The recommended option for most applications is the level of session consistency.
- If you are considering the strong consistency level, we recommend that you use the bonded staleness consistency level because it provides a linearizability guarantee with a configurable delay.
- If you are considering the eventual consistency level, we recommend that you use the consistent prefix consistency level because it provides comparable levels of availability and latency with the advantage of guaranteed read orders.
- Carefully evaluate the strong and eventual consistency levels because they are the most extreme options. In most situations, other consistency levels can provide a better balance between performance, latency, and data consistency.

When you use Cassandra or MongoDB APIs, Cosmos DB maps the consistency levels offered by Cassandra and MongoDB to the consistency level offered by Cosmos DB. The reason for doing this is because when you use these APIs, neither Cassandra nor MongoDB offers a well-defined consistency level. Instead, Cassandra provides write or read consistency levels that map to the Cosmos DB consistency level in the following ways:

- **Cassandra write consistency level**   This level maps to the default Cosmos DB account consistency level.
- **Cassandra read consistency level**   Cosmos DB dynamically maps the consistency level specified by the Cassandra driver client to one of the Cosmos DB consistency levels.

On the other hand, MongoDB allows you to configure the following consistency levels: Write Concern, Read Concern, and Master Directive. Similar to the mapping of Cassandra consistency levels, Cosmos DB consistency levels map to MongoDB consistency levels in the following ways:

- **MongoDB write concern consistency level**   This level maps to the default Cosmos DB account consistency level.

- **MongoDB read concern consistency level**   Cosmos DB dynamically maps the consistency level specified by the MongoDB driver client to one of the Cosmos DB consistency levels.

- **Configuring a master region**   You can configure a region as the MongoDB "master" by configuring the region as the first writable region.

NEED MORE REVIEW? **CASSANDRA AND MONGODB CONSISTENCY LEVEL MAPPINGS**

You can review how the different consistency levels map between Cassandra and MongoDB and Cosmos DB consistency levels in the article "Consistency Levels and Azure Cosmos DB APIs" at *https://docs.microsoft.com/en-us/azure/cosmos-db/consistency-levels-across-apis*.

EXAM TIP

The consistency level impacts the latency and availability of the data. In general terms, you should avoid the most extreme levels as they have a more significant impact on your program that should be carefully evaluated. If you are unsure of which level of consistency should use, you should use the session level, as this is the best-balanced level.

Create Cosmos DB containers

When you are working with Cosmos DB, you have several layers in the hierarchy of entities managed by the Cosmos DB account. The first layer is the Azure Cosmos DB account, where you choose the API that you want to use for accessing your data. Remember that this API has implications about how the data is stored in the databases.

The second layer in the hierarchy is the database. You can create as many databases as you need in your Cosmos DB account. Databases are a way of grouping containers, and you can think in databases like in namespaces. At this level, you can configure the throughput associated to the containers included in the database. Depending on the API that you are using, the database has a different name:

- **SQL API**   Database.
- **Cassandra API**   Keyspace.
- **MongoDB API**   Database.

- **Gremlin API**   Database.
- **Table API**   This concept does not apply to Table API, although under the hood when you create your first Table, Cosmos DB creates a default database for you.

A container in an Azure Cosmos DB account is the unit of scalability for throughput and storage. When you create a new container, you need to set the partition key for establishing the way that the items that are going to be stored in the container are distributed across the different logical and physical partitions. As we reviewed in the "Implement partitioning schemes" section earlier in this chapter, the throughput is distributed across the logical partitions defined by the partition key.

When you create a new container, you can decide if the throughput for the container is one of the two following modes:

- **Dedicated**   All the throughput is provisioned for a container. In this mode, Azure makes a reservation of resources for the container that is backed by SLAs.
- **Shared**   The throughput is shared between all the containers configured in the database, excluding those containers that have been configured as dedicated throughput mode. The shared throughput is configured at the database level.

When you create a Cosmos DB container, there are a set of properties that you can configure. These properties affect different aspects of the container or the way the items are stored or managed. The following list shows those properties of a container that can be configured. Bear in mind that not all properties are available for all APIs:

- **IndexingPolicy**   When you add an item to a container, by default, all the properties of the item are automatically indexed. It doesn't matter if all the items in the collection share the same schema, or each item has its own schema. This property allows you to configure how to index the items in the container. You can configure different types of indexes and include or exclude some properties from the indexes.
- **TimeToLive (TTL)**   You can configure your container to delete items after a period of time automatically. TimeToLive is expressed in seconds. You can configure the TTL value at the container or item level. If you configure the TTL at the container level, all items in the container have the same TTL, except if you configure a TTL for a specific item. A value of -1 in the TTL means that the item does not expire. If you set a TTL value to an item where its container does not have a TTL value configured, then the TTL at item level has no effect.
- **ChangeFeedPolicy**   You can read the changes made to an item in a container. The change feed provides you with the original and modified values of an item. Because the changes are persisted, you can process the changes asynchronously. You can use this feature for triggering notifications or calling APIs when a new item is inserted or an existing item is modified.
- **UniqueKeyPolicy**   You can configure which property of the item is used as the unique key. Using unique keys, you ensure that you cannot insert two items with the same value for the same item. Bear in mind that the uniqueness is scoped to the logical partition.

For example, if your item has the properties email, firstname, lastname, and company, and you define email as the unique key and company as the partition key, you cannot insert an item with the same email and company values. You can also create compound unique keys, like email and firstname. Once you have created a unique key, you cannot change it. You can only define the unique key during the creation process of the container.

> **NOTE CONTAINERS' PROPERTIES**
>
> The properties available to the containers depends on the API that you configured for your Azure Cosmos DB account. For a complete list of properties available for each API please review the article at *https://docs.microsoft.com/en-us/azure/cosmos-db/databases-containers-items#azure-cosmos-containers*.

Use the following procedure to create a new collection in your Cosmos DB account. This procedure could be slightly different depending on the API that you use for your Cosmos DB account. In this procedure, you use a Cosmos DB account configured with the SQL API:

1. Sign in to the Azure portal (*http://portal.azure.com*).
2. In the Search box at the top of the Azure portal, type the name of your Cosmos DB account and click the name of the account.
3. On your Cosmos DB account blade, click Data Explorer.
4. On the Data Explorer blade, click the New Container icon in the top-left corner of the blade.
5. On the Add Container panel, shown in Figure 2-3, provide a name for the new database. If you want to add a container to an existing database, you can select the database by clicking the Use Existing radio button.
6. Ensure that the Provision database throughput check is selected. Using this option, you are configuring this container as a shared throughput container. If you want to create a dedicated throughput container, uncheck this option.
7. Leave the Throughput value set to 400. This is the value for the database throughput if the previous option is checked. Otherwise, this value represents the dedicated through-put reserved for the container.
8. In the Container Id text box, type a name for the container.
9. In the Partition Key text box, type a partition key, starting with the slash character.
10. If you want to create a unique key for this container, click the Add Unique Key button.
11. Click the OK button at the bottom of the panel.

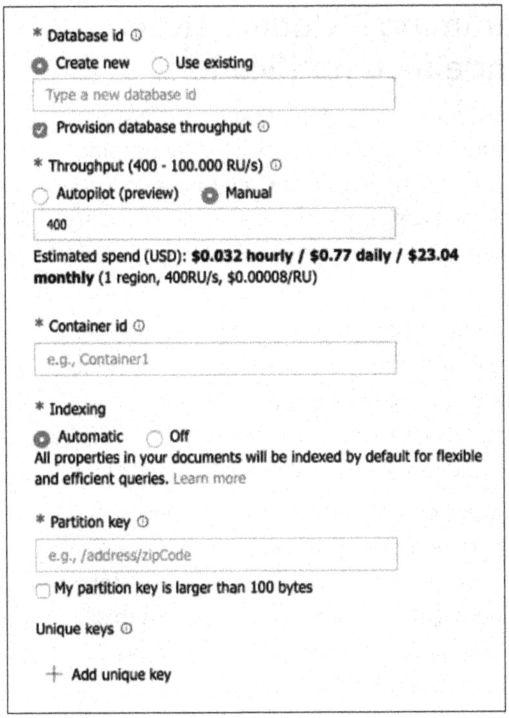

* Database id ⓘ
- ⦿ Create new   ○ Use existing

  [Type a new database id]

☑ Provision database throughput ⓘ

* Throughput (400 - 100.000 RU/s) ⓘ
- ○ Autopilot (preview)   ⦿ Manual

  [400]

Estimated spend (USD): **$0.032 hourly / $0.77 daily / $23.04 monthly** (1 region, 400RU/s, $0.00008/RU)

* Container id ⓘ

[e.g., Container1]

* Indexing
- ⦿ Automatic   ○ Off

All properties in your documents will be indexed by default for flexible and efficient queries. Learn more

* Partition key ⓘ

[e.g., /address/zipCode]

☐ My partition key is larger than 100 bytes

Unique keys ⓘ

  ＋ Add unique key

FIGURE 2-3 Creating a new collection

NEED MORE REVIEW? **TIME TO LIVE, INDEXES, AND CHANGES FEED**

You can review the details of how to configure the Time To Live, Index Policies, and Changes Feed by reading the following articles:

- **Configure Time to Live in Azure Cosmos DB** *https://docs.microsoft.com/en-us/azure/cosmos-db/how-to-time-to-live*

- **Unique Key Constraints in Azure Cosmos DB** *https://docs.microsoft.com/en-us/azure/cosmos-db/unique-keys*

- **Change Feed Design Patterns in Azure Cosmos DB** *https://docs.microsoft.com/en-us/azure/cosmos-db/change-feed-design-patterns*

EXAM TIP

You need to plan carefully how to create a new container in Azure Cosmos DB. You can set some of the properties that you can configure only during the creation process. Once you have created the container if you need to modify those properties, you need to create a new container with the needed values and migrate the data to the new container.

Implement server-side programming including stored procedures, triggers, and change feed notifications

When you work with Cosmos DB API, Azure allows you to write your triggers, stored procedures, and user-defined functions. You can write these procedures and functions using JavaScript. Before you can call a stored procedure, trigger, or user-defined function, you need to register it. You can use the Azure portal, the JavaScript language integrated query API in Cosmos DB, or the Cosmos DB SQL API client SDK for creating and calling your stored procedures, triggers, and user-defined functions.

Any stored procedure, trigger, or user-defined function that you write is registered on a container basis. That means that you need to register the stored procedure on each container where you want to execute your stored procedure. You also need to consider that stored procedures and triggers are scoped to partitions. Any item with a partition key value different from the partition key of the item that fired the trigger or the stored procedure is not visible.

When you are writing a stored procedure, trigger, or user-defined function, you need to create a reference to the execution context. This context gives you access to the requests that fired the stored procedure or trigger and allows you to work with the responses and items that you want to insert into the database. In general terms, the context gives you access to all the operations that you can perform in the Azure Cosmos DB database. The following procedure shows how to create a stored procedure in an Azure Cosmos DB SQL API account:

1. Open the Azure portal (*https://portal.azure.com*).

2. In the Search text box in the top area of the portal, type the name of your Cosmos DB account. Remember that this needs to be an SQL API Cosmos DB account.

3. On your Cosmos DB SQL API account, click Data Explorer.

4. Click an existing database. If you don't have any database, create a new one for testing purposes.

5. Click an existing container, or you can create a testing container following the procedure that we reviewed in a previous section.

6. Click the New Stored Procedure button. This button creates a new sample stored procedure that you can use as a template for your stored procedures.

7. In the Stored Procedure Id text box, provide a name for the stored procedure.

8. Replace the content of the New Stored Procedure tab with the content of Listing 2-6.

LISTING 2-6   Cosmos DB SQL API stored procedure

```
//JavaScript
function createNewDocument(docToCreate) {
    var context = getContext();
    var container = context.getCollection();
    var response = context.getResponse();

    console.log(docToCreate);
```

```
    var accepted = container.createDocument(container.getSelfLink(),
        docToCreate,
        function (err, docCreated) {
            if (err) throw new Error('Error creating a new document: ' + err.message);
            response.setBody(docCreated);
        });

    if (!accepted) return;

}
```

9. Click the Save button.

10. Click the Execute button. This button opens the Input Parameters blade.

11. In the Input Parameters blade, in the Partition Key Value section, change the type from Custom to String.

12. In the Partition Key Value section, in the Value text box, type a value to the partition key. Remember that this partition key is the one that you have defined for the container where you are creating this stored procedure.

13. In the Type drop-down menu in the Enter Input Parameters section, ensure that the value String is selected.

14. In the Param text box, type the document in JSON format that you want to insert. For the sake of simplicity, use a string with a structure similar to {"id": "12345", "key": "value"}.

15. Click the Execute button at the bottom of the Input Parameters panel.

16. In the Data Explorer navigation tree, click on the Items leaf below the container where you are creating the stored procedure.

17. Ensure that the new document has been correctly inserted in your container.

> *NOTE* **BADREQUEST ERROR**
>
> If you get a BadRequest error when you execute the previous example, review the values of the input parameters. Remember that you cannot insert a document in a different partition from the one that you select in the Partition Key Value. For example, if your partition key is the field "city" and the value you provide is "Seville", you need to include this value in the Enter Input Parameters section. For this example, your document should look similar to { "country": "Spain", "city": "Seville"}.

Although the previous example is quite simple, there are some interesting points that we should review. One of the essential points that you need to consider when programming your stored procedures, user-defined functions or trigger, is the fact that the input parameters always have the string type. This means that if you need to pass an object to the stored procedure, you need to stringify the object, and then convert back to a JSON object by using the JSON.parse() method.

As you can see, we use the global getContext() method for getting a reference to the context. That context gives us access to the features of the Cosmos DB account. Then we got a reference to the current container by using the getContainer() method in the context. We also use the getResponse() method from the context for sending back information to the client.

Because we are going to create a new document in the container, we need to use the createDocument() method in the container. This method requires a link to the container where we are going to insert the document, and the document itself. Because the methods require a JSON document, if the value of the input parameter is not a valid JSON string, you get a JSON parse error here. We also provided an optional anonymous function for managing any error that may arise during the creation of the document. If you don't provide a callback function, any error is thrown as an exception.

Creating a trigger is quite similar to create a stored procedure. The concepts are equivalent, but you need to consider when you need to execute the action of your trigger. If you need to make an operation before the item is inserted into the container, you need to use a **pre-trigger**. If you need to make an action after the item has been successfully inserted in the container, you need to use a **post-trigger**.

Pre-triggers cannot have input parameters. Because the item is not actually in the database, you need to work with the request that fired the trigger. This request contains the information needed for inserting the new item into the collection. You can get a reference to the request by using the getRequest() method from the context object. Once you have made your modifications to the original item, you can send the modified item to the database by using the request. setBody() method.

NEED MORE REVIEW? **MORE SAMPLES**

Although the sample that we reviewed in this section could seem simplistic, it covers some important points that you need to be aware of when programming your server-side items. The following articles provide more detailed examples of how to create and register stored procedures, user-defined functions, or triggers using JavaScript or C#:

- **How to write stored procedures, triggers, and user-defined functions in Azure Cosmos DB** *https://docs.microsoft.com/en-us/azure/cosmos-db/ how-to-write-stored-procedures-triggers-udfs*

- **How to write stored procedures and triggers in Azure Cosmos DB by using the JavaScript query API** *https://docs.microsoft.com/en-us/azure/cosmos-db/ how-to-write-javascript-query-api*

- **How to register and use stored procedures, triggers, and user-defined functions in Azure Cosmos DB** *https://docs.microsoft.com/en-us/azure/cosmos-db/ how-to-use-stored-procedures-triggers-udfs*

NEED MORE REVIEW? **CHANGE FEEDS**

Every change, insertion, or deletion made to an item in a collection is automatically registered and stored in the Change Feed. You can use these operations as triggers for Azure Functions that allow you to send notifications to other services or perform any other action that you consider. You can review the details of how to integrate your Azure Functions with Cosmos DB Change feed by reviewing the following articles:

- **How to configure the connection policy used by Azure Functions trigger for Cosmos DB** *https://docs.microsoft.com/en-us/azure/cosmos-db/how-to-configure-cosmos-db-trigger-connection-policy*

- **Change feed in Azure Cosmos DB** *https://docs.microsoft.com/en-us/azure/cosmos-db/change-feed*

Skill 2.2: Develop solutions that use Blob Storage

Storing information in SQL or NoSQL databases is a great way to save that information when you need to save schemaless documents or if you need to guarantee the integrity of the data. The drawback of these services is that they are relatively expensive for storing data that doesn't have such requirements.

Azure Blob Storage allows you to store information that doesn't fit the characteristics of SQL and NoSQL storage in the cloud. This information can be images, videos, office documents, or more. The Azure Blob Storage still provides high-availability features that make it an ideal service for storing a large amount of data but at a lower price compared to the other data storage solutions that we reviewed earlier in this chapter.

This skill covers how to

- Move items in Blob Storage between Storage Accounts or containers
- Set and retrieve properties and metadata
- Interact with data using the appropriate SDK
- Implement data archiving and retention
- Implement hot, cool, and archive storage

Move items in Blob Storage between Storage Accounts or containers

When you are working with Azure Blob Storage, there can be situations in which you may need to move blobs from one Storage Account to another or between containers. For particular situations, there are several tools that you can use for performing these tasks:

- **Azure Storage Explorer**   Is a graphical tool that allows you to manage the different operations with the storage services like Azure Storage, Azure Data Lake Storage, Azure Cosmos DB, and virtual disks.

- **AzCopy**   Is a command-line tool for performing bulk copy operations between different sources and Azure Storage accounts.

- **Python**   Using the azure-storage-blob package, you can manage your Azure Storage Account using Python.

- **SSIS**   The SQL Server Integration Service Feature Pack for Azure allows you to transfer data between your on-premises data sources and your Azure Storage Account.

One of the things that all these options have in common is that they don't provide the move operation as an option. If you need to move blobs or containers between different locations, you need to perform a copy operation, and then delete the source blob or container once the copy operation finishes successfully.

The following example shows how to move a blob called testing.zip between two different containers in different Azure Storage Accounts using Azure Storage Explorer. For this example, you need to create two Azure Storage Accounts with two different containers. Then upload a blob to one of the storage accounts.

1. Open Azure Storage Explorer. You can download it from *https://azure.microsoft.com/en-us/features/storage-explorer/*.

2. On the Azure Storage Explorer, on the left side of the window, click the Manage Accounts button.

3. On the Account Management section, click the Add An Account link.

4. On the Connect To Azure Storage window, shown in Figure 2-4, ensure that the option Add An Azure Account is selected, and in the Azure Environment drop-down menu, the Azure option is selected.

5. Click Next.

6. Log into your Azure subscription.

7. Once you are logged in your Azure subscription, your Azure account should appear in the Account Management.

8. Click Apply. This would automatically switch to the Explorer section.

9. On the Explorer section, in the navigation tree on the left side of the Azure Storage Explorer window, navigate to your source Storage Account.

10. Expand the leaf representing your source Storage Account.

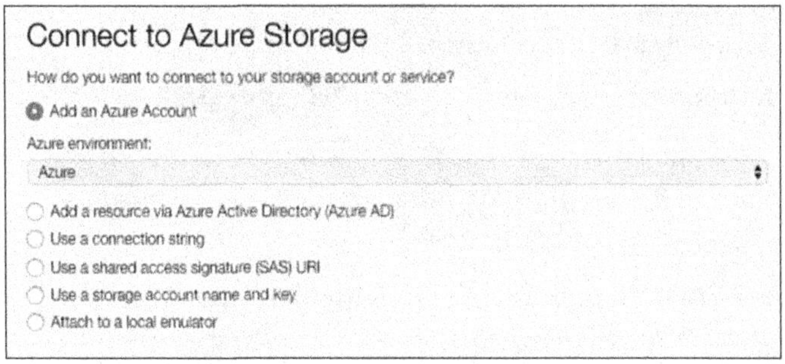

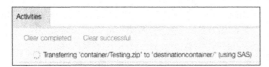

Connect to Azure Storage

How do you want to connect to your storage account or service?

○ Add an Azure Account

Azure environment:

Azure

○ Add a resource via Azure Active Directory (Azure AD)
○ Use a connection string
○ Use a shared access signature (SAS) URI
○ Use a storage account name and key
○ Attach to a local emulator

FIGURE 2-4 Creating a new Collection

11. Expand the Blob Containers leaf below your source Storage Account leaf.

12. Click the leaf representing the container with the blob that you want to move. This action opens a new tab in the Azure Storage Explorer window with the name of your container.

13. Click the blob that you want to move.

14. Click the Copy button on the menu bar on the top side of the container's tab.

15. Navigate to the destination container and click on the leaf representing the destination container.

16. On the tab for the destination container, click the button Paste in the menu bar.

17. Ensure that on the Activities tab at the bottom of the Azure Storage Explorer window appears a message similar to the one shown in Figure 2-5.

Activities

Clear completed   Clear successful

Transferring 'container/Testing.zip' to 'destinationcontainer/' (using SAS)

FIGURE 2-5 Creating a new Collection

18. Click on the source container's tab.

19. Select the blob that you want to move.

20. Click the Delete button on the menu bar in the container's tab.

21. On the Microsoft Azure Storage Explorer – Delete dialog box, click Delete.

The procedure for performing the same move action using other tools like Python or AzCopy is similar to the one shown in the previous example. You need to first copy the blob to the destination container and once the copy finishes successfully, you can remove the original blob.

The AzCopy tool is ideal for doing incremental copy scenarios or copying an entire account into another account. You can use the following command for copying blob items between containers in different Storage Accounts:

```
azcopy copy <URL_Source_Item><Source_SASToken> <URL_Target_Container><Target_SASToken>
```

EXAM TIP

When you are performing copy or move operations on containers or blobs, you are not limited to the same storage account. You can copy blobs and containers between Storage Accounts in different regions or even subscriptions, as long as you have enough privileges for accessing to both accounts.

Set and retrieve properties and metadata

When you work with Azure Storage services, you can work with some additional information assigned to your blobs. This additional information is stored in the form of system properties and user-defined metadata:

- **System properties** This is information that the Storage services automatically adds to each storage resource. You can modify some of these system properties, while others are read-only. Some of these system properties correspond with some HTTP headers. You don't need to worry about maintaining these system properties because the Azure Storage client libraries automatically make any needed modification for you.

- **User-defined metadata** You can assign key-value pairs to an Azure Storage resource. These metadata are for your own purposes and don't affect the behavior of the Azure Storage service. You need to take care of updating the value of these metadata according to your needs.

When working with blob metadata, you can use the appropriate SDK from your preferred language, or you can use the command az storage blob metadata from the Azure CLI. The following example shows how to work with properties and metadata using the .NET SDK:

1. Open Visual Studio Code and create a folder for your project.

2. In the Visual Studio Code Window, open a new terminal.

3. Use the following command to create a new console project:

```
dotnet new console
```

4. Use the following command to install NuGet packages:

```
dotnet add package <NuGet_package_name>
```

5. Install the following NuGet packages:

   - Microsoft.Azure.Storage.Blob
   - Microsoft.Azure.Storage.Common
   - Microsoft.Extensions.Configuration
   - Microsoft.Extensions.Configuration.Binder
   - Microsoft.Extensions.Configuration.Json

6. In the project folder, create a new JSON file and name it **AppSettings.json**. Copy the content from Listing 2-7 to the JSON file and replace the value of the variables with the values of your storage accounts.

7. Create a C# class file and name it **AppSettings.cs**.

8. Replace the contents of the AppSettings.cs file with the contents of Listing 2-8. Change the name of the namespace to match your project's name.

9. Create a C# class file and name it **Common.cs**.

10. Replace the contents of the Common.cs file with the contents of Listing 2-9.

11. Change the name of the namespace to match your project's name.

12. Replace the contents of the Program.cs file with the contents of Listing 2-10. Change the name of the namespace to match your project's name.

13. Edit your .csproj project file and add the following code inside the ItemGroup section:

```
<None Update="AppSettings.json">
    <CopyToOutputDirectory>PreserveNewest</CopyToOutputDirectory>
</None>
```

14. At this point, you can set some breakpoints in the Program.cs file to see, step by step, how the code moves the blob items between the different containers and Storage Accounts.

15. In the Visual Studio Window, press F5 to build and run your code.

LISTING 2-7 AppSettings.json configuration file

```
{
    "SASToken": "<SASToken_from_your_first_storage_account>",
    "AccountName": "<name_of_your_first_storage_account>",
    "ContainerName": "<source_container_name>"
}
```

LISTING 2-8 AppSettings.cs C# class

```csharp
//C# .NET Core

using Microsoft.Extensions.Configuration;

namespace ch2_2_2
{
    public class AppSettings
    {
        public string SASToken { get; set; }
        public string AccountName { get; set; }
        public string ContainerName { get; set; }

        public static AppSettings LoadAppSettings()
        {
            IConfigurationRoot configRoot = new ConfigurationBuilder()
                .AddJsonFile("AppSettings.json",false)
                .Build();
            AppSettings appSettings = configRoot.Get<AppSettings>();
            return appSettings;
        }
    }
}
```

LISTING 2-9 Common.cs C# class

```csharp
//C# .NET Core

using System;
using Microsoft.Azure.Storage;
using Microsoft.Azure.Storage.Auth;
using Microsoft.Azure.Storage.Blob;

namespace ch2_2_2
{
    public class Common
    {

        public static CloudBlobClient CreateBlobClientStorageFromSAS(string SAStoken,
string accountName)
        {
            CloudStorageAccount storageAccount;
            CloudBlobClient blobClient;
            try
            {
                bool useHttps = true;
```

```csharp
                StorageCredentials storageCredentials =
                new StorageCredentials(SAStoken);
                storageAccount = new CloudStorageAccount(storageCredentials,
accountName, null, useHttps);
                blobClient = storageAccount.CreateCloudBlobClient();
            }
            catch (System.Exception)
            {
                throw;
            }

            return blobClient;

        }
    }
}
```

Listing 2-10 shows how to create a new container and get a list of some system properties assigned automatically to the container when you create it.

LISTING 2-10 Program.cs C# class

```csharp
//C# .NET Core
// Getting system properties from a storage resource
using System;
using System.Threading.Tasks;
using Microsoft.Azure.Storage.Blob;

namespace ch2_2_2
{
    class Program
    {
        static void Main(string[] args)
        {
            Console.WriteLine("Getting System properties Demo!");

            AppSettings appSettings = AppSettings.LoadAppSettings();

            //Create a CloudBlobClient for working with the Storage Account
            CloudBlobClient blobClient = Common.CreateBlobClientStorageFromSAS
              (appSettings.SASToken, appSettings.AccountName);

            //Get a container reference for the new container.
            CloudBlobContainer container = blobClient.GetContainerReference
              (appSettings.ContainerName);
```

```
                //Create the container if not already exists
                container.CreateIfNotExists();

                //You need to fetch the container properties before getting their values
                container.FetchAttributes();
                Console.WriteLine($"Properties for container {container.StorageUri.
PrimaryUri.ToString()}");
                System.Console.WriteLine($"ETag: {container.Properties.ETag}");
                System.Console.WriteLine($"LastModifiedUTC: {container.Properties.
LastModified.ToString()}");
                System.Console.WriteLine($"Lease status: {container.Properties.LeaseStatus.
ToString()}");
                System.Console.WriteLine();
        }
    }
}
```

As you can see in the previous code in Listing 2-10, you need to use the FetchAttributes() or FetchAttributesAsync() method before you can read the properties from the container, stored in the Properties property of the CloudBlobContainer or CloudBlockBlob objects. If you get null values for system properties, ensure that you called the FetchAttributes() method before accessing the system property.

Working with user-defined metadata is quite similar to working with system properties. The main difference is that you can add your custom key pairs to the storage resource. These user-defined metadata are stored in the Metadata property of the storage resource. Listing 2-11 extends the example in Listing 2-10 and shows how to set and read user-defined metadata in the container that you created in Listing 2-10. Copy the content from Listing 2-11 and insert the code in the Program.cs file after the last System.Console.WriteLine().

LISTING 2-11   Setting user-defined metadata

```
//C# .NET Core
//Add some metadata to the container that we created before
                container.Metadata.Add("department", "Technical");
                container.Metadata["category"] = "Knowledge Base";
                container.Metadata.Add("docType", "pdfDocuments");

                //Save the containers metadata in Azure
                container.SetMetadata();

                //List newly added metadata. We need to fetch all attributes before being
                //able to read if not, we could get nulls or weird values
                container.FetchAttributes();
```

```
System.Console.WriteLine("Container's metadata:");
foreach (var item in container.Metadata)
{
    System.Console.Write($"\tKey: {item.Key}\t");
    System.Console.WriteLine($"\tValue: {item.Value}");
}
```

You can find a complete list of system properties in the Microsoft.Azure.Storage.Blob .NET client reference at *https://docs.microsoft.com/en-us/dotnet/api/microsoft.azure.storage.blob. blobcontainerproperties*. The BlobContainerProperties and BlobProperties classes are responsible for storing the system properties for the storage resources in a Blob Storage account.

You can also view and edit system properties and user-defined metadata by using the Azure portal, using the Properties and Metadata sections in the Settings section of your container, or clicking on the ellipsis next to the blob item and selecting the Blob Properties option in the contextual menu.

Interact with data using the appropriate SDK

Although using any of the options that we reviewed at the beginning of the skill may be appropriate for some situations, you may need to get more fine-grained control of the items that you need to move between containers or even Storage Accounts.

Microsoft provides several SDKs for working with data in your Storage Accounts. You can find SDKs for the main programming languages supported by Microsoft, like .NET, Java, Python, JavaScript (Node.js or browser), Go, PHP, or Ruby.

The following example written in .NET Core shows how to move a blob item between two containers in the same Storage Account and how to move a blob item between two containers in different Storage Accounts. Before you can run this example, you need to create two Storage Accounts with two blob containers. For the sake of simplicity, you should create the two containers with the same name in the two different Storage Accounts. Also, you need to upload two control files as blob items to one of the containers in one Storage Account:

1. Open Visual Studio Code and create a folder for your project.
2. In the Visual Studio Code Window, open a new terminal.
3. Use the following command to create a new console project:
   ```
   dotnet new console
   ```
4. Use the following command to install NuGet packages:
   ```
   dotnet add package <NuGet_package_name>
   ```
5. Install the following NuGet packages:
   - Azure.Storage.Blobs
   - Azure.Storage.Common
   - Microsoft.Extensions.Configuration
   - Microsoft.Extensions.Configuration.Binder
   - Microsoft.Extensions.Configuration.Json

6. In the project folder, create a new JSON file and name it **AppSettings.json**. Copy the content from Listing 2-12 to the JSON file.

7. Create a C# class file and name it **AppSettings.cs**.

8. Replace the contents of the AppSettings.cs file with the contents of Listing 2-13. Change the name of the namespace to match your project's name.

9. Create a C# class file and name it **Common.cs**.

10. Replace the contents of the Common.cs file with the contents of Listing 2-14.

11. Change the name of the namespace to match your project's name.

12. Replace the contents of the Program.cs file with the contents of Listing 2-15. Change the name of the namespace to match your project's name.

13. Edit your .csproj project file and add the following code inside the ItemGroup section:

```
<None Update="AppSettings.json">
    <CopyToOutputDirectory>PreserveNewest</CopyToOutputDirectory>
</None>
```

14. At this point, you can set some breakpoints in the Program.cs file to see, step by step, how the code moves the blob items between the different containers and Storage Accounts.

15. In the Visual Studio Window, press F5 to build and run your code. You can use the Azure portal or the Microsoft Azure Storage Explorer desktop application to review how your blob items change their locations.

LISTING 2-12 AppSettings.json configuration file

```
{
    "SourceSASConnectionString": "<SASConnectionString_from_your_first_storage_
account>",
    "SourceAccountName": "<name_of_your_first_storage_account>",
    "SourceContainerName": "<source_container_name>",
    "DestinationSASConnectionString": "<SASConnectionString_from_your_second_storage_
account>",
    "DestinationAccountName": "<name_of_your_second_storage_account>",
    "DestinationContainerName": "<destination_container_name>"
}
```

LISTING 2-13 AppSettings.cs C# class

```
//C# .NET Core
using Microsoft.Extensions.Configuration;

namespace ch2_2_3
{
    public class AppSettings
    {
```

```
    public string SourceSASConnectionString { get; set; }
    public string SourceAccountName { get; set; }
    public string SourceContainerName { get; set; }
    public string DestinationSASConnectionString { get; set; }
    public string DestinationAccountName { get; set; }
    public string DestinationContainerName { get; set; }

    public static AppSettings LoadAppSettings()
    {
        IConfigurationRoot configRoot = new ConfigurationBuilder()
            .AddJsonFile("AppSettings.json",false)
            .Build();
        AppSettings appSettings = configRoot.Get<AppSettings>();
        return appSettings;
    }
    }
}
```

LISTING 2-14 Common.cs C# class

```
//C# .NET Core
using Azure.Storage.Blobs;

namespace ch2_2_3
{
    public class Common
    {

        public static BlobServiceClient CreateBlobClientStorageFromSAS(string
SASConnectionString)
        {
            BlobServiceClient blobClient;
            try
            {
                blobClient = new BlobServiceClient(SASConnectionString);
            }
            catch (System.Exception)
            {
                throw;
            }

            return blobClient;

        }
    }
}
```

In Listing 2-15, portions of the code that are significant to the process of working with the Azure Blob Storage service are shown in bold.

LISTING 2-15   Program.cs C# class

```
//C# .NET Core
using System.Threading.Tasks;
using System;
using Azure.Storage.Blobs;
using Azure.Storage.Blobs.Models;

namespace ch2_2_3
{
    class Program
    {
        static void Main(string[] args)
        {
            Console.WriteLine("Copy items between Containers Demo!");
            Task.Run(async () => await StartContainersDemo()).Wait();
            Console.WriteLine("Move items between Storage Accounts Demo!");
            Task.Run(async () => await StartAccountDemo()).Wait();
        }

        public static async Task StartContainersDemo()
        {
            string sourceBlobFileName = "Testing.zip";
            AppSettings appSettings = AppSettings.LoadAppSettings();

            //Get a cloud client for the source Storage Account
            BlobServiceClient sourceClient = Common.CreateBlobClientStorageFromSAS
(appSettings.SourceSASConnectionString);

            //Get a reference for each container
            var sourceContainerReference = sourceClient.GetBlobContainerClient
(appSettings.SourceContainerName);
            var destinationContainerReference = sourceClient.GetBlobContainer
Client(appSettings.DestinationContainerName);

            //Get a reference for the source blob
            var sourceBlobReference = sourceContainerReference.GetBlobClient
(sourceBlobFileName);
            var destinationBlobReference = destinationContainerReference.
GetBlobClient(sourceBlobFileName);

            //Copy the blob from the source container to the destination container
```

```
                await destinationBlobReference.StartCopyFromUriAsync(sourceBlob
Reference.Uri);


        }

        public static async Task StartAccountDemo()
        {
            string sourceBlobFileName = "Testing.zip";
            AppSettings appSettings = AppSettings.LoadAppSettings();

            //Get a cloud client for the source Storage Account
            BlobServiceClient sourceClient = Common.CreateBlobClientStorageFromSAS
(appSettings.SourceSASConnectionString);
            //Get a cloud client for the destination Storage Account
            BlobServiceClient destinationClient = Common.CreateBlobClientStorage
FromSAS(appSettings.DestinationSASConnectionString);

            //Get a reference for each container
            var sourceContainerReference = sourceClient.GetBlobContainerClient
(appSettings.SourceContainerName);
            var destinationContainerReference = destinationClient.GetBlobContainer
Client(appSettings.DestinationContainerName);

            //Get a reference for the source blob
            var sourceBlobReference = sourceContainerReference.GetBlobClient
(sourceBlobFileName);
            var destinationBlobReference = destinationContainerReference.
GetBlobClient(sourceBlobFileName);

            //Move the blob from the source container to the destination container
            await destinationBlobReference.StartCopyFromUriAsync(sourceBlob
Reference.Uri);
            await sourceBlobReference.DeleteAsync();
        }
    }
}
```

In this example, you made two different operations—a copy between containers in the same Storage Account and a movement between containers in different Storage Accounts. As you can see in the code shown previously in Listing 2-15, the high-level procedure for moving blob items between containers is

1. Create a BlobServiceClient instance for each Storage Account that is involved in the blob item movement.

2. Create a reference for each container. If you need to move a blob item between containers in a different Storage Account, you need to use the BlobServiceClient object that represents each Storage Account.

3. Create a reference for each blob item. You need a reference to the source blob item because this is the item that you are going to move. You use the destination blob item reference for performing the actual copy operation.

4. Once you are done with the copy, you can delete the source blob item by using the DeleteAsync() method.

Although this code is quite straightforward, it has a critical problem that you can solve in the following sections. If someone else modifies the source blob item while the write operation is pending, the copy operation fails with an HTTP status code 412. We are going to fix this later in this section.

You may notice that the code in this example uses a different SDK from the code in the previous sections. The reason for this is that, at the time of this writing, there are available two different versions of the .NET SDK for working with Azure Storage:

- **Microsoft.Azure.Storage.Blob**   This is the SDK version 11. You can configure permissions on the blobs using this version.
- **Azure.Storage.Blobs**   This is the SDK version 12. This version simplifies the way of working with Azure Storage Blobs but does not offer the full set of features that has version 11. You cannot set permissions using this version.

NEED MORE REVIEW?   **CROSS-ACCOUNT BLOB COPY**

You can review the details of how the asynchronous copy between Storage Accounts works by reading this MSDN article, "Introducing Asynchronous Cross-Account Copy Blob" at *https:// blogs.msdn.microsoft.com/windowsazurestorage/2012/06/12/introducing-asynchronous-cross-account-copy-blob/.*

EXAM TIP

When you need to move a blob to any destination, container, or Storage Account, remember that you need first to perform a copy operation and then delete the source blob. There is no such move method in the CloudBlockBlob class.

When you are working with the Blob Storage service—in which several users or processes can simultaneously access the same Storage Account—you can face a problem when two users or processes are trying to access the same blob. Azure provides a leasing mechanism for solving this kind of situation. A lease is a short block that the blob service sets on a blob or container item for granting exclusive access to that item. When you acquire a lease to a blob, you get exclusive write and delete access to that blob. If you acquire a lease in a container, you get exclusive delete access to the container.

When you acquire a lease for a storage item, you need to include the active lease ID on each write operation that you want to perform on the blob with the lease. You can choose the duration for the lease time when you request it. This duration can last from 15 to 60 seconds or forever. Each lease can be in one of the following five states:

- **Available** The lease is unlocked, and you can acquire a new lease.

- **Leased** There is a lease granted to the resource, and the lease is locked. You can acquire a new lease if you use the same ID that you got when you created the lease. You can also release, change, renew, or break the lease when it is in this status.

- **Expired** The duration configured for the lease has expired. When you have a lease on this status, you can acquire, renew, release, or break the lease.

- **Breaking** You have broken the lease, but it's still locked until the break period expires. In this status, you can release or break the lease.

- **Broken** The break period has expired, and the lease has been broken. In this status, you can acquire, release, and break a lease. You need to break a lease when the process that acquired the lease finishes suddenly, such as when network connectivity issues or any other condition results in the lease not being released correctly. In these situations, you may end up with an orphaned lease, and you cannot write or delete the blob with the orphaned lease. In this situation, the only solution is to break the lease. You may also want to break a lease when you need to force the release of the lease manually.

You use the Azure portal for managing the lease status of a container or blob item, or you use it programmatically with the Azure Blob Storage client SDK. In the example shown in Listings 2-12 to 2-15, in which we reviewed how to copy and move items between containers or Storage Accounts, we saw that if some other process or user modifies the blob while our process is copying the data, we get an error. You can avoid that situation by acquiring a lease for the blob that you want to move. Listing 2-16 shows in bold the modification that you need to add to the code in Listing 2-15 so that you can acquire a lease for the blob item.

LISTING 2-16 Program.cs modification

```
//C# .NET Core
//Add lines in bold to StartContainersDemo method on Listing 2-15
//Add the following using statement to the beginning of the file:
//using Azure.Storage.Blobs.Specialized;
public static async Task StartContainersDemo()
        {
            string sourceBlobFileName = "Testing.zip";
            AppSettings appSettings = AppSettings.LoadAppSettings();

            //Get a cloud client for the source Storage Account
            BlobServiceClient sourceClient = Common.CreateBlobClientStorageFromSAS
(appSettings.SourceSASConnectionString);

            //Get a reference for each container
            var sourceContainerReference = sourceClient.GetBlobContainerClient
(appSettings.SourceContainerName);
```

```
                var destinationContainerReference = sourceClient.GetBlobContainerClient
(appSettings.DestinationContainerName);

                //Get a reference for the source blob
                var sourceBlobReference = sourceContainerReference.GetBlobClient
(sourceBlobFileName);
                var destinationBlobReference = destinationContainerReference.GetBlobClient(
sourceBlobFileName);

                //Get the lease status of the source blob
                BlobProperties sourceBlobProperties = await sourceBlobReference.
GetPropertiesAsync();
                System.Console.WriteLine($"Lease status: {sourceBlobProperties.
LeaseStatus}" +
                        $"\tstate: {sourceBlobProperties.LeaseState}" +
                        $"\tduration: {sourceBlobProperties.LeaseDuration}");

                //Acquire an infinite lease. If you want to set a duration for the lease
                //use
                //TimeSpan.FromSeconds(seconds). Remember that seconds should be a value
                //between 15 and 60.
                //We need to save the lease ID automatically generated by Azure for release
                //the lease later.
                string leaseID = Guid.NewGuid().ToString();
                BlobLeaseClient sourceLease = sourceBlobReference.
GetBlobLeaseClient(leaseID);

                sourceLease.Acquire(new TimeSpan(-1));

                sourceBlobProperties = await sourceBlobReference.GetPropertiesAsync();
                System.Console.WriteLine($"Lease status: {sourceBlobProperties.
LeaseStatus}" +
                        $"\tstate: {sourceBlobProperties.LeaseState}" +
                        $"\tduration: {sourceBlobProperties.LeaseDuration}");

                //Copy the blob from the source container to the destination container
                await destinationBlobReference.StartCopyFromUriAsync
(sourceBlobReference.Uri);

                //Release the lease acquired previously
                sourceLease.Release();

        }
```

As you can see in the previous example, you need to get a reference to a BlobLeaseClient. This object allows you to acquire new leases by invoking the method Acquire(). In this example, we created an infinite lease because we used a TimeSpan with the value -1. Once we have copied the blob, we need to release the lease by using the Release() method of the BlobLeaseClient.

> **NEED MORE REVIEW?** **LEASING BLOBS AND CONTAINERS**
>
> You can review the details of how leasing works for blobs and containers by consulting the following articles:
>
> - **Lease Blob** *https://docs.microsoft.com/en-us/rest/api/storageservices/lease-blob*
>
> - **Lease Container** *https://docs.microsoft.com/en-us/rest/api/storageservices/lease-container*

EXAM TIP

Leasing is the mechanism that you need to use to ensure that no other users or processes can access a blob while you are working with it. You can create timed or infinite leases. Remember that you need to release infinite leases manually.

Implement data archiving and retention

When you are working with data, the requirements for accessing the data change during the lifetime of the data. Data that has been recently placed on your storage system usually is accessed more frequently and requires faster access than older data. If you are using the same type of storage for all your data, that means you are using storage for data that is rarely accessed. If your storage is based on SSD disk or any other technology that provides proper performance levels, this means that you can be potentially wasting expensive storage for data that is rarely accessed. A solution to this situation is to move less-frequently accessed data to a cheaper storage system. The drawback of this solution is that you need to implement a system for tracking the last time data has been accessed and moving it to the right storage system.

Azure Blob Storage provides you with the ability to set different levels of access to your data. These different access levels, or tiers, provide different levels of performance when accessing the data. Each different access level has a different price. Following are the available access tiers:

- **Hot**   You use this tier for data that you need to access more frequently. This is the default tier that you use when you create a new Storage Account.
- **Cool**   You can use this tier for data that is less frequently accessed and is stored for at least 30 days.
- **Archive**   You use this tier for storing data that is rarely accessed and is stored for at least 180 days. This access tier is available only at the blob level. You cannot configure a Storage Account with this access tier.

The different access tiers have the following performance and pricing implications:

- Cool tier provides slightly lower availability, reflected in the service-level agreement (SLA) because of lower storage costs; however, it has higher access costs.

- Hot and cool tiers have similar characteristics in terms of time-to-access and throughput.

- Archive storage is offline storage. It has the lowest storage cost rates but has higher access costs.

- The lower the storage costs, the higher the access costs.

- You can use storage tiering only on General Purpose v2 (GPv2) Storage Accounts.

- If you want to use storage tiering with a General Purpose v1 (GPv1) Storage Account, you need to convert to a GPv2 Storage Account.

Moving between the different access tiers is a transparent process for the user, but it has some implications in terms of pricing. In general, when you are moving from a warmer tier to a cooler tier—hot to cool or hot to archive—you are charged for the write operations to the destination tier. When you move from a cooler tier to a warmer tier—from the archive to cold or from cold to hot—you are charged for the read operations from the source tier. Another essential thing to bear in mind is how the data is moved when you change your data tier from archive to any other access tier. Because data in the archive tier is saved into offline storage, when you move data out of the access tier, the storage service needs to move the data back to online storage. This process is known as blob rehydration and can take up to 15 hours.

If you don't manually configure the access tier for a blob, it inherits the access from its container or Storage Account. Although you can change the access tier manually using the Azure portal, this process creates an administrative overload that could also lead to human errors. Instead of manually monitoring the different criteria for moving a blob from one tier to another, you can implement policies that make that movement based on the criteria that you define. You use these policies for defining the lifecycle management of your data. You can create these lifecycle management policies by using the Azure portal, Azure PowerShell, Azure CLI, or REST API.

A lifecycle management policy is a JSON document in which you define several rules that you want to apply to the different containers or blob types. Each rule consists of a filter set and an action set.

- **Filter set** The filter set limits the actions to only a group of items that match the filter criteria.

- **Action set** You use this set to define the actions that are performed on the items that matched the filter.

The following procedure for adding a new policy using the Azure portal:

1. Sign in to the Azure portal (*http://portal.azure.com*).

2. In the Search box at the top of the Azure portal, type the name of your Storage Account.

3. On the Blob service section, click Lifecycle Management.

4. Copy the content from Listing 2-17 and paste it into the Lifecycle Management panel.

5. Click the Save button on the top-left corner of the panel.

LISTING 2-17   Lifecycle management policy definition

```
{
    "rules": [
        {
            "enabled": true,
            "name": "rule1",
            "type": "Lifecycle",
            "definition": {
                "actions": {
                    "baseBlob": {
                        "tierToCool": {
                            "daysAfterModificationGreaterThan": 30
                        },
                        "tierToArchive": {
                            "daysAfterModificationGreaterThan": 90
                        },
                        "delete": {
                            "daysAfterModificationGreaterThan": 2555
                        }
                    },
                    "snapshot": {
                        "delete": {
                            "daysAfterCreationGreaterThan": 90
                        }
                    }
                },
                "filters": {
                    "blobTypes": [
                        "blockBlob"
                    ],
                    "prefixMatch": [
                        "container-a"
                    ]
                }
            }
        }
    ]
}
```

The previous policy applies to all blobs under the container named container-a, as stated by the prefixMatch in the filters section. In the actions sections, you can see the following things:

- Blobs that are not modified in 30 days or more are moved to the cool tier.
- Blobs that are not modified in 90 days or more are moved to the archive tier.
- Blobs that are not modified in 2,555 days or more are deleted from the Storage Account.

Snapshots that are older than 90 days are also deleted. The lifecycle management engine process the policies every 24 hours. This means that it is possible that you won't see your changes reflected on your Storage Account until several hours after you made the changes.

> **NEED MORE REVIEW?** **STORAGE ACCESS TIERS AND LIFECYCLE MANAGEMENT POLICIES**
>
> You can extend your knowledge about storage access tiers and lifecycle management by reviewing the following articles from Microsoft Docs:
>
> - **Azure Blob Storage: Hot, Cool, and Archive Access Tiers** *https://docs.microsoft.com/en-us/azure/storage/blobs/storage-blob-storage-tiers*
>
> - **Manage the Azure Blob Storage Lifecycle** *https://docs.microsoft.com/en-us/azure/storage/blobs/storage-lifecycle-management-concepts*

Implement hot, cool, and archive storage

In the previous section, we reviewed how to configure archiving and retention policies in your Storage Accounts. In this section, we are going to review how to work with the different performance tiers using the Azure Storage SDK.

The following example shows how to switch a blob between the different access tiers:

1. Open Visual Studio Code and create a folder for your project.

2. In the Visual Studio Code Window, open a new terminal.

3. Use the following command to create a new console project:

   ```
   dotnet new console
   ```

4. Use the following command to install NuGet packages:

   ```
   dotnet add package <NuGet_package_name>
   ```

5. Install the following NuGet packages:

   - Azure.Storage.Blobs

   - Azure.Storage.Common

   - Microsoft.Extensions.Configuration

   - Microsoft.Extensions.Configuration.Binder

   - Microsoft.Extensions.Configuration.Json

6. In the project folder, create a new JSON file and name it **AppSettings.json**. Copy the content from Listing 2-18 to the JSON file.

7. Create a C# class file and name it **AppSettings.cs**.

8. Replace the contents of the AppSettings.cs file with the contents of Listing 2-19. Change the name of the namespace to match your project's name.

9. Create a C# class file and name it **Common.cs**.

10. Replace the contents of the Common.cs file with the contents of Listing 2-20.

11. Change the name of the namespace to match your project's name.

12. Replace the contents of the Program.cs file with the contents of Listing 2-21. Change the name of the namespace to match your project's name.

13. Edit your .csproj project file and add the following code inside the ItemGroup section:

```
<None Update="AppSettings.json">
    <CopyToOutputDirectory>PreserveNewest</CopyToOutputDirectory>
</None>
```

14. At this point, you can set some breakpoints in the Program.cs file to see, step by step, how the code moves the blob items between the different containers and Storage Accounts.

15. In the Visual Studio Window, press F5 to build and run your code. You can use the Azure portal or the Microsoft Azure Storage Explorer desktop application to review how your blob items change their locations.

LISTING 2-18   AppSettings.json configuration file

```
{
    "SASConnectionString": "<SASConnectionString_from_your_first_storage_account>",
    "AccountName": "<name_of_your_first_storage_account>",
    "ContainerName": "<source_container_name>"
}
```

LISTING 2-19   AppSettings.cs C# class

```
//C# .NET Core
using Microsoft.Extensions.Configuration;

namespace ch2_2_6
{
    public class AppSettings
    {
        public string SASConnectionString { get; set; }
        public string AccountName { get; set; }
        public string ContainerName { get; set; }

        public static AppSettings LoadAppSettings()
        {
            IConfigurationRoot configRoot = new ConfigurationBuilder()
                .AddJsonFile("AppSettings.json",false)
                .Build();
            AppSettings appSettings = configRoot.Get<AppSettings>();
            return appSettings;
        }
    }
}
```

LISTING 2-20 Common.cs C# class

```
//C# .NET Core
using Azure.Storage.Blobs;

namespace ch2_2_6
{
    public class Common
    {

        public static BlobServiceClient CreateBlobClientStorageFromSAS(string
SASConnectionString)
        {
            BlobServiceClient blobClient;
            try
            {
                blobClient = new BlobServiceClient(SASConnectionString);
            }
            catch (System.Exception)
            {
                throw;
            }

            return blobClient;

        }
    }
}
```

In Listing 2-21, portions of the code that are significant to the process of working with the different Access Tiers are shown in bold.

LISTING 2-21 Program.cs C# class

```
//C# .NET Core
using System.Threading.Tasks;
using System;
using Azure.Storage.Blobs;
using Azure.Storage.Blobs.Models;
using Azure.Storage.Blobs.Specialized;

namespace ch2_2_6
{
    class Program
    {
        static void Main(string[] args)
        {
```

```
            Console.WriteLine("Moving blobs between Access Tiers");
            Task.Run(async () => await StartContainersDemo()).Wait();
        }

        public static async Task StartContainersDemo()
        {
            string BlobFileName = "Testing.zip";
            AppSettings appSettings = AppSettings.LoadAppSettings();

            //Get a cloud client for the  Storage Account
            BlobServiceClient blobClient = Common.CreateBlobClientStorageFromSAS
(appSettings.SASConnectionString);

            //Get a reference for each container
            var containerReference = blobClient.GetBlobContainerClient(appSettings.
ContainerName);

            //Get a reference for the  blob
            var blobReference = containerReference.GetBlobClient(BlobFileName);

            //Get current Access Tier
            BlobProperties blobProperties = await blobReference.GetPropertiesAsync();
            System.Console.WriteLine($"Access Tier: {blobProperties.AccessTier}\t" +
                    $"Inferred: {blobProperties.AccessTierInferred}\t" +
                    $"Date last Access Tier change: {blobProperties.
AccessTierChangedOn}");

            //Change Access Tier to Cool
            blobReference.SetAccessTier(AccessTier.Cool);

            //Get current Access Tier
            blobProperties = await blobReference.GetPropertiesAsync();
            System.Console.WriteLine($"Access Tier: {blobProperties.AccessTier}\t" +
                    $"Inferred: {blobProperties.AccessTierInferred}\t" +
                    $"Date last Access Tier change: {blobProperties.
AccessTierChangedOn}");

            //Change Access Tier to Archive
            blobReference.SetAccessTier(AccessTier.Archive);

            //Get current Access Tier
            blobProperties = await blobReference.GetPropertiesAsync();
            System.Console.WriteLine($"Access Tier: {blobProperties.AccessTier}\t" +
                    $"Inferred: {blobProperties.AccessTierInferred}\t" +
                    $"Date last Access Tier change: {blobProperties.
AccessTierChangedOn}");
```

```
            //Change Access Tier to Hot
            blobReference.SetAccessTier(AccessTier.Hot);

            //Get current Access Tier
            blobProperties = await blobReference.GetPropertiesAsync();
            System.Console.WriteLine($"Access Tier: {blobProperties.AccessTier}\t" +
                        $"Inferred: {blobProperties.AccessTierInferred}\t" +
                        $"Date last Access Tier change: {blobProperties.
AccessTierChangedOn}\t" +
                        $"Archive Status: {blobProperties.ArchiveStatus}" );
        }
    }
}
```

As you can see, you can change to the different access tiers by using the SetAccessTier()
method from the BlobClient object representing the blob that you are working with. You
should also use the metadata property AccessTier from the blob for getting, which is the
current access tier where the blob is stored. You should pay special attention to the Archive-
Status property. If you try to change the access tier for a blob that is being rehydrated from
the archive tier, you get an exception. The AccessTierInferred property is also essential, as it
indicates if the current access tier is inherited from the container or is configured in the blob.

EXAM TIP

You should not try to change the access tier for a blob that is stored in an Azure Storage
Account Gen1. Only Azure Storage Account Gen2 allows working with access tiers. If you try
to use the SetAccessTier() method with a blob in an Azure Storage Account Gen1, you get an
exception.

EXAM TIP

You can move from hot to cool and vice versa to access tiers without needing to wait for
rehydration. The rehydration process only happens when you move a blob from the archive
to any other access tier.

Chapter summary

- Cosmos DB is a premium storage service that provides low-latency access to data dis-
  tributed across the globe.
- The PartitionKey system property defines the partition where the entity is stored.
- Choosing the correct PartitionKey is critical for achieving the right performance level.

- You can access Cosmos DB using different APIs: SQL, Table, Gremlin (Graph), MongoDB, and Cassandra.
- You can create your custom indexes in Cosmos DB.
- You can choose the property that is used as the partition key.
- You should avoid selecting partition keys that create too many or too few logical partitions.
- A logical partition has a limit of 20 GB of storage.
- Consistency levels define how the data is replicated between the different regions in a Cosmos DB account.
- There are five consistency levels: strong, bounded staleness, session, consistent prefix, and eventual.
- Strong consistency level provides a higher level of consistency but also has a higher latency.
- Eventual consistency level provides lower latency and lower data consistency.
- You can move blob items between containers in the same Storage Account or containers in different Storage Accounts.
- Azure Blob Storage service offers three different access tiers with different prices for storage and accessing data.
- You can move less frequently accessed data to cool or archive access tiers to save money.
- You can automatically manage the movement between access tiers by implementing lifecycle management policies.

Thought experiment

In this thought experiment, you can demonstrate your skills and knowledge about the topics covered in this chapter. You can find the answers to this thought experiment in the next section.

You are developing a web application that needs to work with information with a structure that can change during the lifetime of the development process. You need to query this information using different criteria. You need to ensure that your application returns the results of the queries as fast as possible. Your application needs to get information from an external system. The external system uploads information to an Azure Blob Storage Gen1 account.

With this information in mind, answer the following questions:

1. During the testing phases, you realize that the partition key is creating "hot spots." What should you do to solve the situation?

2. The information provided by the external system should be stored for several years due to legal reasons. Once the information is processed by your application, the information is no longer needed. You need to provide a secure and cost-effective solution.

Thought experiment answers

This section contains the solutions to the thought experiment.

1. A "hot spot" appears in a Cosmos DB container when you choose a partition key that stores most of the items in the same logical partition. You can solve the "hot spot" by changing the partition key and choosing a partition key that distributes the items evenly across the different logical partitions. Unfortunately, you cannot modify a partition key once you have created the container. In this scenario, you need to create a new container with the new partition key, and then migrate all the data to the new container using the AzCopy tool.

2. Because you need to keep the data for several years, you need to use the Storage Account Access Tiers. Because you are using a Gen1 Storage Account, you cannot use access tiers in that Storage Account. You need to upgrade your Blob Storage account to a Gen2. Once you have your Gen2 Storage Account, you can configure a lifecycle management policy for automatically moving to the archive tier for those files that have not been accessed for some time.

## CHAPTER 3

Implement Azure security

Regardless of the application, most of them have a standard requirement—protect the information that it manages. With regard to security, you need to think about the five dimensions of information security awareness: integrity, availability, confidentiality, authorization, and no-repudiation. Each of these dimensions is useful for evaluating the different risks and the countermeasures that you need to implement for mitigating the associated risks.

Implementing the appropriate security mechanism on your application can be tedious and potentially error-prone. Azure offers several mechanisms for adding security measures to your applications, controlling the different security aspects for accessing your data, and controlling the services that depend on your applications.

Skills covered in this chapter:

- Skill 3.1: Implement user authentication and authorization
- Skill 3.2: Implement secure cloud solutions

Skill 3.1: Implement user authentication and authorization

When a user wants to access your application, the user needs to prove that he or is the person he or she claims to be. Authentication is the action that the user performs to prove his or her identity. The user proves his or her identity using information known only to the user. An authentication system needs to address how to protect that information so only the appropriate user can access it while nobody else—not even the authorization system—can access it. A solution for this problem is to allow the user to access his or her data by using two different mechanisms for proving his or her identity—information that only the user knows and showing something, a token, only the user has. This approach is known as *multifactor authentication*.

Azure provides a secure mechanism for integrating authentication into your applications. You can use single-factor or multifactor authentication systems without worrying about the intricate details of implementing this kind of system.

Authenticating users before they can access your application is only part of the equation. Once your users have been authenticated, you need to decide if any user can access any part of your application, or if some parts of your application are restricted. The authorization controls which actions or sections the user can perform once he or she has been authorized.

Implement OAuth2 authentication

The authentication process requires the user to provide evidence that the user is the person he or she claims to be. In the real world, you can find multiple examples of authentication; for example, every time that you show your driver's license to a police officer, you are actually authenticating against the police officer. In the digital world, this authentication happens by providing some information that only you know, such as a secret word (a password), a digital certificate, or any kind of token that only you possess.

You have a range of options for implementing such an authentication mechanism in your application. Each implementation has its pros and cons, and the appropriate authentication mechanism depends on the level of security that you require for your application.

The most basic way of authenticating a user is form-based authentication. When you use this mechanism, you need to program a web form that asks the user for a username and a password. Once the user submits the form, the information in the form is compared to the values stored in your storage system. This storage system can be a relational database, a NoSQL database, or even a simple file with different formats stored on a server. If the information provided by the user matches the information stored in your system, the application sends a cookie to the user's browser. This cookie stores a key or some type of ID for authenticating subsequent requests to access your application without repeatedly asking the user for his or her username and password.

One of the most significant drawbacks of using form-based authentication is the authentication mechanism's dependency on cookies. Another inconvenience is that this is stateful, which requires that your server keeps an authentication session for tracking the activity between the server and the client. This dependency on cookies and authentication session management makes it more difficult to scale solutions using form-based authentication. One additional point to consider is that cookies don't work well (or it's challenging to work with them) on mobile apps. Fortunately, there are alternatives to form-based authentication that are more suitable for the requirements that have mobile or IoT scenarios; also, there are alternatives that can improve the scalability of your web application.

Token-based authentication is the most extended authentication mechanism for environments and scenarios that require high scalability or do not support the usage of cookies. Token-based authentication consists of a signed token that your application uses for authenticating requests and granting access to the resources in your application. The token does not contain the username and password of your user. Instead, the token stores some information about the authenticated user that your server can use for granting access to your application's resources.

When you use token-based authentication, you follow a workflow similar to the one shown in Figure 3-1:

1. An unauthenticated user connects to your web application.

2. Your web application redirects the user to the login page. This login page can be provided by your web application acting as a security server or by an external security server.

3. The security server validates the information provided by the user—typically, the username and password—and generates a JWT token.

4. The security server sends the JWT token to the user. The browser or mobile app that the user used to connect to your application is responsible for storing this JWT token for reusing it in the following requests.

5. The browsers or mobile app provides the JWT token to your web application on each following request.

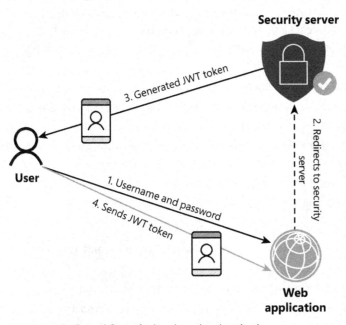

FIGURE 3-1 Basic workflow of token-based authentication

There are several token implementations, but the most extended one is JSON Web Token or JWT. A JWT token consists of

- **Header** The header contains the name of the algorithm used for signing the token.

- **Body or Payload** The body or payload contains different information about the token and the purpose of this token. The body contains several standard fields or claims that are defined in the RFC 7519 and any other custom field that you may need for your application.

- **Cryptographic signature** This is a string that validates your token and ensures that the token has not been corrupted or incorrectly manipulated.

One of the main advantages of using token-based authentication is that you can delegate the process of managing the identity of the users to external security servers. Thanks to this delegation, you can abstract from the implementation of managing and storing JWT tokens and usernames and passwords. That is what you do when you want to allow your users to access your application by using their Facebook, Google, or Twitter accounts. Your application trusts the identification and authentication processes made by these external security servers or identity managers, and you grant access to your application based on the information stored in the JWT token provided by the security server. You still need to store some information about the user. Still, there is no need to know anything about the password or any other information that the user needed to provide to the security server for authentication.

Microsoft provides the Identity Framework for working with authentication. You can use the Identity Framework for adding token-based authentication to your application. As previously mentioned, you can implement your own token-based authentication or use an external authentication provider that performs the verification of the user's login and password. The following example shows how to create a simple web application with Google authentication enabled. You can use a similar procedure for enabling another social login to your application, such as Facebook, Twitter, or Microsoft accounts.

1. Open Visual Studio 2019 on your computer.

2. In the welcome window of Visual Studio 2019, on the Get Started column, click Create A New Project.

3. On the Create A New Project window, on the All Languages drop-down menu, select C#.

4. In the Search For Templates text box, type **asp.net**.

5. On the result list, click ASP.NET Web Application (.NET Framework).

6. Click the Next button at the bottom-right corner of the window.

7. On the Configure Your New Project, type a Project Name, a Location, and a Solution Name for your project.

8. Click the Create button at the bottom-right corner of the window.

9. On the Create A New ASP.NET Web Application window, select MVC template from the template list in the middle of the left side of the window. MVC is for Model-View-Controller.

10. On the right side of the Create A New ASP.NET Web Application window, in the Authentication section, click the Change link.

11. On the Change Authentication window, select Individual User Accounts from the available options in the left column.

12. Click the OK button for closing the Change Authentication window.

13. Click the Create button at the bottom-right corner of the window.

At this point, you have created a basic ASP.NET web application configured for using form-based authentication. Now, you can check that the basic authentication in this application works. At this point, you are not using OAuth2 authentication:

1. Press F5 to run the project.

2. In the top-right corner of your application's web browser, click Register.

3. On the Register form, enter an email address and password.

4. Click the Register button at the bottom of the form.

Once you have registered, you are automatically logged on, and you can log off and log in again to ensure everything works properly.

Now, use the following steps for modifying the newly created web application for adding OAuth2 authentication:

1. In the Solution Explorer, click the name of your project and press F4.

2. In the Development Server section, ensure the value of the SSL Enabled setting is set to True.

3. Copy the SSL URL below the SSL Enabled setting, and close the Properties window.

4. In the Solution Explorer, right-click the project's name and click Properties at the bottom of the contextual menu. This opens your project's csproj file in a new tab.

5. On your project's csproj file tab, select the Web tab and paste the SSL URL in the Project Url text box in the Servers section.

6. Open the HomeController.cs file and add the `RequireHttps` attribute to the `HomeController` class:

```
[RequireHttps]
public class HomeController : Controller
{
    public ActionResult Index()
```

7. Create a Google Project for integrating your web application with Google's authentication platform. You need a Google account for these steps:

   a. Log in to your Google account.

   b. Navigate to *https://developers.google.com/identity/sign-in/web/devconsole-project*.

   c. Click Configure A Project.

   d. On the Configure A Project For Google Sign-In dialog box, select Create A New Project from the drop-down menu.

   e. Enter a name for your project and click Next at the bottom-left corner of the dialog box.

   f. On the Configure Your OAuth Client dialog box, type the name of your web application. This name is shown in the consent window that appears to the user during login.

   g. Click Next at the bottom-left corner of the dialog box.

h. On the Configure Your OAuth Client dialog box, select Web Server in the Where Are You Calling From? drop-down menu.

i. In the Authorized Redirect URIs text box, use the URL SSL that you copied in step 4 and create a redirect URI with this structure:

`<YOUR_URL_SSL>/signin-google`

Use the following example for your reference:

`https://localhost:44395/signin-google`

j. Click Create in the bottom-left corner of the dialog box.

k. On the You're All Set! dialog box, click the Download Client Configuration button. Alternatively, you can copy the Client ID and Client Secret fields. You need these values in a later step.

l. Click the API Console link at the bottom of the dialog box.

m. On the left side of the Google Console, click Library.

n. In the Search For APIs & Services text box, type **Google+**.

o. In the result list, click Google+ API.

p. In the Google+ API window, click the Enable button.

8. In the App_Start/Startup.Auth.cs file, in the `ConfigureAuth` method, uncomment the following lines:

```
app.UseGoogleAuthentication(new GoogleOAuth2AuthenticationOptions()
{
    ClientId = "",
    ClientSecret = ""
});
```

9. Use the Client ID and Client Secret values that you copied in step 7k and assign the value to the corresponding variable in the preceding code. (Note that these items need to be placed inside quotation marks.)

10. Press F5 for running the application.

11. Click Log In in the top-left corner of the web application.

12. Under the Use Another Service To Log In option on the left side of the page, click the Google button.

13. Log in using your Google account.

14. Click the Register button. Once you are logged in with Google, you are redirected to the web application. Because your Google account does not exist on your application's database, you get a registration form.

15. You are registered and logged in to your application using a Google account.

Once you have logged in to the application using your Google account, you can review the database and look for the new login information. You can view the database connections in the SQL Server Object Explorer. You can open the SQL Server Object Explorer from the View menu. You can see in the AspNetUsers table that there is a new entry for your new Google account login, but the PasswordHash field is empty. You can also review the AspNetUserLogins table. This table contains all the logins from external authorization providers, such as Google, that have been registered in your application.

The previous example reviewed how you can use third-party identity servers, like Google, for authenticating users in your application using the OAuth2 protocol. Now, we are going to review how to create your OAuth2 server. You usually add this type of authentication when you need these third-party applications to access some services or resources of your code. You can grant access to these applications by creating a token that authenticates the third-party application and grants access to specific parts of your HTTP service.

The OAuth protocol addresses the need to secure access to resources and information in your application by the third party's process. Without OAuth, if you want to grant access to an external application to the resources of your application, you need to use a username and password. If the third-party application is compromised, then the username and password are also compromised, and your resources are exposed. The OAuth protocol defines four different roles:

- **Resource owner** This is the person or entity that can grant access to the resources. If the resource owner is a person, it can also be referred to as the user.
- **Resource server** This is the server that hosts the resources that you want to share. This server needs to be able to accept and respond to the access codes used for accessing the resource.
- **Client** This is the third-party application that needs to access the resource. The client makes the needed requests to the resource server on behalf of the resource owner. The term "client" does not necessarily imply any specific implementation, like a server, a desktop, or any other kind of device.
- **Authorization server** This is the server that issues the access token to the client for accessing the resources. The client needs to be authenticated before it can get the correct token.

Figure 3-2 shows the basic authentication flow for OAuth.

As you can see in Figure 3-2, the process of acquiring a token for accessing a protected resource consists of the following steps:

- **Authentication request** The client requests access to the protected resource. The resource owner, based on the privileges of the client, grants access to the client for accessing the resource. The authentication of the client can be directly done by the resource owner or preferably by the authentication server.

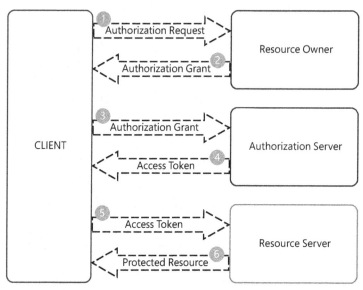

FIGURE 3-2 OAuth basic authentication flow

- **Authentication grant**   When the resource owner grants the client access to the resource, the client sends an authentication grant, which is a code or credential that represents the permission to access the resource, which has been granted by the resource owner. The client uses this authentication grant credential to request an access token to the authorization server. There are four different mechanisms for handling this authentication:

  - **Authorization code**   The client instructs the resource owner to request authentication to the authentication server. Once the resource owner is authenticated, the authentication server creates an authorization code that the resource owner sends back to the client. The client uses this authorization code as the grant for requesting the access token.

  - **Implicit**   Using this authentication grant flow, the authentication server does not authenticate the client. Instead, the client gets the access token without needing to authenticate to the resource server using an authentication grant. This implicit flow is a simplified authorization code flow. To improve security in this flow, the resource server uses the redirect URI provided by the client.

  - **Resource owner credentials**   Instead of using an authorization code or implicit authentication, the client uses the credentials of the resource owner for authenticating against the resource server. This type of authentication grant should be used only when there is a high level of trust between the client and the resource owner.

  - **Client credentials**   The client provides his or her credentials for accessing the resource. This authentication grant is useful for scenarios in which the client needs access to resources that are protected by the same authorization server as the client and are under the control of the client. This type of authentication grant is also useful if the resource server and the client arranged the same authorization for the resources and the client.

- **Access token** The client requests an access token from the authorization server that allows the client to access the resource on the resource server. The client sends this access token to the resource server with each request to access the resource. This access token has an expiration date. Once the access token is expired, the token is invalid, and the client needs to request another access token. To ease the process of renewing the access token, the authentication server provides two different tokens—the actual access token and a refresh token. The client uses the refresh token when it needs to renew an expired access token.

- **Protected resource** This is the resource that the client wants to access. The resource server protects the resource. The client needs to send the access token to the resource server every time it needs to access the resource.

NEED MORE REVIEW? **THE OAUTH 2.0 AUTHORIZATION FRAMEWORK**

You can get more information about the details of how the OAuth 2.0 Authorization Framework works by reviewing the official RFC 6749 at *https://tools.ietf.org/html/rfc6749*.

The following example shows how to implement OAuth 2.0 authentication in your Web API application. In this example, you are going to create an authorization server, a resource server, and a client that can request an access token before accessing the resource. For the sake of readability, we have split the steps for implementing this example into different parts. The following steps show how to create the authorization server:

1. Open Visual Studio 2019.
2. Click File > New > Project.
3. On the Create A New Project window, on the All Languages drop-down menu, select C#.
4. On the Search For Templates text box type **asp.net**.
5. On the result list, click ASP.NET Web Application (.NET Framework).
6. Click the Next button at the bottom-right corner of the window.
7. In the Configure Your New Project window, type a Project Name, a Location, and a Solution Name for your project.
8. Click the Create button at the bottom-right corner of the window.
9. In the Create A New ASP.NET Web Application window, click the MVC template.
10. Click the Change link in the Authentication section on the right side of the window.
11. On the Change Authentication window, click the Individual User Accounts option.
12. Click the OK button on the Change Authentication window.
13. Click the Create button on the Create A New ASP.NET Web Application window.

14. In Visual Studio, open the file at App_Start > Startup.Auth.cs, and add the following line to the beginning of the file:

```
using Microsoft.Owin.Security.OAuth;
```

15. Add the code shown in Listing 3-1 to the Startup.Auth.cs file. You need to add this code to the `ConfigureAuth()` method, after the line

```
app.UseTwoFactorRememberBrowserCookie(DefaultAuthenticationTypes.
TwoFactorRememberBrowserCookie);
```

16. Ensure the following using statements exist in the Startup.Auth.cs file for avoiding compilation errors:

- `using System;`
- `using Microsoft.AspNet.Identity;`
- `using Microsoft.AspNet.Identity.Owin;`
- `using Owin;`
- `using Microsoft.Owin;`
- `using Microsoft.Owin.Security.Cookies;`
- `using Microsoft.Owin.Security.OAuth;`
- `using Microsoft.Owin.Security.Infrastructure;`
- `using AuthorizationServer.Constants;`
- `using System.Threading.Tasks;`
- `using System.Collections.Concurrent;`
- `using System.Security.Claims;`
- `using System.Security.Principal;`
- `using System.Linq;`
- `using <your_project's_name>.Models;`

LISTING 3-1 Adding OAuth Authorization Server

```
// C#. ASP.NET.
//Setup the Authorization Server
            app.UseOAuthAuthorizationServer(new OAuthAuthorizationServerOptions
            {
                AuthorizeEndpointPath = new PathString(Paths.AuthorizePath),
                TokenEndpointPath = new PathString (Paths.TokenPath),
                ApplicationCanDisplayErrors = true,
#if DEBUG
                AllowInsecureHttp = true,
#endif
                Provider = new OAuthAuthorizationServerProvider
                {
                    OnValidateClientRedirectUri = ValidateClientRedirectUri,
```

```
                    OnValidateClientAuthentication = ValidateClientAuthentication,
                    OnGrantResourceOwnerCredentials = GrantResourceOwnerCredentials,
                    OnGrantClientCredentials = GrantClientCredentials
                },

// The authorization code provider is the object in charge of creating and receiving
// the authorization code.
        AuthorizationCodeProvider = new AuthenticationTokenProvider
        {
            OnCreate = CreateAuthenticationCode,
            OnReceive = ReceiveAuthenticationCode,
        },

        // The refresh token provider is in charge in creating and receiving refresh
        // token.
        RefreshTokenProvider = new AuthenticationTokenProvider
        {
            OnCreate = CreateRefreshToken,
            OnReceive = ReceiveRefreshToken,
        }
                });

                //Protect the resources on this server.
                app.UseOAuthBearerAuthentication(new OAuthBearerAuthenticationOptions
                {
                });
```

This code configures the OAuth Authentication Server by using the `UseOAuthAuthoriza-tionServer()` method. This method accepts an `OAuthAuthorizationServerOptions` object for configuring several useful endpoints:

- **AuthorizeEndpointPath**   The authorize endpoint is the path in the authorization server to which the client application redirects the user-agent to obtain the user or resource owner's consent to access the resource. With this consent, the client application can request an access token.

- **TokenEndpointPath**   This is the path in the authorization server that the client uses to obtain an access token. If the client is configured with a client secret, the client needs to provide this client secret on the request for obtaining a new token.

- **AllowInsecureHttp**   This setting allows the client to make requests to the authorize and token endpoints by using HTTP URIs instead of HTTPS URIs.

- **Provider**   Your authorization server application needs to provide the needed delegated methods for processing the different events that arise during the OAuth authorization flow. You can do this by implementing the `OAuthAuthorization-ServerProvider` interface or using the default implementation provided by the

OAuthAuthorizationServerProvider object. In this example, you use the OAuthAuthorizationServerProvider object and provide four delegate functions for the different events. Listings 3-2 to 3-5 show the different delegate methods that you use for the events managed by this provider.

- **AuthorizationCodeProvider**   When the authorization server authenticates the client, the server needs to send an authorization code to the server. This provider manages the events that arise during the management of the authentication code. Listings 3-6 and 3-7 show the delegate methods that manage the events of creating or receiving a code.

- **RefreshTokenProvider**   This object controls the events that happen when the client requests a refresh of an access token. Listings 3-8 and 3-9 show the delegate methods that control the events of creating and receiving a request of refreshing an access token.

17. Add the content from Listings 3-2 to 3-9 to the Startup.Auth.cs file. Add these methods to the Startup class. The implementation of these delegates is not suitable for production environments. For example, the validation of the client redirect URI, and the authentication of the clients are based on a hard-coded value stored in the Client class. In a real-world scenario, you should have these entities stored in a database. In this example, the creation of the access token, shown in Listing 3-4, is stored in an in-memory dictionary. In a real-world scenario, you should save in a database the access tokens that you grant to the clients.

LISTING 3-2   OnValidateClientRedirectUri delegate

```
// C#. ASP.NET.
private Task ValidateClientRedirectUri(OAuthValidateClientRedirectUriContext context)
    {
        if (context.ClientId == Clients.Client1.Id)
        {
            context.Validated(Clients.Client1.RedirectUrl);
        }
        else if (context.ClientId == Clients.Client2.Id)
        {
            context.Validated(Clients.Client2.RedirectUrl);
        }
        return Task.FromResult(0);
    }
```

LISTING 3-3   OnValidateClientAuthentication delegate

```
// C#. ASP.NET.
private Task ValidateClientAuthentication(OAuthValidateClientAuthenticationContext
context)
```

```
        {
            string clientId;
            string clientSecret;
            if (context.TryGetBasicCredentials(out clientId, out clientSecret) ||
                context.TryGetFormCredentials(out clientId, out clientSecret))
            {

                if (clientId == Clients.Client1.Id && clientSecret == Clients.Client1.
                    Secret)
                {
                    context.Validated();
                }

                else if (clientId == Clients.Client2.Id && clientSecret == Clients.
                        Client2.Secret)
                {
                    context.Validated();
                }
            }
            return Task.FromResult(0);

        }
```

LISTING 3-4   OnGrantResourceOwnerCredentials delegate

```
// C#. ASP.NET.
private Task GrantResourceOwnerCredentials(OAuthGrantResourceOwnerCredentialsContext
context)
        {

            ClaimsIdentity identity = new ClaimsIdentity(new GenericIdentity(context.
            UserName, OAuthDefaults.AuthenticationType), context.Scope.Select(x =>
            new Claim("urn:oauth:scope", x)));

            context.Validated(identity);

            return Task.FromResult(0);
        }
```

LISTING 3-5   OnGrantClientCredentials delegate

```
// C#. ASP.NET.
private Task GrantClientCredentials(OAuthGrantClientCredentialsContext context)
        {

            var identity = new ClaimsIdentity(new GenericIdentity(context.ClientId,
```

```
        OAuthDefaults.AuthenticationType), context.Scope.Select(x =>
        new Claim("urn:oauth:scope", x)));

        context.Validated(identity);

        return Task.FromResult(0);
    }
```

LISTING 3-6 Authorization code for OnCreate delegate

```
// C#. ASP.NET.
private void CreateAuthenticationCode(AuthenticationTokenCreateContext context)
    {
        context.SetToken(Guid.NewGuid().ToString("n") + Guid.NewGuid().
        ToString("n"));
        authenticationCodes[context.Token] = context.SerializeTicket();
    }
```

LISTING 3-7 Authorization code for OnReceive delegate

```
// C#. ASP.NET.
private void ReceiveAuthenticationCode(AuthenticationTokenReceiveContext context)
    {
        string value;
        if (_authenticationCodes.TryRemove(context.Token, out value))
        {
            context.DeserializeTicket(value);
        }
    }
```

LISTING 3-8 Refresh token for OnCreate delegate

```
// C#. ASP.NET.
private void CreateRefreshToken(AuthenticationTokenCreateContext context)
    {
        context.SetToken(context.SerializeTicket());
    }
```

LISTING 3-9 Refresh token for OnReceive delegate

```
// C#. ASP.NET.
private void ReceiveRefreshToken(AuthenticationTokenReceiveContext context)
    {
        context.DeserializeTicket(context.Token);
    }
```

18. Add the following private property to the Startup class in the Startup.Auth.cs file:

```
private readonly ConcurrentDictionary<string, string> _authenticationCodes =
            new ConcurrentDictionary<string, string>(StringComparer.Ordinal);
```

19. On the Solution Explorer window, add a new folder to your project called Constants.

20. On the Solution Explorer window, right-click the Constants folder and click Add > New Item.

21. On the New Item window, on the tree control on the left side of the window, click Installed > Visual C# > Code.

22. Click the template named Class.

23. At the bottom of the Add New Item window, type **Clients.cs** in the Name text box.

24. Click the Add button in the bottom-right corner of the window.

25. Replace the content of the Clients.cs file with the content in Listing 3-10. Change the namespace to match your project's name.

LISTING 3-10   Clients.cs

```
// C#. ASP.NET.

namespace <YOUR_PROJECT'S_NAME>.Constants
{
    public class Clients
    {
        public readonly static Client Client1 = new Client
        {
            Id = "123456",
            Secret = "abcdef",
            RedirectUrl = Paths.AuthorizeCodeCallBackPath
        };

        public readonly static Client Client2 = new Client
        {
            Id = "78901",
            Secret = "aasdasdef",
            RedirectUrl = Paths.ImplicitGrantCallBackPath
        };

    }

    public class Client
    {
        public string Id { get; set; }
```

```
            public string Secret { get; set; }

            public string RedirectUrl { get; set; }
        }
    }
```

26. On the Solution Explorer window, click your project's name and press F4.

27. On your project's properties window, ensure the value of SSL Enabled is set to True.

28. Copy the value of the SSL URL setting.

29. Right-click the project's name and click the Properties menu item at the bottom of the contextual menu.

30. On the project's properties tab in Visual Studio, click the Web element on the left side of the window.

31. In the Servers section, paste the SSL URL value that you copied in step 28 in the Project URL text box.

32. Add a new empty C# class to the Constants folder and name it **Paths.cs**. You can repeat the steps 20–24 to create a new C# class.

33. Replace the content of the file Paths.cs with the code shown in Listing 3-11.

34. Paste the value of the SSL URL that you copied on step 28 on the following constants:

   - **AuthorizationServerBaseAddress**

   - **ResourceServerBaseAddress**

   - **ImplicitGrantCallBackPath**   Ensure that you don't delete the URI part. This constant should look like <SSL URL>/Home/SignIn.

   - **AuthorizeCodeCallBackPath**   Ensure that you don't delete the URI part. This constant should look like <SSL URL>/Manage.

LISTING 3-11   Paths.cs

```
// C#. ASP.NET.
namespace <YOUR_PROJECT'S_NAME>.Constants
{
    public class Paths
    {
        public const string AuthorizationServerBaseAddress = "https://localhost:44317";
        public const string ResourceServerBaseAddress = "https://localhost:44317";
        public const string ImplicitGrantCallBackPath =
        "https://localhost:44317/Home/SignIn";
        public const string AuthorizeCodeCallBackPath = "https://localhost:44317/Manage";
```

```
        public const string AuthorizePath = "/OAuth/Authorize";
        public const string TokenPath = "/OAuth/Token";
        public const string LoginPath = "/Account/Login";
        public const string LogoutPath = "/Account/Logout";
        public const string MePath = "/api/Me";
    }
}
```

At this point, you need to create the API Controller that manages the requests to the Authorize and Token endpoint. When you configured the Authentication Server, you used the following code snippet for setting the endpoints that the server uses for attending OAuth requests:

```
app.UseOAuthAuthorizationServer(new OAuthAuthorizationServerOptions
        {
                AuthorizeEndpointPath = new PathString(Paths.AuthorizePath),
                TokenEndpointPath = new PathString(Paths.TokenPath),
```

If you review the value of the parameters AuthorizePath and TokenPath in your Paths class, you can see that their values are /OAuth/Authorize and /OAuth/Token, respectively. Now, you need to create the controller that manages the requests to these endpoints.

35. In the Solution Explorer window, right-click the Controllers folders in your project, and then choose Add > Controller.

36. On the Add Scaffold window, choose MVC 5 Controller – Empty.

37. Click the Add button.

38. On the Add Controller window, type **OAuthController**.

39. Open the OAuthController.cs file and replace the content of the file with the code shown in Listing 3-12.

LISTING 3-12 OAuthController.cs

```
// C#. ASP.NET.
using System.Security.Claims;
using System.Web;
using System.Web.Mvc;

namespace <your_project's_name>.Controllers
{
    public class OAuthController : Controller
    {

        // GET: OAuth/Authorize
        public ActionResult Authorize()
        {
            if (Response.StatusCode != 200)
```

```
            {
                return View("AuthorizeError");
            }

            var authentication = HttpContext.GetOwinContext().Authentication;
            var ticket = authentication.AuthenticateAsync("ApplicationCookie").Result;
            var identity = ticket != null ? ticket.Identity : null;
            if (identity == null)
            {
                authentication.Challenge("ApplicationCookie");
                return new HttpUnauthorizedResult();
            }

            var scopes = (Request.QueryString.Get("scope") ?? "").Split(' ');

            if (Request.HttpMethod == "POST")
            {
                if (!string.IsNullOrEmpty(Request.Form.Get("submit.Grant")))
                {

                    identity = new ClaimsIdentity(identity.Claims, "Bearer", identity.
                    NameClaimType, identity.RoleClaimType);
                    foreach (var scope in scopes)
                    {
                        identity.AddClaim(new Claim("urn:oauth:scope", scope));
                    }
                    authentication.SignIn(identity);
                }
                if (!string.IsNullOrEmpty(Request.Form.Get("submit.Login")))
                {
                    authentication.SignOut("ApplicationCookie");
                    authentication.Challenge("ApplicationCookie");
                    return new HttpUnauthorizedResult();
                }
            }

            return View();
        }
    }
}
```

40. On the Solution Explorer, right-click Views > OAuth, and then select Add > View.

41. On the Add View window, on the View Name field, type **Authorize**.

42. Click Add.

43. Replace the content of the file Authorize.cshtml with the code shown in Listing 3-13:

LISTING 3-13   Authorize.cshtml

```
// C#. ASP.NET.
@{
    ViewBag.Title = "Authorize";
}

@using System.Security.Claims
@using System.Web
@{
    var authentication = Context.GetOwinContext().Authentication;
    var ticket = authentication.AuthenticateAsync("ApplicationCookie").Result;
    var identity = ticket != null ? ticket.Identity : null;
    var scopes = (Request.QueryString.Get("scope") ?? "").Split(' ');
}
<!DOCTYPE html>
<html xmlns="http://www.w3.org/1999/xhtml">
<head>
    <title>@ViewBag.Title</title>
</head>
<body>
    <h1>Authorization Server</h1>
    <h2>OAuth2 Authorize</h2>
    <form method="POST">
        <p>Hello, @identity.Name</p>
        <p>A third party application wants to do the following on your behalf:</p>
        <ul>
            @foreach (var scope in scopes)
            {
                <li>@scope</li>
            }
        </ul>
        <p>
          <input type="submit" name="submit.Grant" value="Grant" />
          <input type="submit" name="submit.Login" value="Sign in as different user" />
        </p>
    </form>
</body>
</html>
```

44. Add another empty view named **AuthorizeError**.

45. Replace the content of the file AuthorizeError.cshtml with the code shown in Listing 3-14:

LISTING 3-14 AuthorizeError.cshtml

```
// C#. ASP.NET.
@{
    ViewBag.Title = "AuthorizeError";
}
@using System
@using System.Security.Claims
@using System.Web
@using Microsoft.Owin
@{
    IOwinContext owinContext = Context.GetOwinContext();
    var error = owinContext.Get<string>("oauth.Error");
    var errorDescription = owinContext.Get<string>("oauth.ErrorDescription");
    var errorUri = owinContext.Get<string>("oauth.ErrorUri");
}
<!DOCTYPE html>
<html xmlns="http://www.w3.org/1999/xhtml">
<head>
    <title>@ViewBag.Title</title>
</head>
<body>
    <h1>Katana.Sandbox.WebServer</h1>
    <h2>OAuth2 Authorize Error</h2>
    <p>Error: @error</p>
    <p>@errorDescription</p>
</body>
</html>
```

This example only provides an implementation for the Authorize endpoint for the sake of simplicity. An authorized user in your application needs to grant access to the resources in your application explicitly. When the user grants those privileges, the application automatically creates an in-memory OAuth token that you can use to make a request to the protected resources. In a real-world scenario, this process should be separated in the two different endpoints—Authorize and Token. You should use the Token endpoint for creating or refreshing the access token issued by the authorization server.

Now that you have created and configured your authorization server, you can create the resource server. In this example, you are going to create the resource server on the same application where you implemented the authorization server. In a real-world scenario, you can use the same application, or you can use a different application deployed by a different server or Azure App Service.

1. On the Solution Explorer window, right-click the Controllers folder in your project and click Add > Controller.

2. On the Add New Scaffolded Item window, select the Web API 2 Controller — Empty template.

3. Click the Add button.

4. In the Add Controller window, type **MeController** and click the Add button.

5. Replace the content of the MeController.cs file with the code shown in Listing 3-15. This controller is quite simple and only returns the information stored in the token that you provide to the resource server when you try to access the resource.

LISTING 3-15 MeController.cs

```
// C#. ASP.NET.
using System.Collections.Generic;
using System.Linq;
using System.Security.Claims;
using System.Web.Http;

namespace <your_project's_name>.Controllers
{
    [Authorize]
    public class MeController : ApiController
    {
        // GET api/<controller>
        public IEnumerable<object> Get()
        {
            var identity = User.Identity as ClaimsIdentity;
            return identity.Claims.Select(c => new
            {
                Type = c.Type,
                Value = c.Value
            });
        }
    }
}
```

6. On the Solution Explorer window, in the App_Start folder, rename the file WebApiConfig.cs to Startup.WebApi.cs.

7. In the Visual Studio window, click Tools > NuGet Package Manager > Manage NuGet Packages For Solution.

8. On the NuGet Package Manager tab, click Browse.

9. Type **Microsoft asp.net web api owin** and press Enter.

10. Click the Microsoft.AspNet.WebApi.Owin package.

11. On the right side of the NuGet Manager tab, click the check box beside your project.

12. Click the Install button.

13. On the Preview Changes window, click OK.

14. On the License Acceptance, click the I Accept button.

15. Open the Startup.WebApi.cs file and change the content of the file with the content shown in Listing 3-16.

LISTING 3-16 Startup.WebApi.cs

```
// C#. ASP.NET.
using Microsoft.Owin.Security.OAuth;
using Owin;
using System.Web.Http;

namespace <your_project's_name>
{
    public partial class Startup
    {
        public void ConfigureWebApi(IAppBuilder app)
        {
            var config = new HttpConfiguration();
            // Web API configuration and services
            // Configure Web API to use only bearer token authentication.
            config.SuppressDefaultHostAuthentication();
            config.Filters.Add(new HostAuthenticationFilter(OAuthDefaults
                            .AuthenticationType));

            // Web API routes
            config.MapHttpAttributeRoutes();

            config.Routes.MapHttpRoute(
                name: "DefaultApi",
                routeTemplate: "api/{controller}/{id}",
                defaults: new { id = RouteParameter.Optional }
            );

            app.UseWebApi(config);
        }
    }
}
```

16. Open the Startup.cs file and add the following line at the end of the Configuration() method:

```
ConfigureWebApi(app);
```

Once you have implemented the resource server in your application, you should be able to make requests to the authorization server to get access to the resource published by the resource server. As you saw in the OAuth workflow, you need to get authenticated by the authorization server before you can get an access token. This means that you need to be logged in to the application before being able to make any requests to the /OAuth/Authorize endpoint.

Now you can create your client application that makes requests to the authorization server and resource server. That client application can be the same application that you used for implementing the authorization and resource servers. You are going to modify the default MVC template for making requests to the Authorization and Resource servers.

1. In the Visual Studio window, click Tools > NuGet Package Manager > Manage NuGet Packages For Solution.

2. In the NuGet Package Manager tab, click Browse.

3. Type **DotNetOpenAuth.OAuth2.Client** and press Enter.

4. Click the DotNetOpenAuth.OAuth2.Client package. This NuGet package eases the interaction with OAuth servers.

5. On the right side of the NuGet Manager tab, click the check box beside your project.

6. Click the Install button.

7. On the Preview Changes window, click OK.

8. Open the ManageController.cs file.

9. Add the following using statements to the ManageController.cs file:

   - **using System;**
   - **using System.Linq;**
   - **using System.Threading.Tasks;**
   - **using System.Web;**
   - **using System.Web.Mvc;**
   - **using Microsoft.AspNet.Identity;**
   - **using Microsoft.AspNet.Identity.Owin;**
   - **using Microsoft.Owin.Security;**
   - **using AuthorizationServer.Models;**
   - **using AuthorizationServer.Constants;**
   - **using DotNetOpenAuth.OAuth2;**
   - **using System.Net.Http;**

10. Replace the Index() method with the code shown in Listing 3-17.

LISTING 3-17   Index method in ManageController.cs

```csharp
// C#. ASP.NET.
public async Task<ActionResult> Index(ManageMessageId? message)
    {
        ViewBag.StatusMessage =
        message == ManageMessageId.ChangePasswordSuccess ? "Your password has been
                changed."
        : message == ManageMessageId.SetPasswordSuccess ? "Your password has been
                set."
        : message == ManageMessageId.SetTwoFactorSuccess ? "Your two-factor
                authentication provider has been set."
        : message == ManageMessageId.Error ? "An error has occurred."
        : message == ManageMessageId.AddPhoneSuccess ? "Your phone number was
                added."
        : message == ManageMessageId.RemovePhoneSuccess ? "Your phone number was
                removed."
        : "";

        var userId = User.Identity.GetUserId();
        var model = new IndexViewModel
        {
            HasPassword = HasPassword(),
            PhoneNumber = await UserManager.GetPhoneNumberAsync(userId),
            TwoFactor = await UserManager.GetTwoFactorEnabledAsync(userId),
            Logins = await UserManager.GetLoginsAsync(userId),
            BrowserRemembered = await AuthenticationManager.
                            TwoFactorBrowserRememberedAsync(userId)
        };

        ViewBag.AccessToken = Request.Form["AccessToken"] ?? "";
        ViewBag.RefreshToken = Request.Form["RefreshToken"] ?? "";
        ViewBag.Action = "";
        ViewBag.ApiResponse = "";

        InitializeWebServerClient();
        var accessToken = Request.Form["AccessToken"];
        if (string.IsNullOrEmpty(accessToken))
        {

            var authorizationState = _webServerClient.ProcessUserAuthorization(
                            Request);
            if (authorizationState != null)
            {
                ViewBag.AccessToken = authorizationState.AccessToken;
                ViewBag.RefreshToken = authorizationState.RefreshToken;
                ViewBag.Action = Request.Path;
```

```
        }
    }

    if (!string.IsNullOrEmpty(Request.Form.Get("submit.Authorize")))
    {

        var userAuthorization = _webServerClient.PrepareRequestUserAuthorization(
        new[] { "bio", "notes" });
            userAuthorization.Send(HttpContext);
            Response.End();
    }
    else if (!string.IsNullOrEmpty(Request.Form.Get("submit.Refresh")))
    {
        var state = new AuthorizationState
        {
            AccessToken = Request.Form["AccessToken"],
            RefreshToken = Request.Form["RefreshToken"]
        };
        if (_webServerClient.RefreshAuthorization(state))
        {
            ViewBag.AccessToken = state.AccessToken;
            ViewBag.RefreshToken = state.RefreshToken;
        }
    }
    else if (!string.IsNullOrEmpty(Request.Form.Get("submit.CallApi")))
    {
        var resourceServerUri = new Uri(Paths.ResourceServerBaseAddress);
        var client = new HttpClient(_webServerClient.CreateAuthorizingHandler
                    (accessToken));
        var body = client.GetStringAsync(new Uri(resourceServerUri,
                    Paths.MePath)).Result;
        ViewBag.ApiResponse = body;
    }

    return View(model);
}
```

11. Add the following property to the `ManageController` class:

```
private WebServerClient _webServerClient;
```

12. Add the following helper method to the `ManageController` class:

```
private void InitializeWebServerClient()
{
    var authorizationServerUri = new Uri(Paths.AuthorizationServerBaseAddress);
    var authorizationServer = new AuthorizationServerDescription
    {
```

```
                AuthorizationEndpoint = new Uri(authorizationServerUri, Paths.AuthorizePath),
                TokenEndpoint = new Uri(authorizationServerUri, Paths.TokenPath)
        };

    _webServerClient = new WebServerClient(authorizationServer, Clients.Client1.Id,
    Clients.Client1.Secret);
    }
```

13. On the `Application_Start()` method in the Global.asax.cs file, add the following line:

```
AntiForgeryConfig.SuppressXFrameOptionsHeader = true;
```

14. Add the following using statement to the Global.asax.cs file:

```
using System.Web.Helpers;
```

15. In the Solution Explorer window, click Views > Manage > Index.cshtml.

16. Add the code shown in Listing 3-18 after the section Two-Factor Authentication in the Index.cshtml file.

LISTING 3-18 Authorization Code Grant section

```
// C#. ASP.NET.
<dt>Authorization Code Grant Client:</dt>
        <dd>
            <form id="form1" action="@ViewBag.Action" method="POST">
                <div>
                    Access Token<br />
                    <input id="AccessToken" name="AccessToken" width="604" type="text"
                            value="@ViewBag.AccessToken" />

                    <input id="Authorize" name="submit.Authorize" value="Authorize"
                    type="submit" />
                    <br />
                    <br />
                    Refresh Token<br />
                    <input id="RefreshToken" name="RefreshToken" width="604"
                    type="text" value="@ViewBag.RefreshToken" />
                    <input id="Refresh" name="submit.Refresh" value="Refresh"
                    type="submit" />
                    <br />
                    <br />
                    <input id="CallApi" name="submit.CallApi" value="Access Protected
                    Resource API" type="submit" />
                </div>
                <div>
                    @ViewBag.ApiResponse
                </div>
            </form>
        </dd>
```

At this point, your example application is ready for testing the implementation of the different actors that take part in the OAuth workflow. The following steps show how to test your OAuth implementation to ensure that it works correctly:

1. Open the example project in Visual Studio and press F5 to run the project.

2. A new web browser window should open with your web application. Click the Register link located on the top-left corner of the page.

3. On the Register page, add an email address and password and confirm the password. Then click the Register button. You are going to use this user to grant privileges to the OAuth client for making requests to the /OAuth/Me endpoint.

4. Once you have registered the new user, you are automatically logged on and redirected to the Home page.

5. On the Home page, click your user's email link at the top-left corner of the Home page.

6. On the Manage page, click the Authorize button, which redirects you to the Authorization Server page.

7. On the Authorization Server page, review the information provided and click the Grant button. After you grant access to the OAuth client application, you get the access and refresh token shown in Figure 3-3, which is needed to make requests to the resource server.

8. Click the Access Protected Resource API to make a request to the /OAuth/Me endpoint. You should get all information stored in the identity claim that you use for making this request, including the scopes bio and notes.

FIGURE 3-3 OAuth Access and Refresh Token

> **NEED MORE REVIEW? OAUTH AUTHORIZATION SERVER**
>
> In this example, you reviewed how to implement the authorization and resource server, the client, and the resource owner on the same web application. Although this is a valid scenario, you usually would find that these roles are implemented on a separate application. The code we reviewed is based on the example explained in the Microsoft Docs article at *https://docs.microsoft.com/en-us/aspnet/aspnet/overview/owin-and-katana/owin-oauth-20-authorization-server*. In that article, you can review how to implement each role in separate applications.

EXAM TIP

When you are working with OAuth2 authentication, remember that you don't need to store the username and password information in your system. You can delegate that task in specialized authentication servers. Once the user has been authenticated successfully, the authentication server sends an access token that you can use for confirming the identity of the client. This access token needs to be refreshed once the token expires. The OAuth2 can use a refresh token for requesting a new access token without asking the user again for his or her credentials.

Create and implement shared access signatures

Until now, all the protection and access control mechanisms that reviewed in this section had to do with protecting the information managed directly by your application. These mechanisms are good if your application manages and presents the information to the user. Still, they are not appropriate for other services that can also store information managed by your application. If your application uses Azure Storage accounts for storing some reports, images, or documents in a table, and you want to grant access to third parties to that information, none of the previously reviewed mechanisms are appropriate for this scenario.

When you are working with storage, you need to control who and how much time a process, person, or application can access your data. Azure Storage allows you to control this access based on several levels of protection:

- **Shared Key Authorization** You use one of the two access keys configured at the Azure Storage account level to construct the correct request for accessing the Azure Storage account resources. You need to use the Authorization Header for using the access key in your request. The access key provides access to the entire Azure Storage account and all its containers, such as blobs, files, queues, and tables. You can consider Azure Storage account keys to be like the root password of the Azure Storage account.

- **Shared Access Signatures** You use Shared Access Signatures (SAS) for narrowing the access to specific containers inside the Storage Account. The advantage of using SAS is that you don't need to share the Azure Storage account's access key. You can also configure a higher level of granularity when setting access to your data.

The drawback of using shared access keys is that if either of the two access keys is exposed, the Azure Storage account and all the containers and data in the Azure Storage account are also exposed. The access keys also allow us to create or delete elements in the Azure Storage account.

Shared access signatures provide you with a mechanism for sharing access with clients or applications to your Azure Storage account without exposing the entire account. You can configure each SAS with a different level of access to each of the following:

- **Services** You can configure SAS for granting access only to the services that you require, such as blob, file, queue, or table.

- **Resource types**   You can configure access to a service, container, or object. For the Blob service, this means that you can configure the access to API calls at the service level, such as list containers. If you configure the SAS token at the container level, you can make API calls like getting or setting container metadata or creating new blobs. If you decide to configure the access at the object level, you can make API calls like creating or updating blobs in the container.

- **Permissions**   Configure the action or actions that the user is allowed to perform in the configured resources and services.

- **Date expiration**   You can configure the period for which the configured SAS is valid for accessing the data.

- **IP addresses**   You can configure a single IP address or range of IP addresses that are allowed to access your storage.

- **Protocols**   You can configure whether the access to your storage is performed using HTTPS-only or HTTP and HTTPS protocols. You cannot grant access to the HTTP-only protocol.

Azure Storage uses the values of previous parameters for constructing the signature that grants access to your storage. You can configure three different types of SAS:

- **User delegation SAS**   This type of SAS applies only to Blob Storage. You use an Azure Active Directory user account for securing the SAS token

- **Account SAS**   Account SAS controls access to the entire Storage Account. You can also control access to operations at the service level, like getting service stats or getting or setting service properties. You need to use the storage account key for securing this kind of SAS.

- **Service SAS**   Service SAS delegates access to only specific services inside the Storage Account. You need to use the storage account key for securing this kind of SAS.

Regardless of the SAS type, you need to construct a SAS token for access. You append this SAS token to the URL that you use for accessing your storage resource. One of the parameters of a SAS token is the signature. The Azure Storage Account service uses this signature to authorize access to the storage resources. The way you create this signature depends on the SAS type that you are using.

For user delegation SAS, you need to use a user delegation key created using Azure Active Directory (Azure AD) credentials. The user used for creating this delegation key needs to have granted the `Microsoft.Storage/storageAccounts/blobServices/generateUserDelegationKey/action` Role-Base Access Control permission. We review role-based access control authorization in the "Control access to resources by using role-based access controls (RBAC)" later in this chapter.

For service or account SAS, you need to use the Azure Storage Account key for creating the signature that you have to include in the SAS token. For constructing the SAS URI for an Account SAS, you need to use the parameters shown in Table 3-1.

TABLE 3-1 Account SAS URI parameters

Parameter Name	URI Parameter	Required	Description
api-version	api-version	NO	You can set the version of the storage service API that processes your request.
SignedVersion	sv	YES	Sets the version of the signed storage service used to authenticate your request. This version should be 2015-04-05 or later.
SignedServices	ss	YES	Sets the services to which you grant access. You can grant access to more than one service by combining the allowed values: ■ **Blob** You need to use the value (b) in the SAS URI. ■ **Queue** You need to use the value (q) in the SAS URI. ■ **Table** You need to use the value (t) in the SAS URI. ■ **File** You need to use the value (f) in the SAS URI.
SignedResourceTypes	Srt	YES	Sets the resource type to which you grant access. You can configure more than one resource type simultaneously by combining more than one of the allowed values: ■ **Service** You need to use the value (s) in the SAS URI. ■ **Container** You need to use the value (c) in the SAS URI. ■ **Object** You need to use the value (o) in the SAS URI.
SignedPermission	sp	YES	Configures the permissions that you grant to the resource types and services configured on previous parameters. Not all permissions apply to all resource types and services. The following list only shows the permissions that apply to the Blob service: ■ **Read** You need to use the value (r) in the SAS URI. ■ **Write** You need to use the value (w) in the SAS URI. ■ **Delete** You need to use the value (d) in the SAS URI. ■ **List** You need to use the value (l) in the SAS URI. ■ **Add** You need to use the value (a) in the SAS URI. ■ **Create** You need to use the value (c) in the SAS URI. If you set a permission that is meaningful only for a service or resource type that you didn't set on the previous parameters, the permission is silently ignored.

Parameter Name	URI Parameter	Required	Description
SignedStart	st	NO	Sets the time and date at which the SAS token is valid. It must be expressed in UTC using ISO 8601 format: ■ YYYY-MM-DD ■ YYYY-MM-DDThh:mmTZD ■ YYYY-MM-DDThh:mm:ssTZD
SignedExpiry	se	YES	Sets the time and date in which the SAS token becomes invalid. It must be expressed in UTC using ISO 8601 format.
SignedIP	sip	NO	Sets the IP or range of IP addresses from which the storage service accepts requests. When using ranges of IPs, the limits are included in the range.
SignedProtocol	spr	NO	Sets the protocol allowed to request the API. Correct values are ■ HTTPS only (https) ■ HTTP and HTTPS (https, http)
Signature	sig	YES	This is an HMAC-SHA256–computed string encoded using Base64 that the API uses for authenticating your request. You calculate the signature based on the parameters that you provided in the SAS URI. This signature must be valid to process your request.

Use the following procedure for constructing and testing your own account SAS token:

1. Sign in to the management portal (*http://portal.azure.com*).

2. In the search box at the top of the Azure portal, type the name of your Storage Account.

3. On the Storage Account blade, click Shared Access Signature in the Settings section.

4. On the Shared Access Signature panel, deselect the File, Table, and Queue check boxes under Allowed Services, as shown in Figure 3-4. Leave the Blob check box selected.

5. Ensure that all options in Allowed Resource Types and Allowed Permissions are checked, as shown in Figure 3-4.

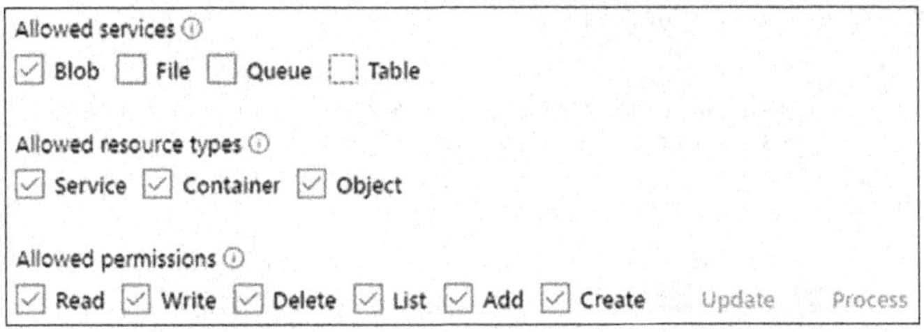

FIGURE 3-4 Configuring the Account SAS policy

6. In the Start And Expiry Date/Time section, set a date for a start and ending date and time during which the Azure Storage Account accepts requests using this token.

7. Ensure that Allowed IP addresses have no value in the text box, and HTTPS Only is selected in the Allowed Protocols section.

8. In the Signing Key drop-down menu, make sure that you have selected the Key1 value.

9. Click the Generate SAS And Connection String button at the bottom of the panel.

10. Copy the Blob Service SAS URL. Now you can test your SAS token, using a tool such as Postman, curl, a web browser, or Microsoft Azure Storage Explorer.

11. Open Microsoft Azure Storage Explorer. If you don't have this tool installed, you can download it from *https://azure.microsoft.com/en-us/features/storage-explorer/*.

12. On the Microsoft Azure Storage Explorer window, on the left side of the window, click the button with a plug icon. This button opens the Connect dialog box.

13. In the Connect dialog box, select the Use A Shared Access Signature (SAS) URI option.

14. Click the Next button on the bottom side of the dialog box.

15. In the Attach With SAS URI, type a name for your connection in the Display Name text box.

16. In the URI text box, paste the URL that you copied in step 10.

17. Click the Next button.

18. Click the Connect button.

Once the connection is created, you should be able to view your Blob Storage service and create new containers or blobs inside the containers.

If you need to narrow the access to your resources and limit it only to tables or entities, you can create a Service SAS. This type of SAS token is quite similar to an Account SAS; you need to create a URI that you append to the URL that you use to request your Blob Storage service. Account and Service SAS share most of the URI parameters, although some parameters are specific to the service, and you need to consider them when creating your Service SAS token. Table 3-2 shows the parameters that you need to set for creating a Blob Service SAS. Other Azure Storage services require different parameters.

TABLE 3-2 BLOB Service SAS URI parameters

Parameter Name	URI Parameter	Required	Description
SignedVersion	Sv	YES	Sets the version of the signed storage service used to authenticate your request. This version should be 2015-04-05 or later.
SignedResource	sr	YES	Sets the type of shared resource: ■ **Blob** You need to use the value (b) in the SAS URI. ■ **Container** You need to use the value (c) in the SAS URI.
SignedPermission	Sp	YES	Configures the permissions that you grant to the shared resource. You need to omit this parameter if you decide to use a Stored Access Policy.

Parameter Name	URI Parameter	Required	Description
SignedStart	st	NO	Sets the time and date at which the SAS token is valid. It must be expressed in UTC using ISO 8601 format: ■ YYYY-MM-DD ■ YYYY-MM-DDThh:mmTZD ■ YYYY-MM-DDThh:mm:ssTZD If you use an API version 2012-02-12 or later, the difference between signedstart and signedexpiry cannot be greater than one hour unless you are using a container policy.
SignedExpiry	se	YES	Sets the time and date in which the SAS token becomes invalid. It must be expressed in UTC using ISO 8601 format. You need to omit this parameter if you decide to use a Stored Access Policy.
SignedIP	sip	NO	Sets the IP or range of IP addresses from which the storage service accepts requests. When using ranges of IPs, the limits are included in the range. You need to omit this parameter if you decide to use a Stored Access Policy.
SignedProtocol	spr	NO	Sets the protocol allowed to request the API. Valid values are ■ HTTPS only (https) ■ HTTP and HTTPS (https, http)
SignedIdentifier	Si	NO	Relates the SAS URI that you are constructing with a Stored Access Policy on your Storage Account. Using Stored Access Policies provides a greater level of security.
Signature	sig	YES	This is an HMAC-SHA256 computed string encoded using Base64 that the API uses for authenticating your request. You calculate the signature based on the parameters that you provided in the SAS URI. This signature must be valid to process your request.
Cache-Control	rscc	NO	Requires version (sv) set to 2013-08-15 or later for Blob service and 2015-02-21 or later for File service.
Content-Disposition	rscd	NO	Requires version (sv) set to 2013-08-15 or later for Blob service and 2015-02-21 or later for File service.
Content-Encoding	rsce	NO	Requires version (sv) set to 2013-08-15 or later for Blob service and 2015-02-21 or later for File service.
Content-Language	rscl	NO	Requires version (sv) set to 2013-08-15 or later for Blob service and 2015-02-21 or later for File service.
Content-Type	rsct	NO	Requires version (sv) set to 2013-08-15 or later for Blob service and 2015-02-21 or later for File service.

The following example shows how to create a Shared Access Signature for a blob container. This SAS token grants access to the blob container and all blobs stored inside the blob container. For this example, you need an Azure Storage Account with a blob container that is configured with the private access level:

1. Open the Azure portal (*https://portal.azure.com*).

2. In the search text box at the top of the Azure portal, type the name of your Azure Storage Account.

3. In the Results list, click the name of your Azure Storage Account.

4. On your Azure Storage Account's blade, click StorageExplorer (preview) in the navigation menu on the left side of the blade.

5. On the Storage Explorer (preview) panel shown in Figure 3-5, expand the Blob Containers node and right-click the container, which you need to grant access.

FIGURE 3-5 Storage services in the Storage Explorer (preview)

6. In the contextual menu over your blob container, click Get Shared Access Signature.

7. In the Shared Access Signature panel shown in Figure 3-6, configure the Start Time, Expiry Time, and Permissions that you want to grant to the SAS token.

8. Click the Create button at the bottom of the panel.

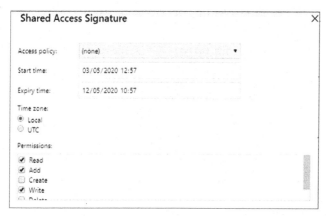

FIGURE 3-6 Creating a Shared Access Signature

9. On the Shared Access Signature panel, copy the URL of the newly generated SAS. You can share this SAS URL with any third party who needs to access this specific blob.

You can use these same steps for creating a SAS token for a single blob in a container. Just navigate using the Storage Explorer to the blob that you want to share, right-click the blob, and click Get Shared Access Signature in the contextual menu.

As you can imagine, one drawback of using this approach is that anyone who has access to the SAS URL can access the information protected by that SAS. You can improve the security of the SAS tokens by creating a Stored Access Policy and attaching the policy to the SAS token. Stored Access Policies allows you to define access policies that are associated and stored with the table that you want to protect. When you define a Stored Access Policy, you provide an identifier to the policy. Then you use this identifier when you construct the Service SAS token. You need to include this identifier when you construct the signature that authenticates the token and is part of the SAS itself.

The advantage of using a Stored Access Policy is that you define and control the validity and expiration of the policy without needing to modify the Service SAS token. Using a Stored Access Policy also improves security by hiding the details of the Access Policy from the user, as you just provide the name of the Stored Access Policy. You can associate up to five different stored access policies.

> **NEED MORE REVIEW?** **WORKING WITH STORED ACCESS POLICIES**
>
> Working with Stored Access Policies is similar to working with ad-hoc access policies. You can review how to work with Stored Access Policies by reviewing the following articles:
>
> - *https://docs.microsoft.com/en-us/rest/api/storageservices/define-stored-access-policy*
>
> - *https://docs.microsoft.com/en-us/azure/storage/common/storage-stored-access-policy-define-dotnet*

The following example shows how to create a user delegation SAS token using a .NET Core console application:

1. Open Visual Studio Code and create a folder for your project.

2. In the Visual Studio Code Window, open a new terminal.

3. Use the following command to create a new console project:

    ```
    dotnet new console
    ```

4. Use the following command to install NuGet packages:

    ```
    dotnet add package <NuGet_package_name>
    ```

5. Install the following NuGet packages:

    - Azure.Storage.Blobs
    - Azure.Identity

6. Open the Program.cs file and replace the content with the code shown in Listing 3-19.

LISTING 3-19   Program.cs

```
// C#. ASP.NET.
using System;
using Azure.Storage.Blobs;
using Azure.Storage.Blobs.Models;
using Azure.Storage.Sas;
using Azure;
using Azure.Identity;


namespace ch3_1_2
{
    class Program
    {
        static void Main(string[] args)
        {
            string storageAccount = "az204testing";

            DateTimeOffset startTimeKey = DateTimeOffset.UtcNow;
            DateTimeOffset endTimeKey = DateTimeOffset.UtcNow.AddDays(7);
            DateTimeOffset startTimeSAS = startTimeKey;
            DateTimeOffset endTimeSAS = startTimeSAS.AddDays(1);

            Uri blobEndpointUri = new Uri($"https://{storageAccount}.blob.core.windows.
                            net");

            var defaultCredentials = new DefaultAzureCredential(true);

            BlobServiceClient blobClient = new BlobServiceClient(blobEndpointUri,
                                defaultCredentials);

            //Get the key. We are going to use this key for creating the SAS
            UserDelegationKey key = blobClient.GetUserDelegationKey(startTimeKey,
            endTimeKey);

            System.Console.WriteLine($"User Key Starts on: {key.SignedStartsOn}");
            System.Console.WriteLine($"User Key Expires on: {key.SignedExpiresOn}");
            System.Console.WriteLine($"User Key Service: {key.SignedService}");
            System.Console.WriteLine($"User Key Version: {key.SignedVersion}");

            //We need to use the BlobSasBuilder for creating the SAS
            BlobSasBuilder blobSasBuilder = new BlobSasBuilder()
            {
                StartsOn = startTimeSAS,
                ExpiresOn = endTimeSAS
            };
```

```
                //We set the permissions Create, List, Add, Read, and Write
                blobSasBuilder.SetPermissions("clarw");

                string sasToken = blobSasBuilder.ToSasQueryParameters
                (key, storageAccount).ToString();

                System.Console.WriteLine($"SAS Token: {sasToken}");
            }
        }
    }
}
```

As you can see in the piece of code in bold in Listing 3-19, you use the `GetUserDelegation-Key()` method for getting a user delegation key for your Azure Storage Account. The user you are using for getting this key needs to have assigned the `Microsoft.Storage/storageAccounts/blobServices/generateUserDelegationKey/action` permission, otherwise you get an exception.

Once you have your user delegation key, you use the `BlobSasBuilder` class for creating an object that constructs the SAS token for you. Using the instance of the `BlobSasBuilder` class, you can configure the permissions that you need for accessing the container. In this case, you use the `SetPermission()` method with the parameter `clarw` that matches with the permissions shown in Table 3-1. In this example, because we didn't set any container name, we get a SAS token for the Azure Blob Storage Account.

Using the `ToSasQueryParameters()` method from the `BlobSasBuilder` class, you get the actual SAS token. You need to provide the user delegation key that you obtained previously to this method for getting the SAS token.

Once you get your SAS token, you can use it for accessing your Azure Storage Account. The code in Listing 3-20 shows how to interact with your Azure Storage Account, using the SAS token that you created in Listing 3-19. If you want to test this code, just replace the content of the Program.cs file that you created in the previous example, with the content in Listing 3-20. Before replacing your code, you need to add the System.IO NuGet Package by running the following command in your Visual Studio Code terminal window:

```
dotnet add package System.IO
```

LISTING 3-20   Program.cs extension

```
// C#. ASP.NET.
using System;
using Azure.Storage.Blobs;
using Azure.Storage.Blobs.Models;
using Azure.Storage.Sas;
using Azure;
using Azure.Identity;
using System.IO;


namespace ch3_1_2
{
    class Program
    {
        static void Main(string[] args)
        {
            string storageAccount = "az204testing";
            string containerName = "az204-blob-testing";
            string blobName = System.IO.Path.GetRandomFileName();

            DateTimeOffset startTimeKey = DateTimeOffset.UtcNow;
            DateTimeOffset endTimeKey = DateTimeOffset.UtcNow.AddDays(7);
            DateTimeOffset startTimeSAS = startTimeKey;
            DateTimeOffset endTimeSAS = startTimeSAS.AddYears(1);

            Uri blobEndpointUri = new Uri($"https://{storageAccount}.blob.core.
                              windows.net");

            var defaultCredentials = new DefaultAzureCredential(true);

            BlobServiceClient blobClient = new BlobServiceClient(blobEndpointUri,
                                    defaultCredentials);

            //Get the key. We are going to use this key for creating the SAS
            UserDelegationKey key = blobClient.GetUserDelegationKey(startTimeKey,
            endTimeKey);

            Console.WriteLine($"User Key Starts on: {key.SignedStartsOn}");
            Console.WriteLine($"User Key Expires on: {key.SignedExpiresOn}");
            Console.WriteLine($"User Key Service: {key.SignedService}");
            Console.WriteLine($"User Key Version: {key.SignedVersion}");

            //We need to use the BlobSasBuilder for creating the SAS
            BlobSasBuilder blobSasBuilder = new BlobSasBuilder()
            {
                BlobContainerName = containerName,
```

```
        BlobName = blobName,
        Resource = "b",
        StartsOn = startTimeSAS,
        ExpiresOn = endTimeSAS,
        Protocol = Azure.Storage.Sas.SasProtocol.Https
};

//We set the permissions Create, List, Add, Read, and Write
blobSasBuilder.SetPermissions(BlobSasPermissions.All);

string sasToken = blobSasBuilder.ToSasQueryParameters
(key, storageAccount).ToString();

Console.WriteLine($"SAS Token: {sasToken}");

//We construct the full URI for accessing the Azure Storage Account
UriBuilder blobUri = new UriBuilder()
{
    Scheme = "https",
    Host = $"{storageAccount}.blob.core.windows.net",
    Path = $"{containerName}/{blobName}",
    Query = sasToken
};

//We create a random text file
using (System.IO.StreamWriter sw = System.IO.File.CreateText(blobName))
{
    sw.Write("This is a testing blob for uploading using user delegated SAS
    tokens");
}

BlobClient testingBlob = new BlobClient(blobUri.Uri);
testingBlob.Upload(blobName);

//Now we download the blob again and print the content.

Console.WriteLine($"Reading content from testing blob {blobName}");
Console.WriteLine();

BlobDownloadInfo downloadInfo = testingBlob.Download();

using (StreamReader sr = new StreamReader(downloadInfo.Content, true))
{
    string line;
    while ((line = sr.ReadLine()) != null)
    {
```

```
                    Console.WriteLine(line);
                }
            }

            Console.WriteLine();
            Console.WriteLine("Finished reading content from testing blob");

        }
    }
}
```

We have put the essential parts in bold in Listing 3-20. When you need to use the SAS token for working Azure Storage accounts, you need to construct the correct SAS token for the element that you are working with. This means, if you are going to work with a container, then you need to create a SAS token for that container and get a reference to the container using the BlobContainerClient. Once you have the reference to the container, you can keep working with other child elements without needing to create a new SAS token for each element inside the container.

In the example in Listing 3-20, we create a random text file with some content that we uploaded to the container and then downloaded again. Then we created a SAS token for uploading the random text file. Notice that we created the SAS token pointing to a blob doesn't even exist. Once we have the correct SAS token, with the correct permissions, we created a BlobClient object using the URI pointing to the final location in the Azure Blob Storage account inside the container. We use the SAS token as the query parameter of the URI. Once we have our BlobClient object representing the blob, we can perform all the needed operations without needing the create a new SAS token for the same blob, as long as the token has not expired.

> **NEED MORE REVIEW?** **SHARED ACCESS SIGNATURES**
>
> If you want to read more about how to work with Shared Access Signatures, not only with the Azure Blob Storage service, but with other Azure Storage services, like Tables, Queue, or Files, you can review the article at *https://docs.microsoft.com/en-us/rest/api/storageservices/delegate-access-with-shared-access-signature.*

 EXAM TIP

If you plan to work with user delegation SAS, you need to consider that this type of SAS is available only for Azure Blob Storage and Azure Data Lake Storage Gen2. You cannot use either Stored Access Policies when working with user delegation SAS.

Register apps and use Azure Active Directory to authenticate users

You can secure access to the information managed by your application by using several mechanisms, like form-based authentication, SSL authentication, Windows authentication, or OAuth2 authentication, among others. Each of these mechanisms has advantages and disadvantages.

The "Implement OAuth2 authentication" section earlier in this chapter reviewed how to use OAuth2 authentication with a basic web application. When we reviewed the OAuth2 concepts in that section, you saw that in the OAuth2 authentication flow, there is a security server that takes care of providing the security mechanisms for authenticating the users. Once the security server authenticates, the server emits a token that your application can validate and use for authenticating the request from your application's client. When working with the security server, you can use your own implementation of an OAuth2 server, or you can rely on third-party security services, like Facebook, Google, or LinkedIn, among others.

Microsoft also provides the ability to use its services for OAuth2 authentication. Microsoft provides OAuth2 authentication through its Azure Active Directory identity service. On its most basic layer, this is a free service that you can use if you want your application's users to be able to log in using Microsoft Outlook.com accounts for personal accounts or the Azure Active Directory accounts for professional accounts.

Before your application can use the Azure Active Directory service for authenticating your application's users, you need to register the application in your Azure Active Directory tenant. When you are registering your application, there are some points that you need to consider before proceeding to the registration:

- **Supported account types**   You need to consider whether the users of your application would be
  - **Users from your organization only**   Any person that have an user account in your Azure Active Directory tenant would be able to use your application.
  - **Users from any organization**   You use this option when you want any user with a professional or educational Azure Active Directory account to be able to log into your application.
  - **Users from any organization or Microsoft accounts**   You use this option if you want your users to log into your application by using professional, educational, or any of the freely available Microsoft accounts.
- **Platform**   The OAuth2 authentication is not limited to web applications. You can also use this type of authentication with mobile platforms, like iOS or Android, or desktop platforms, like macOS, Console, IoT, Windows, or UWP.

The following procedure shows how to register a web application in the Azure Active Directory:

1. Open the Azure portal (*https://portal.azure.com*),

2. On the Search resources, services, and docs text box on the middle-top of the Azure Portal, type **Azure Active Directory**.

3. On the result list, in the Services section, click Azure Active Directory.

4. On the Azure Active Directory page, in the Manage section, click App Registrations.

5. In the App Registrations blade, click the New Registration button on the top-left corner of the panel.

6. In the Register An Application blade, type the name of your application in the Name text box.

7. In the Supported Account Types option control, select Accounts In This Organizational Directory Only.

8. Click the Register button at the bottom-left corner of the blade.

The previous procedure shows how to make a simple app registration. Now you need to configure your app registration according to your app needs. One of the most critical sets of settings that you need to configure correctly is the Authentication settings, shown in Figure 3-7. You use the Authentication settings for managing the authentication options for your application. In this case, you configure the redirect URLs used by Azure Active Directory for authenticating your application's requests. If the redirect URL provided by your application doesn't match with any of the URLs configured in this section, the authentication fails.

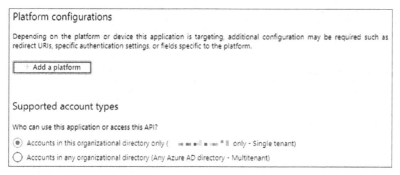

FIGURE 3-7 Authentication settings

The other two critical sets of settings that you need to consider are Certificates & Secrets and API Permissions. Certificates & Secrets enables you to manage the Certificates and the Secrets that your application needs to use to provide the application's identity when requesting a token. You use the API Permissions for configuring the needed permission for calling other APIs, either from Microsoft, your organization, or other third-party APIs. The following example shows how to create a simple web application that uses Azure Active Directory authentication. Although you could register the app for this example directly from the wizard in Visual Studio 2019, we prefer to show you how to make an app registration directly from the Azure portal. In this example, you are going to use the app that you registered in the previous procedure. If you didn't follow that procedure, you should review and follow it before you can proceed with the following example:

1. Open Visual Studio 2019.

2. In the welcome window of Visual Studio 2019, on the Get Started column, click Create A New Project.

3. On the Create A New Project window, on All Languages drop-down menu, select C#.

4. In the Search For Templates text box, type **asp.net**.

5. In the result list, click ASP.NET Web Application (.NET Framework).

6. Click the Next button at the bottom-right corner of the window.

7. On the Configure Your New Project window, type a Project Name, a Location, and a Solution Name for your project.

8. Click the Create button at the bottom-right corner of the window.

9. In the Create A New ASP.NET Web Application window, select the MVC template on the template list in the middle of the left side of the window. MVC is for Model-View-Controller.

10. On the right side of the Create A New ASP.NET Web Application window, on the Authentication section, ensure the Authentication is set to No Authentication.

11. Click the Create button at the bottom-right corner of the window.

12. Open the Azure portal (*https://portal.azure.com*) and navigate to the app that you registered in the previous example.

13. In the Overview blade of your app in the Azure portal, copy the value of the parameter Application (client) ID. You need this value for a later step.

14. In the Manage section on the left side of your App blade, click Certificates & Secrets.

15. On the Certificates & Secrets blade, in the Client Secrets area, click the New Client Secret button.

16. Type a description in the text box for this client secret.

17. Click the Add button.

18. In the Client Secrets area, on the list of client secrets, copy the value of the client secret that you just created. You need this value in a later step.

19. On the Solution Explorer window in your Visual Studio 2019 window, right-click the Connected Services node.

20. Click Add Connected Service in the contextual menu.

21. In the Connected Services Windows, click Authentication with Azure Active Directory.

22. In the Configure Azure AD Authentication window, in the Introduction section, click the Next button at the bottom right of the window.

23. In the Single Sign-On section, in the Domain drop-down menu, type the name of your tenant. You can find this information in the Azure portal, in the Overview blade of your Azure Active Directory tenant.

24. On the Configuration Settings area, select Use Settings From An Existing Azure AD Application To Configure Your Project.

25. In the Client ID text box, paste the value that you copied in step 13.

26. Leave Redirect URI blank.

27. Click the Next button at the bottom right of the window.

28. In the Directory Access section, check the Read Directory Data option.

29. In the Client Secret text box, copy the client secret that you created in step 18.

30. Click the Finish button.

31. In the Azure AD Authentication window, wait for the wizard to add all the needed code to your application.

32. In the Solution Explorer, click the name of your project and press F4.

33. In the Properties window, copy the value of the SSL URL setting. You need this value in a later step.

34. Open the Azure portal and navigate to your registered app in your Azure Active Directory tenant.

35. On your registered app blade, in the Manage section, click Authentication.

36. On the Authentication blade, in the Platform Configurations area, click the Add A Platform button.

37. On the Configure Platforms panel, in the Web Applications section, click Web.

38. On the Redirect URI text box, copy the value of the SSL URL setting that you copied in step 33.

39. In the Implicit Grant section, check ID Tokens.

40. Click the Configure button.

41. In your Visual Studio 2019 window, press F5 for running your project.

Once you execute the web application, a generic Microsoft login page should appear in your browser. You need to provide a valid user account from your tenant to log in. At this point, your application uses the Azure Active Directory for authenticating users. Additionally, you can also read information from your tenant.

When you run the Authentication with the Azure Active Directory wizard, there are some code changes that you should understand. The wizard adds some properties to the appSettings section in the web.config file. These properties represent relevant settings needed for connecting to your Azure Active Directory tenant:

- **ida:ClientId** This is the ID representing your registered application in your Azure Active Directory tenant.

- **ida:AADInstance** Provides the instance that you are going to use for authentication. In most situations, you use general public instances. You only need to change this value if your tenant is hosted in isolated instances like Government, China, or Germany.

- **ida:Domain** This is your Azure Active Directory tenant, where you registered your app.

- **ida:TenantId**   This is the ID representing the tenant where you registered your app.

- **ida:PostLogoutRedirectUri**   This is the URL where Microsoft redirects the user once the authentication process finished successfully. This value must match with the value configured in your app registration in the Azure portal.

- **ida:ClientSecret**   The client secret is similar to the password that your application uses for authenticating against the Azure Active Directory service before it can interact with the APIs protected by the identity service.

As with any other authorization system in C#, you need to add the [Authorized] attribute to any resource that you want to protect. In this case, the wizard adds this attribute to any existing controller in your application. Finally, the most critical piece of code is the one used for configuring the OpenID/OAuth2 authentication. Listing 3-21 shows the code snippet added to your Startup.Auth.cs file for connecting your application with Azure Active Directory.

LISTING 3-21   Program.cs extension

```
// C#. ASP.NET.
app.UseOpenIdConnectAuthentication(
            new OpenIdConnectAuthenticationOptions
            {
                ClientId = clientId,
                Authority = Authority,
                PostLogoutRedirectUri = postLogoutRedirectUri,

                Notifications = new OpenIdConnectAuthenticationNotifications()
                {
                    // If there is a code in the OpenID Connect response, redeem //
                    it for an access token and refresh token, and store those
                    // away.
                    AuthorizationCodeReceived = (context) =>
                    {
                        var code = context.Code;
                        ClientCredential credential = new ClientCredential
                                                (clientId, appKey);
                        string signedInUserID = context.AuthenticationTicket
                                        .Identity.FindFirst(ClaimTypes
                                        .NameIdentifier).Value;
                        AuthenticationContext authContext =
                        new AuthenticationContext(Authority,
                        new ADALTokenCache(signedInUserID));
                        return authContext.AcquireTokenByAuthorizationCodeAsync(
                            code, new Uri(HttpContext.Current.Request.Url
                            .GetLeftPart(UriPartial.Path)), credential,
                            graphResourceId);
                    }
                }
            });
```

EXAM TIP

When you are registering a new application in your Azure Active Directory tenant, you need to consider which will be your target user. If you need for any user from any Azure Active Directory organization to be able to log into your application, you need to configure a multitenant app. In those multitenant scenarios, the app registration and management is always performed in your tenant and not in any other external tenant.

Control access to resources by using role-based access controls (RBAC)

When you are working with your Azure subscription, there are situations where you need to grant access to other users. These users may need access only to specific resources inside your subscription, like a specific resource group or to an Azure SQL Database. You can achieve this level of granularity by using role-based access controls (RBAC).

Built on top of the Azure Resource Manager, RBAC provides fine-grained access control to the different resources in an Azure subscription. When working with RBAC, you need to consider the following concepts:

- **Security principal** This is the entity that requests permission for doing an action. A security principal can be one of the following:
  - **User** This is an individual who has a profile in an Azure Active Directory tenant. You are not limited to your own tenant. You can assign a role to users in other tenants as well.
  - **Group** This is a set of users.
  - **Service principal** This is like a user for an application. A service principal represents an application inside the tenant.
  - **Managed identity** This kind of identity represents cloud applications that need to access resources in your Azure tenant. Azure automatically manages this kind of identity.
- **Permission** This is the action that you can perform with a resource. An example of an action would be requesting a user delegation key for creating a SAS token. Another example of an action is listing the content of a container. You cannot directly assign a role to a security principal. You always need to use a role or role definition.

- **Role definition** Usually known as just role for short, a role definition is a collection of permissions. You assign a role to a security principal. There are a lot of predefined roles in Azure that you can use for managing access to the resources. There are four fundamental roles:

  - **Owner** Grants full access to all resources in the scope.

  - **Contributor** Grants modify access to all resources in the scope. You can perform all modification operations, including deleting, with the resources in the scope. You cannot grant roles to other security principals.

  - **Reader** Grants read access to all resources in the scope.

  - **User Access Administrator** Useful only for managing user access to Azure resources.

  Aside from these four fundamental built-in roles, there are roles specific to each service, like Virtual Machine Contributor or Cosmos DB Account Reader.

- **Scope** This is the group of resources where you assign the role. You can set a role at four different levels: management group (a group of subscriptions), subscription, resource group, and resource. These four levels are organized in a parent-child relationship where the management group is the highest level and resource is the lowest. When you assign a role to level, those permission are inherited by the lower levels. That means that if you grant the Owner role to a user at the subscription level, that user has the Owner privileges in all the resource groups and resources in that subscription.

- **Role assignment** This is the junction between the different pieces of RBAC. A role assignment connects a security principal with a role and a scope. Figure 3-8 shows the relationship between the different RBAC elements.

The following procedure shows how to grant the Contributor role to a resource group:

1. Open the Azure portal (*https://portal.azure.com*).

2. In the Search Resources, Services, And Docs text box, type the name of the resource group where you want to grant the Contributor role.

3. In the result list, click the name of the resource group.

4. On the Resource Group blade, click Access Control (IAM) on the left side of the control.

5. On the Access Control (IAM) blade, click the Add button on the top-left corner of the blade.

6. On the contextual menu that appears below the Add button, click Add Role Assignment.

7. On the Add Role Assignment blade, on the Role drop-down menu, select Contributor.

8. Leave the Assign Access To drop-down menu set to the default value.

9. In the Select text box, type the name of the user, group, or service principal that you want to assign the Contributor role.

10. On the result list below the Select text box, click the security principal that you want to assign the role.

11. Click the Save button on the bottom-left corner of the Add Role Assignment blade.

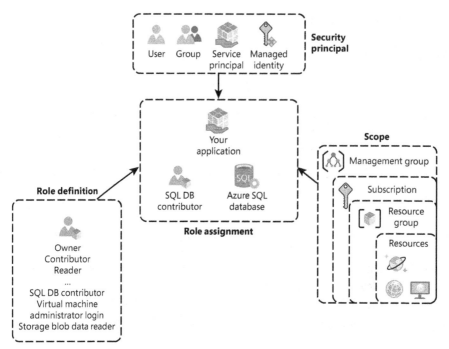

FIGURE 3-8 Role-based access control

Making role assignments to other levels, like management groups, subscriptions, or resources, is similar to the previous procedure. In general, you make the RBAC role association in the Access Control (IAM) section of each level.

NEED MORE REVIEW? **RBAC CUSTOM ROLES**

Although Azure provides a good amount of built-in roles, there could be situations where the built-in roles don't have the right privileges for your needs. In those situations, you can create a custom role. When you define a custom role, you use the role in the same way as you use a built-in role. You need to create a role definition for your role by configuring the needed permissions for your custom role. You can find more information about how to create custom roles by reviewing the article at *https://docs.microsoft.com/en-us/azure/ role-based-access-control/custom-roles*.

EXAM TIP

When you are assigning specific service roles, carefully review the permissions granted by the role. In general, granting access to a resource doesn't grant access to the data managed by that resource. For example, the Storage Account Contributor grants access for managing Storage Accounts but doesn't grant access to the data itself.

Skill 3.2: Implement secure cloud solutions

The previous skill reviewed how to protect access to the data by authenticating and authorizing users who try to access the information managed in your application. This protection is only a portion of the mechanisms that you should put in place for protecting your data. You also need to ensure that all the configuration needed for running your application in the different environments is managed securely. The reason for also securing that configuration is that configuration has the needed passwords, certificates, and secrets for accessing the information managed by your application.

When you encrypt your data, you need to use encryption and decryption keys or secrets for accessing and protecting the data. Storing these secrets and encryption keys is as important as encrypting the data. Losing an encryption or decryption key is similar to losing your house's keys. The Azure Key Vault allows you to securely store these encryption/decryption keys as well as other secrets or certificates that your applications may require in a secured encryption store in Azure. In conjunction with Managed Identities, the Azure Key Vault services allow you to securely store your secrets without needing to store a password, certificate, or any kind of credentials for accessing your secrets.

> **This skill covers how to**
> - Secure app configuration data by using the App Configuration and KeyVault API
> - Manage keys, secrets, and certificates by using the KeyVault API
> - Implement Managed Identities for Azure resources

Secure app configuration data by using the App Configuration and KeyVault API

Most of today's medium to large applications are based on distributed architectures. Independently of whether the infrastructure that executes your application is based on virtual machines, containers, serverless computing, or any other type of computing, you need to share the configuration between the elements that execute the same component of your application. For example, if your application runs on an Internet Information Services cluster behind a load balancer, all the virtual machines hosting the IIS service share the same configuration for running your application.

This kind of scenario is where Azure App Configuration becomes a handy tool. Azure App Configuration allows you to store all the necessary configuration for your cloud application in a single repository. Other Azure services also allow you to manage configuration for your apps, but they have some crucial differences that you should consider:

- **Azure App Service settings** As you know, you can create settings for your Azure App Service. These settings apply to the instance that you are configuring. You can even create different settings values for different deployment slots. On the other hand, the

Azure App Configuration service is a centralized configuration service that allows you to share the same configuration between different Azure App Service instances. You also need to consider that the Azure App Configuration service is not limited to Azure App Service. You can also use it with containerized applications or with applications running inside virtual machines.

■ **Azure Key Vault**   Azure Key Vault allows you to securely store passwords, secrets, and any other setting that your application may need. The encryption is performed using hardware-level encryption, among other interesting features like certificates rotation or granular access policies. Although Azure App Configuration encrypts the value of your configuration, Azure Key Vault still provides higher levels of security. You can use the Azure Key Vault in conjunction with Azure App Configuration by creating references in Azure App Configuration to items stored in the Azure Key Vault.

When you work with Azure App Configuration, you need to deal with two different components: the App Configuration store and the SDK. The Azure App Configuration store is the place where you store your configuration. When you configure your Azure App Configuration store, you can choose between two different pricing tiers: Free and Standard. The main difference between the two pricing tiers is the number of stores that you can create in a subscription. In the Free tier, you are limited to one store per subscription whereas you don't have such a limitation in the Standard tier. Other differences between the two tiers are the maximum size of the store: 10 MB in the Free tier versus 1 GB in the Standard tier, or the size of the key history: 7 days in the Free tier versus 30 days in the Standard tier. You can switch from the Free to the Standard tier at any moment, but you cannot switch back to the Free tier from the Standard tier. The following procedure shows how to create an Azure App Configuration:

1.   Open the Azure portal (*https://portal.azure.com*).

2.   Click the Create A Resource button in the Azure Services section at the top of the Azure portal.

3.   In the New blade, type **app configuration** in the Search The Marketplace text box.

4.   In the result list below the text box, click App Configuration.

5.   In the App Configuration blade, click the Create button.

6.   In the App Configuration blade, type a name for the App Configuration store in the Resource Name text box. The name must contain only alphanumeric ASCII characters or the hyphen (-) character, and it must be between 5 and 50 characters.

7.   Select the subscription where you want to deploy your App Configuration store using the Subscription drop-down menu.

8.   In the Resource Group drop-down menu, select the resource group where you want to deploy your App Configuration store. Alternatively, you can create a new resource group by clicking the Create New link below the Resource Group drop-down menu.

9.   Select a location in the Location drop-down menu.

10. In the Pricing Tier drop-down menu, select Free.

11. Click the Create button at the bottom of the blade.

Once you have created your Azure App Configuration store, you can create the key-value pairs for storing your configuration. Before you create your first key-value pair, you should review how keys work inside the App Configuration store.

A key is an identifier associated with a value stored in the App Configuration store. You use the key for retrieving a value from the store. Keys are case-sensitive, so "appSample204" and "APPSAMPLE204" are different keys. This is important because some languages or frameworks are case-insensitive for settings, so you should not use case-sensitivity for differencing keys. When naming a key, you can use any Unicode character, except the asterisk (*), the comma (,), and the back slash (\). If you need to include any of these reserved characters, you need to prepend the back slash (\) escape character. As a best practice, you should consider using namespace when naming your keys. By using a separator character between the different levels, you can create a hierarchy of settings inside your store. As the Azure App Configuration service doesn't analyze or parse your keys, it is entirely up to you to choose the namespace that better fits your needs. Some examples of keys using namespaces are

```
AppSample:Devel:DbConnection
AppSample:AUS:WelcomeMessage
```

You can also add a label attribute to a key. By default, the label attribute is null. You can use the label for making values different using the same key. This is especially useful when used for deployment environments: The following three examples are different keys because the labels are different:

```
Key = AppSample:DBConnection - Label = Develop
Key = AppSample:DBConnection - Label = Stage
Key = AppSample:DBConnection - Label = Production
```

When creating a new key-value pair, you have a limit of 10,000 for the size of the pair. This limit applies to the size of the key, plus the size of the optional label, plus the size of the value. You should also bear in mind that the same limitations that apply to the string that you use for the key are the same for value. That is, you can use any Unicode character for the value, except asterisk (*), comma (,), and back slash (\). If you need to include any of these reserved characters, you need to prepend the back slash (\) escape character.

> **NEED MORE REVIEW?** **FEATURE MANAGEMENT AND DYNAMIC CONFIGURATION**
>
> You can take advantage of Azure App Configuration for implementing more advanced features like feature management or dynamic configuration. The following articles give you more insight about these features:
>
> - **Feature Management** *https://docs.microsoft.com/en-us/azure/azure-app-configuration/quickstart-feature-flag-aspnet-core*
>
> - **Enable Dynamic configuration** *https://docs.microsoft.com/en-us/azure/azure-app-configuration/enable-dynamic-configuration-aspnet-core*

After you've reviewed the basics of the Azure App Configuration, you can review how to use this service in your code. The following example is based on the code in Chapter 2 in the section "Interact with data using the appropriate SDK." In this example, you are going to modify the code for using an Azure App Container store instead of using an AppSettings JSON file:

1. Open Visual Studio Code and create a folder for your project.
2. In the Visual Studio Code Window, open a new terminal.
3. Use the following command to create a new console project:

    ```
    dotnet new console
    ```

4. Use the following command to install NuGet packages:

    ```
    dotnet add package <NuGet_package_name>
    ```

5. Install the following NuGet packages:

    - Azure.Storage.Blobs
    - Azure.Storage.Common
    - Azure.Identity
    - Microsoft.Extensions.Configuration
    - Microsoft.Extensions.Configuration.AzureAppConfiguration

6. Create a C# class file and name it **AppSettings.cs**.
7. Replace the contents of the AppSettings.cs file with the contents of Listing 3-22. Change the name of the namespace to match your project's name.
8. Create a C# class file and name it **Common.cs**.
9. Replace the contents of the Common.cs file with the contents of Listing 3-23.
10. Change the name of the namespace to match your project's name.
11. Replace the contents of the **Program.cs** file with the contents of Listing 3-24. Change the name of the namespace to match your project's name.

LISTING 3-22 AppSettings.cs

```csharp
// C#. ASP.NET.
using System;
using Microsoft.Extensions.Configuration;

namespace ch3_2_1
{
    public class AppSettings
    {
        public string SourceSASConnectionString { get; set; }
        public string SourceAccountName { get; set; }
        public string SourceContainerName { get; set; }
        public string DestinationSASConnectionString { get; set; }
```

```
        public string DestinationAccountName { get; set; }
        public string DestinationContainerName { get; set; }

        public static AppSettings LoadAppSettings()
        {
            var builder = new ConfigurationBuilder();
            builder.AddAzureAppConfiguration(Environment.GetEnvironmentVariable
            ("ConnectionString"));

            var config = builder.Build();
            AppSettings appSettings = new AppSettings();
            appSettings.SourceSASConnectionString = config["TestAZ204:StorageAccount:
                                              Source:ConnectionString"];
            appSettings.SourceAccountName = config["TestAZ204:StorageAccount:Source:
                                    AccountName"];
            appSettings.SourceContainerName = config["TestAZ204:StorageAccount:
                                         Source:ContainerName"];
            appSettings.DestinationSASConnectionString = config["TestAZ204:Storage
                                                    Account:Destination:
                                                    ConnectionString"];
            appSettings.DestinationAccountName = config["TestAZ204:StorageAccount:
                                            Destination:AccountName"];
            appSettings.DestinationContainerName = config["TestAZ204:StorageAccount:
                                            Destination:ContainerName"];

            return appSettings;
        }
    }
}
```

LISTING 3-23 Common.cs

```
// C#. ASP.NET.
using Azure.Storage.Blobs;

namespace ch3_2_1
{
    public class Common
    {

        public static BlobServiceClient CreateBlobClientStorageFromSAS(
        string SASConnectionString)
        {
            BlobServiceClient blobClient;
            try
            {
                blobClient = new BlobServiceClient(SASConnectionString);
```

```
        }
        catch (System.Exception)
        {
            throw;
        }

        return blobClient;

    }
}
}
```

LISTING 3-24   Program.cs

```
// C#. ASP.NET.
using System.Threading.Tasks;
using System;
using Azure.Storage.Blobs;

namespace ch3_2_1
{
    class Program
    {
        static void Main(string[] args)
        {
            Console.WriteLine("Copy items between Containers Demo!");
            Task.Run(async () => await StartContainersDemo()).Wait();
        }

        public static async Task StartContainersDemo()
        {
            string sourceBlobFileName = "Testing.zip";
            AppSettings appSettings = AppSettings.LoadAppSettings();

            //Get a cloud client for the source Storage Account
            BlobServiceClient sourceClient = Common.CreateBlobClientStorageFromSAS(
                appSettings.SourceSASConnectionString);

            //Get a reference for each container
            var sourceContainerReference = sourceClient.GetBlobContainerClient(app
                Settings.SourceContainerName);
            var destinationContainerReference = sourceClient.GetBlobContainerClient(
                appSettings.DestinationContainerName);
```

```
//Get a reference for the source blob
var sourceBlobReference = sourceContainerReference.GetBlobClient(
                        sourceBlobFileName);
var destinationBlobReference = destinationContainerReference.
                        GetBlobClient(sourceBlobFileName);

//Move the blob from the source container to the destination container
await destinationBlobReference.StartCopyFromUriAsync(sourceBlobReference
                                                    .Uri);


        }
    }
}
```

Listings 3-23 and 3-24 are mostly the same files that you can find in the example in Chapter 2 in the section "Interact with data using the appropriate SDK." The file AppSettings.cs shown in Listing 3-22 contains all the magic for working with the App Configuration service. As with any regular .NET Core application, you need to create a `ConfigurationBuilder` object for managing the configuration of the application. Once you get your builder, you use the `AddAzureAppConfiguration()` extension method for connecting to the App Configuration store. Finally, you use the `Build()` method from the builder object for loading all the settings stored in the App Configuration store. Once you loaded all the settings, you can access each key-value pair by just using the correct key, as you can see in Listing 3-24.

At this point, if you try to run this example, you will get some exceptions because you are not providing the connection string needed for accessing your Azure App Configuration store. You neither defined any key-value pair in your App Configuration store, so even if you were able to access the store, you would get null values. Use the following steps for getting the connection string needed for accessing the App Configuration store and define each of the needed key-value pairs:

1. Open the Azure portal (*https://portal.azure.com*).

2. In the Search Resources, Services, and Docs text box at the top of the Azure portal, type the name of your App Configuration store.

3. In your App Configuration Store blade, click Access Keys in the Settings section.

4. In the Access Keys blade, copy one of the connection strings by clicking the blue icon on the right side next to the Connection String text box.

5. In your Visual Studio Code window, open a new terminal and type the following command. Replace the text *<your_connection_string>* with the value that you copied in step 4:

    ```
    setx ConnectionString "<your_connection_string>"
    ```

6. Restart your Visual Studio Code window. You need to perform this step to ensure that the environment variable that you defined in the previous step is available for your code.

7. In the Azure portal, in your App Configuration store blade, click Configuration Explorer in the Operations section on the left side of the blade.

8. In the Configuration Explorer, click the Create button at the top-left corner of the blade.

9. In the Create panel, shown in Figure 3-9, type the name of the key in the Key text box. Use one of the keys shown in Listing 3-22.

FIGURE 3-9 Create a new key-value

10. In the Value text box, provide the value for the corresponding key. Remember that you are using values from the example in Chapter 2 in the section "Interact with data using the appropriate SDK." The correct values are specific to your scenario, but you can use Listing 2-12 for your reference.

11. Click the Apply button.

12. Repeat steps 8 to 10 until you create a key-value pair for each setting in Listing 3-22. Here is the complete list for your reference:

- TestAZ204:StorageAccount:Source:ConnectionString

- TestAZ204:StorageAccount:Source:AccountName

- TestAZ204:StorageAccount:Source:ContainerName

- TestAZ204:StorageAccount:Destination:ConnectionString

- TestAZ204:StorageAccount:Destination:AccountName

- TestAZ204:StorageAccount:Destination:ContainerName

13. In your Visual Studio Code window, press F5 for running your project. At this point, your code should be able to connect to your Azure App Configuration store and retrieve all the needed settings.

This example shows you the basics for working with Azure App Configuration but also shows some drawbacks that you should consider for production environments. In this example, you defined an environment variable for storing the connection string for connecting to the

App Configuration store. Although this could be a valid configuration for testing or developing environments, there are security implications that you should consider for production environments. You should consider using Managed Service Identity for production environments, instead of using connection strings.

Another security improvement that you should consider is storing connection strings directly as a key-value in your App Configuration store. For this kind of sensitive information, you should store it as a secret in an Azure Key Vault and create an Azure Key Vault Reference in your App Configuration store pointing to the right secret. For the sake of brevity, we didn't include the procedure of how to create Key Vault references, but you can review a complete reference in the article at *https://docs.microsoft.com/en-us/azure/azure-app-configuration/use-key-vault-references-dotnet-core*.

> **NEED MORE REVIEW?   BEST PRACTICES**
>
> You can review some best practices when working with Azure App Configuration by reading the article at *https://docs.microsoft.com/en-us/azure/azure-app-configuration/howto-best-practices*.

EXAM TIP

When you are defining your key-value pair, remember that you are limited to a maximum length of 10,000. Remember also that keys are case-sensitive, so "AppSetting" and "appsetting" are treated as different keys.

Manage keys, secrets, and certificates by using the KeyVault API

Azure Key Vault is the service provided by Microsoft for securely storing secret keys and certificates in a centralized, secure store. By using Azure Key Vault, your developers no longer need to store this sensitive information on their computers while they are developing an application. Thanks to the identity-based access control, you only need to configure a policy for granting access to the needed service or user principals to the secure store. Another advantage is that you can apply fine-grained access control, allowing access to specific secrets only to the needed application or user.

The next example shows how to use the KeyVault API for creating, reading, updating, or deleting the different elements that you can store in the Azure Key Vault. You need an empty Azure App Service and an Azure Key Vault configured in your Azure subscription to run this example.

1. Open the Azure portal at *https://portal.azure.com*.
2. In the search text box on top of the Azure portal, type the name of your Azure Web App.
3. Click the name of your Azure Web App in the result list below the text box.

4. On the Azure Web App Service blade, click the Identity menu item in the Settings section.

5. In the Status switch control, click the On option.

6. Click Save.

7. In the Enable System Assigned Managed Identity dialog box, click Yes.

8. Once you enable the system-assigned managed identity, you get the Principal or Object ID associated with your Azure App Service.

9. In the search text box at the top of the Azure portal, type the name of your Azure Key Vault. Click the name of your Azure Key Vault in the result list.

10. On the Key Vault blade, click Access Policies in the Settings section in the navigation menu.

11. On the Access Policies blade, click the Add Access Policy link.

12. On the Add Access Policy panel, click the Configure From Template drop-down menu and select the Key, Secret, and Certificate Management option.

13. Click Select Principal.

14. On the Principal panel, type the name of your Azure App Service in the Select text box.

15. In the results list, click the name of your Azure App Service.

16. Click the Select button.

17. On the Add Access Policy panel, click the Add button.

18. On the Access Policies blade, click the Save button in the top-left corner of the blade.

19. Repeat steps 10 through 18 and add the user account that you use for accessing your Azure subscription. You need to add this policy to be able to debug your code using Visual Studio. You need to ensure that you add the policy for granting access to the same user account that you use accessing your Azure subscription from Visual Studio.

20. Open Visual Studio 2019.

21. In the welcome window of Visual Studio 2019, on the Get Started column, click Create A New Project.

22. On the Create A New Project window, on the All Languages drop-down menu, select C#.

23. On the Search For Templates text box type **asp.net**.

24. On the result list, click ASP.NET Web Application (.NET Framework).

25. Click the Next button at the bottom right of the window.

26. On the Configure Your New Project, type a Project Name, a Location, and a Solution Name for your project.

27. Click the Create button at the bottom right of the window.

28. On the Create A New ASP.NET Web Application window, select the MVC template on the template list in the middle of the left side of the window. MVC is for Model-View-Controller.

29. On the right side of the Create A New ASP.NET Web Application window, on the Authentication section, ensure the Authentication is set to No Authentication.

30. Click the Create button at the bottom-right corner of the window.

31. In the Visual Studio window, click Tools > NuGet Package Manager > Manage NuGet Packages For Solution.

32. On the NuGet Package Manager tab, click Browse.

33. Type **Microsoft.Azure.Services.AppAuthentication** and press Enter.

34. Click the Microsoft.Azure.Services.AppAuthentication package.

35. On the right side of the NuGet Manager tab, click the check box next to your project.

36. Click the Install button.

37. In the Preview Changes window, click OK.

38. In the License Acceptance window, click the I Accept button.

39. Repeat steps 32 through 38 and install the Microsoft.Azure.KeyVault package.

40. Open the HomeController.cs file in the Controllers folder.

41. Replace the content of the Index() method with the content of Listing 3-25. You may need to add the following namespaces to the HomeController.cs file:

- Microsoft.Azure.KeyVault
- Microsoft.Azure.KeyVault.Models
- Microsoft.Azure.Services.AppAuthentication
- System.Threading
- System.Threading.Tasks

LISTING 3-25 Creating, deleting, updating, and reading Key Vault items

```
// C#. ASP.NET.
public ActionResult Index()
      {
            string keyVaultName = "<YOUR_VAULT's_NAME>";
            string vaultBaseURL = $"https://{keyVaultName}.vault.azure.net";



            //Get a token for accessing the Key Vault.
            var azureServiceTokenProvider = new AzureServiceTokenProvider();

            //Create a Key Vault client for accessing the items in the vault;
            var keyVault = new KeyVaultClient(new KeyVaultClient.AuthenticationCallback
                        (azureServiceTokenProvider.KeyVaultTokenCallback));

            // Manage secrets in the Key Vault.
            // Create a new secret
            string secretName = "secret-az204";

            Task.Run(async () => await keyVault.SetSecretAsync(vaultBaseURL,
                        secretName,
```

```
  "This is a secret testing value")).Wait();
var secret = Task.Run(async () => await keyVault.GetSecretAsync
  ($"{vaultBaseURL}/secrets/{secretName}")).GetAwaiter().GetResult();
// Update an existing secret
Task.Run(async () => await keyVault.SetSecretAsync(vaultBaseURL,
                     secretName,
  "Updated the secret testing value")).Wait();
secret = Task.Run(async () => await keyVault.GetSecretAsync
    ($"{vaultBaseURL}/secrets/{secretName}")).GetAwaiter().GetResult();
// Delete the secret
Task.Run(async () => await keyVault.DeleteSecretAsync(vaultBaseURL,
                     secretName)).Wait();

// Manage certificates in the Key Vault
string certName = "cert-az204";
// Create a new self-signed certificate
var policy = new CertificatePolicy
{
    IssuerParameters = new IssuerParameters
    {
        Name = "Self",
    },
    KeyProperties = new KeyProperties
    {
        Exportable = true,
        KeySize = 2048,
        KeyType = "RSA"
    },
    SecretProperties = new SecretProperties
    {
        ContentType = "application/x-pkcs12"
    },
    X509CertificateProperties = new X509CertificateProperties
    {
        Subject = "CN=AZ204KEYVAULTDEMO"
    }
};

Task.Run(async () => await keyVault.CreateCertificateAsync(vaultBaseURL,
certName, policy, new CertificateAttributes { Enabled = true })).Wait();
// When you create a new certificate in the Key Vault it takes some time
// before it's ready.
// We added some wait time here for the sake of simplicity.
Thread.Sleep(10000);
var certificate = Task.Run(async () => await keyVault.GetCertificateAsync
  (vaultBaseURL, certName)).GetAwaiter().GetResult();
```

```
// Update properties associated with the certificate.
CertificatePolicy updatePolicy = new CertificatePolicy
{
    X509CertificateProperties = new X509CertificateProperties
    {
        SubjectAlternativeNames = new SubjectAlternativeNames
        {
            DnsNames = new[] { "az204.examref.testing" }
        }
    }
};


Task.Run(async () => await keyVault.UpdateCertificatePolicyAsync(
                    vaultBaseURL, certName, updatePolicy)).Wait();
Task.Run(async () => await keyVault.CreateCertificateAsync(vaultBaseURL,
                    certName)).Wait();
Thread.Sleep(10000);


certificate = Task.Run(async () => await keyVault.GetCertificateAsync(
                            vaultBaseURL, certName)).GetAwaiter().
                            GetResult();

Task.Run(async () => await keyVault.UpdateCertificateAsync(certificate.
                        CertificateIdentifier.Identifier, null,
                        new CertificateAttributes { Enabled =
                        false })).Wait();
Thread.Sleep(10000);

// Delete the self-signed certificate.
Task.Run(async () => await keyVault.DeleteCertificateAsync(vaultBaseURL,
                    certName)).Wait();


// Manage keys in the Key Vault
string keyName = "key-az204";
NewKeyParameters keyParameters = new NewKeyParameters
{
    Kty = "EC",
    CurveName = "SECP256K1",
    KeyOps = new[] { "sign", "verify" }
};


Task.Run(async () => await keyVault.CreateKeyAsync(vaultBaseURL, keyName,
                    keyParameters)).Wait();
```

```
            var key = Task.Run(async () => await keyVault.GetKeyAsync(vaultBaseURL,
                                    keyName)).GetAwaiter().GetResult();

            // Update keys in the Key Vault
            Task.Run(async () => await keyVault.UpdateKeyAsync(vaultBaseURL, keyName,
                            null, new KeyAttributes { Expires = DateTime.UtcNow.
                            AddYears(1)})).Wait();
            key = Task.Run(async () => await keyVault.GetKeyAsync(vaultBaseURL,
                                    keyName)).GetAwaiter().GetResult();

            // Delete keys from the Key Vault
            Task.Run(async () => await keyVault.DeleteKeyAsync(vaultBaseURL, keyName)).
                            Wait();


            return View();
        }
```

At this point, you should be able to run the example. Because you didn't make any modifications to any view, you should not be able to see any changes in your Azure Key Vault. To be able to see how this code creates, reads, modifies, and deletes the different item types in your Azure Key Vault, you should set some breakpoints:

1. Add a breakpoint to the following lines:

   ```
   string secretName = "secret-az204";
   string certName = "cert-az204";
   string keyName = "key-az204";
   ```

2. Open your Azure Key Vault in the Azure Portal, as shown in step 9 of the previous procedure.

3. On your Azure Key Vault blade, click Secrets in the Settings section in the navigation menu.

4. In Visual Studio, press F5 to debug your project.

5. When you hit the breakpoint, press F10 and go back to the Azure portal to see the results. You should use the Refresh button to see the changes in your Azure Key Vault.

NOTE FORBIDDEN ACCESS

If you get a Forbidden Access Error while you are debugging your application in Visual Studio, ensure that you created an Access Policy for the user account that you have configured in your Visual Studio for connecting with your Azure subscription. You need to ensure that the Access Policy grants all the needed privileges to the different object types in the Azure Key Vault. Ensure also that the account that you are using for developing is correctly authenticated in Azure Active Directory. Check your development account in Tools > Options > Azure Service Authentication. If there is a Re-Authenticate link below your development account, click the link to authenticate again.

When you work with the KeyVault API, you need to create a `KeyVaultClient` object that is responsible for the communication with the Azure Key Vault services. As described in the example in the "Implement Managed Service Identity (MSI)/Service Principal authentication" section, you need to get an access token for authenticating your service or user principal to the Azure Key Vault. The following code snippet shows how to perform this authentication:

```
var azureServiceTokenProvider = new AzureServiceTokenProvider();
var keyVault = new KeyVaultClient(new KeyVaultClient.AuthenticationCallback(
            azureServiceTokenProvider.KeyVaultTokenCallback));
```

Now you can use the keyVault variable for working with the different item types. The KeyVault API provides specialized methods for each item type. This way, you should use the `SetSecretAsync()` method for creating a new secret in your Azure Key Vault. The following code snippet shows how to create a new secret:

```
Task.Run(async () => await keyVault.SetSecretAsync(vaultBaseURL, secretName, "This is a
secret testing value")).Wait();
```

If you try to create a new secret, key, or certificate using the same name of an object that already exists in the vault, you are creating a new version of that object, as shown in Figure 3-10. The only exception to this rule is if you have enabled soft-deletion in your Azure Key Vault, and you try to create a new secret using the same name as a deleted object. In that situation, you get a collision exception. You can click on each version to review the properties of the object for that version.

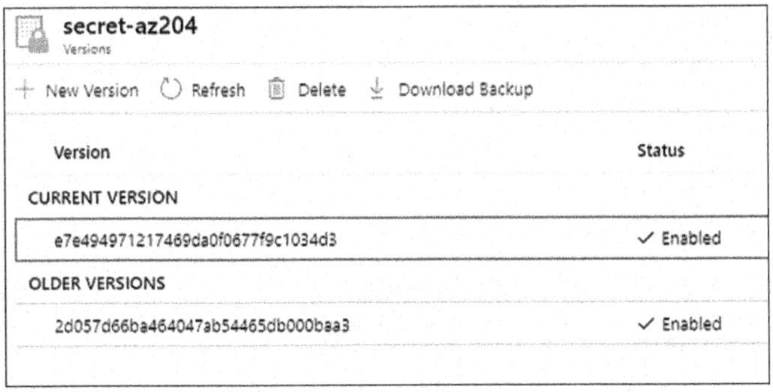

FIGURE 3-10 A secret object with different versions

Most of the methods in the KeyVault API that work with items require the vault URL and the name of the item that you want to access. In this example, you define a variable with the correct value at the beginning of the `Index()` method, as shown in the following code snippet:

```
string keyVaultName = "<YOUR_VAULT's_NAME>";
string vaultBaseURL = $"https://{keyVaultName}.vault.azure.net";
```

These methods are usually overloaded for accepting an object identifier instead of the vault base URL and the object's name. The identifier has the following form:

```
https://{keyvault-name}.vault.azure.net/{object-type}/{object-name}/{object-version}
```

Where:

- *Keyvault-name* is the name of the key vault where the object is stored.
- *Object-type* is the type of object that you want to work with. This value can be secrets, keys, or certificates.
- *Object-name* is the name that you give the object in the vault.
- *Object-version* is the version of the object that you want to access.

Creating a key or certificate uses a slightly different approach from the one that you used for creating a secret. Keys and certificates are more complex objects and require some additional configuration for creating them. The following code snippet extracted from Listing 3-25 shows how to create a new self-signed certificate in the Azure Key Vault:

```
// Create a new self-signed certificate
var policy = new CertificatePolicy
{
    IssuerParameters = new IssuerParameters
    {
        Name = "Self",
    },
    KeyProperties = new KeyProperties
    {
        Exportable = true,
        KeySize = 2048,
        KeyType = "RSA"
    },
    SecretProperties = new SecretProperties
    {
        ContentType = "application/x-pkcs12"
    },
    X509CertificateProperties = new X509CertificateProperties
    {
        Subject = "CN=AZ204KEYVAULTDEMO"
    }
};
Task.Run(async () => await keyVault.CreateCertificateAsync(vaultBaseURL, certName,
policy, new CertificateAttributes { Enabled = true })).Wait();
```

You need to create a CertificatePolicy object before you can create the certificate. A certificate policy is an object that defines the properties of how to create a certificate and any new version associated with the certificate object. You use this certificate policy object as a parameter of the CreateCertificateAsync() method. If you need to modify any property of an existing certificate, you need to define a new certificate policy, update the policy using the UpdateCertificatePolicyAsync() method, and create a new certificate version using the CreateCertificateAsync() method, as shown in the following code snippet:

```
// Update properties associated with the certificate.
CertificatePolicy updatePolicy = new CertificatePolicy
```

```
{
    X509CertificateProperties = new X509CertificateProperties
    {
        SubjectAlternativeNames = new SubjectAlternativeNames
        {
            DnsNames = new[] { "az204.examref.testing" }
        }
    }
};
Task.Run(async () => await keyVault.UpdateCertificatePolicyAsync(vaultBaseURL, certName,
                                updatePolicy)).Wait();
Task.Run(async () => await keyVault.CreateCertificateAsync(vaultBaseURL, certName))
                                .Wait();
```

Deleting an object from the key vault is quite straightforward; you only need to provide the vault base URL and the object's name to the DeleteSecretAsync(), DeleteCertificateAsync(), or DeleteKeyAsync() method. Azure Key Vault also supports soft-delete operations on the protected objects or the vault itself. This option is enabled by default. When you soft delete an object or a vault, the Azure Key Vault provider automatically marks them as deleted but holds the object or vault for a default period of 90 days. This means you can recover the deleted object later if needed.

NEED MORE REVIEW? **MORE DETAILS ABOUT KEYS, SECRETS, AND CERTIFICATES**

You can find more information about the details of the different object types that are available in the Azure Key Vault service by reviewing the article at *https://docs.microsoft.com/ en-us/azure/key-vault/about-keys-secrets-and-certificates.*

EXAM TIP

The kind of information that you usually store in an Azure Key Vault is essential information that needs to keep secret, like passwords, connection strings, private keys, and things like that. When configuring the access to your Key Vault, carefully review the access level you grant to the security principal. As a best practice, you should always apply the principle of least privilege. You grant access to the different levels in a Key Vault by creating Access Policies.

Implement Managed Identities for Azure resources

When you are designing your application, you usually identify the different services or systems on which your application depends. For example, your application may need to connect to an Azure SQL database for storing data or may need to connect to Azure Event Hub for reading messages from other services. In all these situations, there is a common need to authenticate with the service before you can access it. In the Azure SQL database case, you need to use a connection string; if you need to connect to an Azure Event Hub, you need to use a combination of event publishers and Shared Access Signature (SAS) tokens.

The drawback of this approach is that you need to store a security credential, token, or password to be able to authenticate to the service that you want to access. This is a drawback because you might find that this information is stored on developers' computers or is checked in to the source control by mistake. You can address most of these situations by using the Azure Key Vault, but your code still needs to authenticate to Azure Key Vault to get the information for accessing the other services.

Fortunately, Azure Active Directory (Azure AD) provides the Managed Identities for Azure resources (formerly known as Managed Service Identity) that removes the need to use credentials for authenticating your application to any Azure service that supports Azure AD authentication. This feature automatically creates a managed identity that you can use for authenticating to any service that supports Azure AD authentication without needing to provide any credential.

When you work with managed identities, you can work with two different types:

- **System-assigned managed identities** These are identities that Azure automatically enables when you create an Azure service instance, like an Azure virtual machine (VM) or an Azure data lake store. Azure creates an identity associated with the new instance and stores it to the Azure AD tenant associated with the subscription where you created the service instance. If you decide to delete the service instance, then Azure automatically deletes the managed instance associated with the service instance stored in the Azure AD tenant.

- **User-assigned managed identities** You can create your managed identities in the Azure AD tenant associated with your Azure subscription. You can associate this type of managed identity to one or more service instances. The lifecycle of the managed identity is independent of the service instance. This means that if you delete the service instance, the user-assigned managed identity remains in the Azure AD tenant. You need to remove the managed identity manually.

Usually, you use the system-assigned managed identities when your workload is contained within the same Azure resource, or you need to independently identify each of the service instances, like Virtual Machines. On the other hand, if you need to grant access to a workload that is distributed across different resources or you need to pre-authorize a resource as part of a provisioning flow, you should use user-assigned managed identities.

When you work with managed identities, you need to bear in mind three concepts:

- **Client ID** This is a unique identifier generated by Azure AD. This ID associates the application and the service principal during its initial provisioning.

- **Principal ID** This is the ID of the service principal associated with the managed identity. A service principal and a managed identity are tightly coupled, but they are different objects. The service principal is the object that you use to grant role-based access to an Azure resource.

- **Azure Instance Metadata Service (IMDS)** When you use managed identities in an Azure VM, you can use the IMDS for requesting an OAuth Access Token from your application deployed within the VM. The IMDS is a REST endpoint that you can access from your VM using a nonroutable IP address (169.254.169.254).

The following example shows how to create a system-assigned identity in an Azure App Service and how to use this managed identity from your code for accessing an Azure Key Vault. For this example, you need to have an empty Azure App Service, an Azure Key Vault, and at least one item on the Azure Key Vault. You also need to have your Visual Studio connected to the Azure subscription where you have configured the Azure Key Vault.

1. Open the Azure Portal at *https://portal.azure.com*.

2. In the search text box at the top of the Azure portal, type the name of your Azure Web App. If you don't have an Azure Web App, you can create a new Azure Web App by using the procedure at *https://docs.microsoft.com/en-in/azure/app-service/app-service-web-get-started-dotnet*.

3. On the Azure Web App Service blade, click the Identity menu item in the Settings section.

4. On the Status switch control, click the On option.

5. Click the Save button.

6. In the Enable System Assigned Managed Identity dialog box, click the Yes button.

7. Once you enable the system-assigned managed identity, you get the Principal or Object ID, as shown in Figure 3-11.

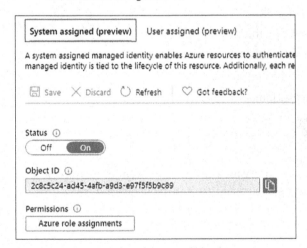

FIGURE 3-11 System assigned managed identity

8. Open Visual Studio 2019.

9. In the welcome window of Visual Studio 2019, on the Get Started column, click Create A New Project.

10. On the Create A New Project window, on the drop-down menu, All Languages drop-down menu, select C#.

11. In the Search For Templates text box type **asp.net**.

12. In the result list, click ASP.NET Web Application (.NET Framework).

13. Click the Next button at the bottom right of the window.

14. In the Configure Your New Project, type a Project Name, a Location, and a Solution Name for your project.

15. Click the Create button at the bottom right of the window.

16. In the Create A New ASP.NET Web Application window, select the MVC template on the template list in the middle of the left side of the window. MVC is for Model-View-Controller.

17. On the right side of the Create A New ASP.NET Web Application window, on the Authentication section, ensure the Authentication is set to No Authentication.

18. Click the Create button at the bottom right of the window.

19. In the Visual Studio window, click Tools > NuGet Package Manager > Manage NuGet Packages For Solution.

20. On the NuGet Package Manager tab, click Browse.

21. Type **Microsoft.Azure.Services.AppAuthentication** and press Enter.

22. Click the Microsoft.Azure.Services.AppAuthentication package.

23. On the right side of the NuGet Manager tab, click the check box next to your project.

24. Click the Install button.

25. In the Preview Changes window, click OK.

26. In the License Acceptance window, click the I Accept button.

27. Repeat steps 20 through 26 and install the Microsoft.Azure.KeyVault package.

28. Open the HomeController.cs file in the Controllers folder.

29. Add the following statements to the HomeController.cs file:

```
using Microsoft.Azure.KeyVault;
using Microsoft.Azure.Services.AppAuthentication;
using System.Threading.Tasks;
```

30. Replace the content of the Index() method with the content of Listing 3-26. The crucial pieces of code related to accessing the Azure Key Vault are highlighted in bold.

LISTING 3-26   Getting a secret from the key vault

```
// C#. ASP.NET.
string keyVaultName = "<PUT_YOUR_KEY_VAULT_NAME_HERE>";
string secretName = "<PUT_YOUR_SECRET_NAME_HERE>";


//Get a token for accessing the Key Vault.
var azureServiceTokenProvider = new AzureServiceTokenProvider();


//Create a Key Vault client for accessing the items in the vault.
var keyVault = new KeyVaultClient(new KeyVaultClient.AuthenticationCallback(
                azureServiceTokenProvider.KeyVaultTokenCallback));
```

```
var secret = Task.Run(async () =>  await keyVault.GetSecretAsync(
                    $"https://{keyVaultName}.vault.azure.net/secrets/{secretName}"))
                    .GetAwaiter().GetResult();

ViewBag.KeyVaultName = keyVaultName;
ViewBag.keyName = secretName;
ViewBag.secret = secret.Value;

return View();
```

As you can see, this code is quite similar to the code in Listing 3-25. The reason is that you used managed identities to get access to the Azure Key Vault in the example in Listing 3-25. Before you can access the Azure Key Vault, you need to get an OAuth token by using the AzureServiceTokenProvider class. Then you can create your Azure Key Vault client and get any item stored in the vault. When you create the Azure Key Vault client, make sure you provide the KeyVaultTokenCallback. Even if you get a valid access token, you still need to grant access to your Azure App Service application in the Azure Key Vault.

1. Open the Views > Home > Index.cshtml file.

2. Append the content of Listing 3-27 to the end of the file.

LISTING 3-27 Adding secret information to the home page

```
// C#. ASP.NET.
<div class="row">
    <div class="col-lg-12">
        <dl class="dl-horizontal">
            <dt>Key Vault Name: </dt>
            <dd>@ViewBag.keyVaultName</dd>
            <dt>Key Name: </dt>
            <dd>@ViewBag.keyName</dd>
            <dt>Key Secret: </dt>
            <dd>@ViewBag.secret</dd>
        </dl>

    </div>
</div>
```

At this point, you could run your project and see the results. Depending on the access policies defined in your Azure Key Vault, your Azure user may already have access to the secrets stored in the key vault. In that case, you should be able to access the secret stored in the Azure Key Vault. If you get an exception when running the web application, there are good chances that you don't have access to the Azure Key Vault. The following steps show how to grant access to your Azure App Service application in the Azure Key Vault.

1. Open the Azure portal (*https://portal.azure.com*).

2. Type the name of your Azure Key Vault in the search text box at the top of the Azure portal. If you don't already have an Azure Key Vault and need to create a new one,

you can use the procedure at *https://docs.microsoft.com/en-us/azure/key-vault/quick-create-portal*.

3. On your Azure Key Vault blade, click Access Policies in the Settings section.

4. On the Access Policies blade, click Add New.

5. On the Add Access Policy page, select Secret Management in the Configure From Template drop-down menu.

6. Click the Select Principal control.

7. In the Principal panel, type the name of your Azure App Service in the Select text box. Your Azure App Service should appear on the list below the text box.

8. Click your App Service name in the list below the Select text box.

9. Click the Select button at the bottom of the panel.

10. Click the Add button at the bottom of the Add Access Policy blade.

11. Click the Save button at the top of the Access Policies blade.

12. In the Visual Studio window, right-click your project's name in the Solution Explorer window.

13. In the contextual menu, click Publish.

14. In the Pick A Publish Target window, ensure that App Service is selected on the left side of the window.

15. In the Azure App Service section, click Select Existing.

16. Click the Create Profile button at the bottom-right corner of the window.

17. In the App Service window, in the tree view at the bottom of the window, look for your App Service and click it.

18. Click the OK button.

At this point, Visual Studio starts publishing your web application to the selected Azure App Service. When the publishing operation finishes, you should be able to see your web application showing the content of the secret stored in your Key Vault.

EXAM TIP

You can configure two different types of managed identities: system- and user-assigned. System-assigned managed identities are tied to the service instance. If you delete the service instance, the system-assigned managed identity is automatically deleted as well. You can assign the same user-assigned managed identities to several service instances.

Chapter summary

- Authentication is the act of proving that a user is who he or she claims to be.
- A user authenticates by providing some information that the user only knows.

- There are several mechanisms of authentication that provide different levels of security.

- Some of the authentication mechanisms are form-based, token-based, or certificate-based.

- Using form-based authentication requires your application to store your users' passwords.

- Form-based authentication requires HTTPS to make the authentication process more secure.

- Using token-based authentication, you can delegate the authorization to third-party authentication providers.

- You can add social logins to your application by using token-based authentication.

- Multifactor authentication is an authentication mechanism that requires the users to provide more than one piece of information that only the user knows.

- You can easily implement multifactor authentication by using Azure Active Directory.

- There are four main actors in OAuth authentication: client, resource server, resource owner, and authentication server.

- The resource owner needs to authenticate the client before sending the authorization grant.

- The access token grants access to the resource hosted on the resource server.

- The authorization grant or authorization code grants the client the needed rights to request an access token to the authorization server.

- The client uses the refresh token to get a new access token when it expires without needing to request a new authorization code.

- The JSON web token is the most extended implementation of OAuth tokens.

- Shared Access Signatures (SAS) is an authentication mechanism for granting access to Azure Storage Accounts without sharing account keys.

- Shared Access Signatures (SAS) tokens must be signed.

- There are three types of SAS token: user delegation, account, and service SAS.

- User delegation SAS tokens are signed using a key assigned to an Azure Active Directory user.

- Account and Service SAS are signed using the Azure Storage account key.

- You can hide the details of the SAS tokens from the URL by using Stored Access Policies.

- Shared access signature tokens provide fine-grained access control to your Azure storage accounts.

- You can create an SAS token for service, container, and item levels.

- You need to register applications in Azure Active Directory for being able to authenticate users using your tenant.

- There are three account types supported for authentication: accounts only in the organizational directory, accounts in any organizational directory, and Microsoft accounts.

- You need to provide a return URL for authenticating your application when requesting user authentication.

- You need to configure a secret or a certificate when your application needs to access information in other APIs.

- Role-Based Access Control (RBAC) authorization provides fine-grained access control to the resources.

- A security principal is an entity to which you can grant privileges.

- Security principals are users, groups, service principals, and managed identities.

- A permission is an action that a security principal can make with a resource.

- A role definition, or role, is a group of permissions.

- A scope is a level where you can assign a role.

- A role association is a relationship between a security principal, a role, and a scope.

- There are four scopes: management groups, subscription, resource group, and resources.

- You can centralize the configuration of your distributed application using Azure App Configuration.

- Azure App Configuration stores the information using key-value pairs.

- Values in the Azure App Configuration are encrypted.

- Azure Key Vault provides better security than the Azure App Configuration service.

- The limit of size for an Azure App Configuration is 10,000, including the key, label, and value.

- You can create references from Azure App Configuration items to Azure Key Vault items.

- Azure Key Vault allows you to store three types of objects: keys, secrets, and certificates.

- You should use managed identities authentication for accessing the Azure Key Vault.

- You need to define a certificate policy before creating a certificate in the Azure Key Vault.

- If you import a certificate into the Azure Key Vault, a default certificate policy is automatically created for you.

Thought experiment

In this thought experiment, demonstrate your skills and knowledge of the topics covered in this chapter. You can find answers to this thought experiment in the next section.

You are developing a web application for your company. The application is in the early stages of development. This application is an internal application that will be used only by the employees of the company. Your company uses Office 365 connected with your company's

Active Directory domain. The application needs to use information from Office 365. Answer the following questions about the security implementation of this application:

1. The employees need to be able to access the application using the same username and password they use for accessing Office 365. What should you do?

2. You are using Azure App Services for developing the application. You need to ensure that the web application can access other Azure services without using credentials in your code. What should you do?

3. You need to ensure that the configuration of your application is stored in central storage. You also need to provide the best security for sensitive information like connection strings and passwords. What should you do?

Thought experiment answers

This section contains the solution to the thought experiment. Each answer explains why the answer choice is correct.

1. You should use OAuth authentication with Azure Active Directory (Azure AD). If you want your application to be able to use Azure AD OAuth authentication, you need to register your application in your Azure AD tenant. Because your application needs access to information in Office 365, you also need to create a client secret before you can access the Microsoft Graph API. When you connect Office 365 with an Active Directory (AD) domain, users in the AD domain can authenticate to Office 365 using the same username and password they use in the AD domain. Office 365 uses an Azure AD tenant for managing the identities of the users in the subscription. Your organization has already configured the synchronization between AD and Office 365 and Azure AD. By using OAuth authentication with Azure AD, your users should be able to access your application using the same username and passwords that they use in the AD domain.

2. You should use the Managed Service Identity (MSI) authentication. Using the feature, Azure authenticates services based on a service principal configured in a service instance. You can use MSI authentication with services that support Azure AD authentication, like Azure Key Vault or Azure SQL Databases. You need to enable a system-assigned or user-assigned managed identity on your Azure App Service. Using MSI, the Azure SQL Database authenticates the identity assigned to your Azure App Service without needing you to provide any password.

3. You should create an Azure App Configuration store. This is the appropriate service for securely storing your app configuration settings in centralized storage. Although the Azure App Configuration store provides secure storage by encrypting the value of the key-value pairs representing your settings, you should use Key Vault references in your Azure App Configuration store for that sensitive information that requires a higher level of security. Azure Key Vault uses hardware-based encryption for storing keys, secrets, and certificates.

## CHAPTER 4

Monitor, troubleshoot, and optimize Azure solutions

Providing a good experience to your users is one of the key factors for the success of your application. Several factors affect the user's experience, such as a good user interface design, ease of use, good performance, and low failure rate. You can ensure that your application will perform well by assigning more resources to your application, but if there are not enough users using your application, you might be wasting resources and money.

To ensure that your application is working correctly, you need to deploy a monitoring mechanism that helps you to get information about your application's behavior. This is especially important during peak usage periods or failures. Azure provides several tools that help you to monitor, troubleshoot, and improve the performance of your application.

Skills covered in this chapter:

- Skill 4.1: Integrate caching and content delivery within solutions
- Skill 4.2: Instrument solutions to support monitoring and logging

Skill 4.1: Integrate caching and content delivery within solutions

Any web application that you implement delivers two types of content—dynamic and static.

- Dynamic content is the type of content that changes depending on user interaction. An example of dynamic content is a dashboard with several graphs or a list of user movements in a banking application.
- Static content is the same for all application users. Images and PDFs are examples of static content (as long as they are not dynamically generated) that users can download from your application.

If the users of your application access it from several locations across the globe, you can improve the performance of the application by delivering the content from the location nearest to the user. For static content, you can improve the performance by copying the content to different cache servers distributed across the globe. Using this technique, users can retrieve the static content from the nearest location with lower latency, which improves the performance of your application.

For dynamic content, you can use cache software to store the most accessed data. This means your application returns the information from the cache, which is faster than reprocessing the data or getting it from the storage system.

> **This skill covers how to**
> - Develop code to implement CDNs in solutions
> - Configure cache and expiration policies for FrontDoor, CDNs, and Redis caches
> - Store and retrieve data in Azure Redis Cache

Develop code to implement CDNs in solutions

A Content Delivery Network (CDN) is a group of servers distributed in different locations across the globe that can deliver web content to users. Because the CDN has servers distributed in several locations, when a user makes a request to the CDN, the CDN delivers the content from the nearest server to the user.

The main advantage of using Azure CDN with your application is that Azure CDN caches your application's static content. When a user makes a request to your application, the CDN stores the static content, such as images, documents, and stylesheet files. When a second user from the same location as the first user accesses your application, the CDN delivers the cached content, relieving your web server from delivering the static content. You can use third-party CDN solutions such as Verizon or Akamai with Azure CDN.

To use Azure CDN with your solution, you need to configure a profile. This profile contains the list of endpoints in your application that would be included in the CDN. The profile also configures the behavior of content delivery and access of each configured endpoint. When you configure an Azure CDN profile, you need to choose between using Microsoft's CDN or using CDNs from Verizon or Akamai.

You can configure as many profiles as you need for grouping your endpoints based on different criteria, such as internet domain, web application, or any other criteria. Bear in mind that Azure CDN pricing tiers are applied at the profile level, so you can configure different profiles with different pricing characteristics. As with any CDN solution in the real world, you need a web application to run the procedures and demonstrations throughout this skill. The following procedure shows how to create a basic web application in Visual Studio and publish it in an Azure Web App. You can use this Azure Web App in all the examples in the rest of this skill:

1. Open Visual Studio 2019 on your computer.
2. In the Visual Studio 2019 home window, in the column named Get Started, click the Continue Without Code link at the bottom of the column.
3. Click the Tools menu and choose Get Tools And Features. Verify that the ASP.NET And Web Development In The Web & Cloud section is checked.

4. In the Visual Studio 2019 window, select File > New > Project to open the New Project window.

5. In the Create a New Project window, select C# in the drop-down menu below the Search For Templates text box at the top right of the window.

6. In the All Project Types drop-down menu, select Web.

7. In the list of templates on the right side of the window, select ASP.NET Core Web Application.

8. In the Configure Your New Project window, complete the following steps:

    a. Select a name for the project.

    b. Enter a path for the location of the solution.

    c. In the Solution drop-down menu, select Create A New Solution.

    d. Enter a name for the solution.

9. Click the Create button in the bottom-right corner of the Configure Your New Project window. This opens the Create A New ASP.NET Core Web Application window.

10. In the Create A New ASP.NET Core Web Application window, ensure that the following values are selected in the two drop-down menus at the top of the window:

    - .NET Core

    - ASP.NET Core 3.1

11. Select Web Application from the Project Templates area in the center of the window.

12. Uncheck the Configure For HTTPS option at the bottom right of the window.

13. Click the Create button in the bottom-right corner of the Create A New ASP.NET Core Web Application window.

14. On the right side of the Visual Studio window, in the Solution Explorer window, right-click the project's name.

15. In the contextual menu, click Publish. This opens the Pick A Publish Target window.

16. In the Pick A Publish Target window, make sure that App Service is selected from the list of Available Targets on the left side of the window.

17. In the Azure App Service section, on the right side of the window, ensure that Create New Option is selected.

18. In the bottom-right corner of the window, click the Create Profile button, which opens the Create App Service window.

19. In the Create App Service window, add a new Azure account. This account needs to have enough privileges in the subscription for creating new resource groups, app services, and an App Service plan.

20. Once you have added a valid account, you can configure the settings for publishing your web application.

21. In the App Name text box, enter a name for the App Service. By default, this name matches the name that you gave to your project.

22. In the Subscription drop-down menu, select the subscription in which you want to create the App Service.

23. In the Resource Group drop-down menu, select the resource group in which you want to create the App Service and the App Service plan. If you need to create a new resource group, you can do so by clicking the New link on the right side of the drop-down menu.

24. To the right of the Hosting Plan drop-down menu, click the New link to open the Configure Hosting Plan window.

25. In the Configure Hosting Plan window, type a name for the App Service plan in the App Service Plan text box.

26. Select a region from the Location drop-down menu.

27. Select a virtual machine size from the Size drop-down menu.

28. Click the OK button in the bottom-right corner of the window. This closes the Configure Hosting Plan window.

29. At the bottom-right corner of the Create App Service window, click the Create button. This starts the creation of the needed resources and the upload of the code to the App Service.

30. Once the publishing process has finished, Visual Studio opens your default web browser with the URL of the newly deployed App Service. This URL will have the structure *https://<your_app_service_name>.azurewebsites.net*.

Once you have created your testing Azure Web App, you can use the URL that you got on step 30 in the previous procedure with the rest of the procedures in this skill. The following procedure shows how to create an Azure CDN profile with one endpoint for caching content from a web application:

1. Open the Azure portal (*https://portal.azure.com*).

2. Click the Create A Resource button in the Azure Services section.

3. On the New blade, in the Search The Marketplace text box, type CDN.

4. In the result list, click CDN.

5. On the CDN blade, click the Create button.

6. On the CDN profile blade, type a Name for the profile.

7. Select an existing Resource Group in the drop-down menu. Alternatively, you can create a new resource group by clicking the Create New link below the Resource Group drop-down menu.

8. In the Pricing Tier drop-down menu, select Standard Microsoft.

9. Click the Create button at the bottom of the CDN profile blade.

10. In the Search text box at the top of the Azure portal, type the name for your CDN profile.

11. In the result list, click the name of your CDN profile.

12. On the CDN profile blade, shown in Figure 4-1, click the Endpoint button.

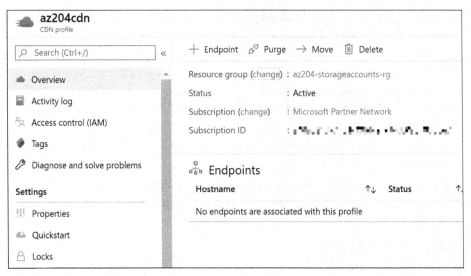

FIGURE 4-1 CDN profile blade

13. In the Add An Endpoint panel, type a Name for the endpoint. Bear in mind that this name needs to be globally unique.

14. In the Origin Type drop-down menu, select Web App.

15. In the Origin Hostname drop-down menu, select the name of your web application.

16. In the Origin Path text box, type the path to the application you need to include in the CDN.

17. Leave the Origin Host header value as is. The Origin Host header value should match the Origin Hostname value.

18. Leave the other options as is they are.

19. Click the Add button.

The propagation of the content through the CDN depends on the type of CDN that you configured. For Standard Microsoft CDN, the propagation usually completes in 10 minutes. Once the propagation of the CDN completes, you can access your web application by using the endpoint that you configured in the previous procedure: *https://<your_endpoint's_name>.azureedge.net*.

Once you have configured the endpoint, you can apply some advanced options to adjust the CDN to your needs:

- **Custom DNS domain** By default, when using the CDN, your users access your application by using the URL *https://<your_endpoint's_name>.azureedge.net*. This URL would not be appropriate for your application. You can assign more appropriate DNS domains to the CDN endpoint, such as *https://app.contoso.com*, which allows your users to access your web application using a URL related to your business and your DNS domain name.

- **Compression** You can configure the CDN endpoint to compress some MIME types. This compression is made on the fly by the CDN when the content is delivered from the cache. Compressing the content allows you to deliver smaller files, improving the overall performance of the application.

- **Caching rules**   You can control how the content is stored in the cache by setting different rules for different paths or content types. By configuring a cache rule, you can modify the cache expiration time, depending on the conditions you configure. Caching rules are only available for profiles from Verizon's Azure CDN Standard and Akamai's Azure CDN Standard.

- **Geo-filtering**   You can block or allow a web application's content to specific countries across the globe.

- **Optimization**   You can configure the CDN for optimizing the delivery of different types of content. Depending on the type of profile, you can optimize your endpoint for

  - General web delivery
  - Dynamic site acceleration
  - General media streaming
  - Video-on-demand media streaming
  - Large file downloads

NOTE   **DYNAMIC SITE ACCELERATION**

Although Dynamic Site Acceleration is part of the features provided by the Azure CDN, this is not strictly a cache solution. If you need to use Dynamic Site Acceleration with Microsoft Azure services, you should use Azure Front Door Service instead of Azure CDN.

If you need to dynamically create new CDN profiles and endpoints, Microsoft provides the Azure CDN Library for .NET and Azure CDN Library for Node.js. Using these libraries, you can automate most of the operations reviewed in this section.

NEED MORE REVIEW?   **HOW CACHING WORKS**

Caching web content involves working with HTTP headers, setting the appropriate expiration times, or deciding which files should be included in the cache. You can review the details of how caching works by reading the article at *https://docs.microsoft.com/en-us/azure/cdn/cdn-how-caching-works*.

EXAM TIP

Content Delivery Networks (CDN) are appropriate for caching static content that changes infrequently. Although Azure CDN from Akamai and Azure CDN from Verizon include Dynamic Site Acceleration (DSA), this feature is not the same as a cache system. You should not confuse Azure CDN DSA optimization with Azure CDN cache.

Configure cache and expiration policies for FrontDoor, CDNs, and Redis caches

When you work with cached content, you need to control the lifetime or validity of that content. Although static content usually has a low rate of change, this kind of content can change. For example, if you are caching the logo of your company and the logo is changed, your users won't see the change in the application until the new logo is loaded in the cache. In this scenario, you can simply purge or remove the old logo from the cache, and the new image will be loaded into the cache as soon as the first user accesses the application.

This mechanism of manually purging the cache could be appropriate for a very specific scenario. Still, in general terms, you should consider using an automatic mechanism for having the freshest content in your cache system. When you add content to a CDN cache, the system automatically assigns a TimeToLive (TTL) value to the content file instead of continuously comparing the file in the cache with the original content on the web server. The cache system checks whether the TTL is lower than the current time. If the TTL is lower than the current time, the CDN considers the content to be fresh and keeps the content in the cache. If the TTL expires, the CDN marks the content as stale or invalid. When the next user tries to access the invalid content file, the CDN compares the cached file with the content in the web server. If both files match, the CDN updates the version of the cached file and makes the file valid again by resetting the expiration time. If the files in the cache and the web server don't match, the CDN removes the file from the cache and updates the content with the freshest content file on the web server.

The cached content can become invalid by deleting the content from the cache or by reaching the expiration time. You can configure the default TTL associated with a site by using the Cache-Control HTTP Header. You set the value for this header in different ways:

- **Default CDN configuration** If you don't configure any value for the TTL, the Azure CDN automatically configures a default value of seven days.

- **Caching rules** You can configure TTL values globally or by using custom matching rules. Global caching rules affect all content in the CDN. Custom caching rules control the TTL for different paths or files in your web application. You can even disable the caching for some parts of your web application.

- **Web.config files** You use the web.config file to set the expiration time of the folder. You can even configure web.config files for different folders by setting different TTL values. Use the following XML code to set the TTL:

```
<configuration>
    <system.webServer>
        <staticContent>
            <clientCache cacheControlMode="UseMaxAge" cacheControlMaxAge=
            "3.00:00:00" />
        </staticContent>
    </system.webServer>
</configuration>
```

- **Programmatically** If you work with ASP.NET, you can control the CDN caching behavior by setting the HttpResponse.Cache property. You can use the following code to set the expiration time of the content to five hours:

```
// Set the caching parameters.
Response.Cache.SetExpires(DateTime.Now.AddHours(5));
Response.Cache.SetCacheability(HttpCacheability.Public);
Response.Cache.SetLastModified(DateTime.Now);
```

Use the following procedure to create caching rules in your Azure CDN. Bear in mind that you can configure caching rules only for Azure CDN for Verizon and Azure CDN for Akamai profiles:

1. Open the Azure portal (*https://portal.azure.com*).
2. Click the Create A Resource button.
3. On the New blade, in the Search The Marketplace text box, type CDN.
4. In the result list, click CDN.
5. On the CDN blade, click the Create button.
6. On the CDN profile blade, type a Name for the profile.
7. Select an existing Resource Group from the drop-down menu. Alternatively, you can create a new resource group by clicking the Create New link below the Resource Group drop-down menu.
8. On the Pricing Tier drop-down menu, select Standard Akamai.
9. Check the Create A New CDN Endpoint Now check box.
10. Type a name for the endpoint in the CDN Endpoint Name text box. Beware that this name cannot be the same as the CDN Profile name.
11. In the Origin Type drop-down menu, select Web App..
12. In the Origin Hostname drop-down menu, select the name of your web application.
13. Click the Create button at the bottom of the CDN Profile blade.
14. In the Search text box at the top of the Azure portal, type the name of your CDN profile.
15. In the result list, click your CDN profile's name.
16. On the Overview panel, on the CDN profile blade, in the Endpoints list, click the existing endpoint.
17. On the Endpoint blade, click Caching Rules in the Settings section of the navigation menu.
18. On the Caching Rules panel, shown in Figure 4-2, set the Caching Behavior drop-down menu to Override in the Global Caching Rules section.
19. Set the Cache Expiration Duration to 15 days.
20. On the Custom Caching Rules list, create a new custom rule. Set the Match Condition drop-down menu to File Extension(s).
21. In the Match Value(s) text box, type **png**.

22. In the Caching Behavior drop-down menu, select Override.

23. In the Days column, type **4**.

24. In the top-left corner of the panel, click the Save button.

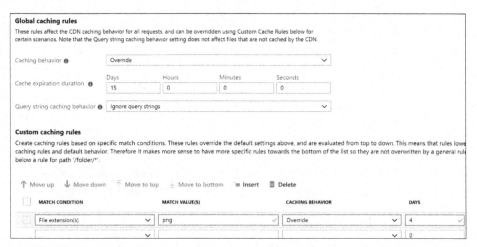

FIGURE 4-2 Configuring Caching Rules

When you work with Azure Cache for Redis, you can also set the TTL for the different values stored in the in-memory database. If you don't set a TTL for the key/value pair, the entry in the cache won't expire. When you create a new entry in the in-memory database, you set the TTL value as a parameter of the StringSet() method. The following code snippet shows how to set a TTL of 5 hours to a String value:

```
_cache.StringSet(key, Serialize(value), new TimeSpan(5, 0, 0));
```

Apart from invalidating the content of the cache by the expiration of the content, you can manually invalidate the content by removing it directly from the CDN or Redis Cache. You can remove a key from the Azure Cache for Redis in-memory database. You can use the following methods:

- **KeyDelete() method**   Use this method for removing a single key from the database. You need to use this method with a database instance.

- **FlushAllDatabases()** method   Use this method to remove all keys from all databases in the Azure Cache for Redis.

For Azure CDN, you can invalidate part or the entire content of the CDN profile by using the Purge option available in the Azure portal. Use the following procedure for purging content from your Azure CDN profile:

1. Open the Azure portal (*https://portal.azure.com*).

2. In the Search text box at the top of the Azure portal, type the name of your CDN profile.

3. On the Overview panel, in your CDN profile blade, click the Purge button.

4. On the Purge panel, shown in Figure 4-3, select the Endpoint you want to purge from the drop-down menu control.

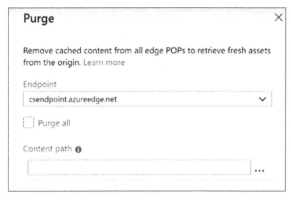

FIGURE 4-3 Purging content from the cache

5. In the Content Path text box, type the path that you want to purge from the cache. If you want to purge all the content from the cache, you need to check the Purge All check box.

> **NOTE** **PURGE ALL AND WILDCARDS IN AZURE CDN FOR AKAMAI**
>
> At the time of this writing, the Purge All and Wildcard options are not available for Akamai CDNs.

Azure CDN is not the only service that Microsoft provides for caching content. The Azure Front Door service allows you to route the traffic efficiently to the closest location to the user. As part of the features offered by the Azure Front Door service, it also allows you to cache content by providing a CDN. As with Azure CDN, you can configure the cache and expiration time for the elements in the cache.

The cache configuration is performed at routing rule level. Using the Azure Front Door service, you can route the traffic for different paths in your URL to different back-end pools hosting your application. A routing rule defines each of these routes. With this structure in mind, you can configure caching for some parts of your application, whereas others remain uncached. The following procedure shows how to enable caching in a routing rule. This procedure assumes that you have already deployed an Azure Front Door. Because we didn't review how to work with Azure Front Door previously in this chapter, you can deploy a demo Front Door by using the quick start guide at *https://docs.microsoft.com/en-us/azure/frontdoor/quickstart-create-front-door.*

1. Open the Azure portal (*https://portal.azure.com*).

2. In the Search Resources, Services, And Docs text box, type the name of your Azure Front Door instance.

3. Click the name of your Azure Front Door instance in the result list.

4. In your Azure Front Door blade, click Front Door Designer in the Settings section on the navigation menu on the left side of the blade.

5. On the Front Door Designer blade, click one of the routing rules inside the green rectangle with the title Routing Rules.

6. On the Update Routing Rule panel, scroll down to the bottom of the panel.

7. Change the Caching switch control from Disabled to Enabled.

8. In the cache settings shown in Figure 4-4, change the value of Cache Duration from 0 Days to 4 Days.

9. Click the Update button.

10. Click the Save button on the top-left corner of the Front Door Designer blade.

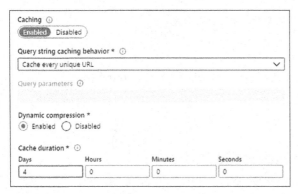

FIGURE 4-4 Configuring Azure Front Door cache

You can also control the cache expiration of an individual item by setting the appropriate cache headers. The following HTTP headers control the cache and expiration of an item in the Azure Front Door cache:

- **Cache-Control: max-age** Expressed in seconds, this header controls how long the item is valid in the cache. For example, if you set this value to 3600, the item can be used up to 60 minutes before the Azure Front Door service makes a request to the back-end pool for a fresh version of the item.

- **Cache-Control: s-maxage** Expressed in seconds, this directive is similar to the previous one but is meaningful only on CDN environments. This directive has precedence over max-age and expires directives.

- **Expires** Expressed using an HTTP-date timestamp, this directive sets the datetime until the item is valid in the cache. The max-age and s-maxage directives take precedence over this directive.

Purging the content of the cache is as simple as in the Azure CDN services. The following steps show how to purge the content of your Azure Front Door:

1. Open the Azure portal (*https://portal.azure.com*).

2. In the Search Resources, Services, And Docs text box, type the name of your Azure Front Door instance.

3. Click the name of your Azure Front Door instance in the result list.

4. In your Azure Front Door blade, click Front Door Designer in the Settings section on the navigation menu on the left side of the blade.

5. On the Front Door Designer blade, click the Purge button on the top left side of the blade.

6. On the Purge panel, mark the Purge All check box. Alternatively, if you want to purge only part of the cached content, type the path of the content that you want to purge in the Content Path text box below the Purge All check box.

7. Click the Purge button at the bottom of the panel.

NEED MORE REVIEW? **AZURE FRONT DOOR CACHING**

Azure Front Door is an advanced routing and caching system. This service allows you to cache big files and compress data on the fly. You can review more details about how Azure Front Door caching works by reading the article at *https://docs.microsoft.com/en-us/azure/frontdoor/front-door-caching*.

Store and retrieve data in Azure Redis Cache

Redis is an open-source cache system that allows you to work *like in* an in-memory data structure store, database cache, or message broker. The Azure Redis Cache or Azure Cache for Redis is a Redis implementation managed by Microsoft. Azure Redis Cache has three pricing layers that provide you with different levels of features:

- **Basic** This is the tier with the fewest features and less throughput and higher latency. You should use this tier only for development or testing purposes. There is no Service Level Agreement (SLA) associated with the Basic tier.

- **Standard** This tier offers a two-node, primary-secondary replicated Redis cache that is managed by Microsoft. This tier has associated a high-availability SLA of 99.9 percent.

- **Premium** This is an enterprise-grade Redis cluster managed by Microsoft. This tier offers the complete group of features with the highest throughput and lower latencies. The Redis cluster is also deployed on more powerful hardware. This tier has a high-availability SLA of 99.9 percent.

NOTE **SCALING THE AZURE REDIS CACHE SERVICE**

You can scale up your existing Azure Redis cache service to a higher tier, but you cannot scale down your current tier to a lower one.

When you are working with Azure Cache for Redis, you can use different implementation patterns that solve different issues, depending on the architecture of your application:

- **Cache-Aside** In most situations, your application stores the data that it manages in a database. Accessing data in a database is a relatively slow operation because it depends on the time to access the disk storage system. A solution would be to load the database in memory, but this approach is costly; in most cases, the database simply doesn't fit on the available memory. One solution to improve the performance of your application in these scenarios is to store the most-accessed data in the cache. When the back-end system changes the data in the database, the same system can also update the data in the cache, which makes the change available to all clients.

- **Content caching** Most web applications use web page templates that use common elements, such as headers, footers, toolbars, menus, stylesheets, images, and so on. These template elements are static elements (or at least don't change often). Storing these elements in Azure Cache for Redis relieves your web servers from serving these elements and improves the time your servers need to generate dynamic content.

- **User session caching** This pattern is a good idea if your application needs to register too much information about the user history or data that you need to associate with cookies. Storing too much information in a session cookie hurts the performance of your application. You can save part of that information in your database and store a pointer or index in the session cookie that points that user to the information in the database. If you use an in-memory database, such as Azure Cache for Redis, instead of a traditional database, your application benefits from the faster access times to the data stored in memory.

- **Job and message queuing** You can use Azure Cache for Redis to implement a distributed queue that executes long-lasting tasks that may negatively affect the performance of your application.

- **Distributed transactions** A transaction is a group of commands that need to complete or fail together. Any transaction needs to ensure that the data is always in a stable state. If your application needs to execute transactions, you can use Azure Cache for Redis for implementing these transactions.

You can work with Azure Cache for Redis using different languages, such as ASP.NET, .NET, .NET Core, Node.js, Java, or Python. Before you can add caching features to your code using Azure Redis Cache, you need to create your Azure Cache for Redis database using the following procedure:

1. Open the Azure portal (*https://portal.azure.com*).
2. Click Create A Resource in the Azure Services section.
3. On the New blade, click Databases on the navigation menu on the left side of the blade.
4. In the list of Database services, shown in Figure 4-5, click the Azure Cache For Redis item.

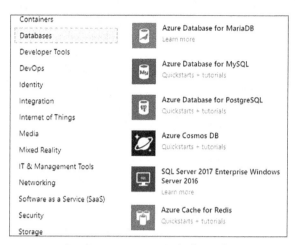

FIGURE 4-5 Creating a new Azure Cache for Redis resource

5. On the New Redis Cache blade, type a DNS Name for your Redis resource.

6. Select the Subscription, Resource Group, and Location from the appropriate drop-down menu that best fits your needs.

7. In the Pricing tier drop-down menu, select the Basic C0 tier.

8. Click the Create button at the bottom of the New Redis Cache blade.

The deployment of your new Azure Cache for Redis takes a few minutes to complete. Once the deployment is complete, you need to get the access keys for your instance of the Azure Cache for Redis. You use this information in your code to connect the Redis service in Azure.

If you are using any of the .NET languages, you can use the StackExchange.Redis client for accessing your Azure Cache for Redis resource. You can also use this Redis client for accessing other Redis implementations. When reading or writing values in the Azure Cache for Redis, you need to create a ConnectionMultiplexer object. This object creates a connection to your Redis server. The ConnectionMultiplexer class is designed to be reused as much as possible.

For this reason, you should store this object and reuse it across all your code, whenever it is possible to reuse. Creating a connection is a costly operation. For this reason, you should not create a ConnectionMultiplexer object for each read or write operation to the Redis cache. Once you have created your ConnectionMultiplexer object, you can use any of the available operations in the StackExchange.Redis package. Following are the basic operations that you can use with Redis:

- **Use Redis as a database** You get a database from Redis, using the GetDatabase() method, for writing and reading values from the database. You use the StringSet() or StringGet() methods for writing and reading.

- **Use Redis as a messaging queue** You get a subscriber object from the Redis client, using the GetSubscriber() method. Then you can publish messages to a queue, using the Publish() method, and read messages from a queue, using the Subscribe() method. Queues in Redis are known as "channels."

The following procedure shows how to connect to an Azure Cache for Redis database and read and write data to and from the database using an ASP.NET application:

1. Open Visual Studio 2019.
2. In the welcome window of Visual Studio 2019, on the Get Started column, click Create A New Project.
3. On the Create A New Project window, on the All Languages drop-down menu, select C#.
4. In the Search For Templates text box type **asp.net**.
5. In the result list, click ASP.NET Web Application (.NET Framework).
6. Click the Next button at the bottom right of the window.
7. On the Configure Your New Project, type a Project Name, a Location, and a Solution Name for your project.
8. Click the Create button at the bottom right of the window.
9. In the Create A New ASP.NET Web Application window, select the MVC template on the template list in the middle left side of the window. MVC is for Model-View-Controller.
10. On the right side of the Create A New ASP.NET Web Application window, in the Authentication section, ensure the Authentication is set to No Authentication.
11. Click the Create button at the bottom-right corner of the window.
12. In the Visual Studio window, select Tools > NuGet Package Manager > Manage NuGet Packages For Solution.
13. On the NuGet Package Manager tab, click Browse.
14. Type **StackExchange.Redis** and press Enter.
15. Click the StackExchange.Redis package.
16. On the right side of the NuGet Manager tab, click the check box next to your project.
17. Click the Install button.
18. In the Preview Changes window, click OK.
19. In the License Acceptance window, click the I Accept button.
20. Open the Azure portal (*https://portal.azure.com*).
21. In the search text box in the top-middle of the portal, type the name of your Azure Cache for Redis that you created in the previous example.
22. Click your Azure Cache for Redis in the results list.
23. On the Azure Cache for Redis blade, click Access Keys in the Settings section in the navigation menu on the left side of the blade.
24. On the Access Keys blade, copy the value of the Primary Connection String (StackExchange.Redis). You need this value on the next steps.
25. In the Visual Studio window, open the Web.config file.
26. In the <appSettings> section, add the following code:

```
<add key="CacheConnection " value="<value_copied_in_step_24>"/>
```

27. Open the HomeController.cs file in the Controllers folder.

28. Add the following using statements to the HomeController.cs file:

```
using System.Configuration;
using StackExchange.Redis;
```

29. Add the code in Listing 4-1 to the HomeController class.

LISTING 4-1 HomeController RedisCache method

```
// C#. ASP.NET.
public ActionResult RedisCache()
{
    ViewBag.Message = "A simple example with Azure Cache for Redis on ASP.NET.";

    var lazyConnection = new Lazy<ConnectionMultiplexer>(() =>
    {

        string cacheConnection = ConfigurationManager.AppSettings["CacheConnection"]
                                                     .ToString();
        return ConnectionMultiplexer.Connect(cacheConnection);
    });
    // You need to create a ConnectionMultiplexer object for accessing the Redis
    // cache.
    // Then you can get an instance of a database.
    IDatabase cache = lazyConnection.Value.GetDatabase();

    // Perform cache operations using the cache object...

    // Run a simple Redis command
    ViewBag.command1 = "PING";
    ViewBag.command1Result = cache.Execute(ViewBag.command1).ToString();

    // Simple get and put of integral data types into the cache
    ViewBag.command2 = "GET Message";
    ViewBag.command2Result = cache.StringGet("Message").ToString();
```

```
    // Write a new value to the database.
    ViewBag.command3 = "SET Message \"Hello! The cache is working from ASP.NET!\"";
    ViewBag.command3Result = cache.StringSet("Message", "Hello! The cache is working
                                                 from ASP.NET!").ToString();


    // Get the message that we wrote on the previous step
    ViewBag.command4 = "GET Message";
    ViewBag.command4Result = cache.StringGet("Message").ToString();


    // Get the client list, useful to see if the connection list is growing...
    ViewBag.command5 = "CLIENT LIST";

    ViewBag.command5Result = cache.Execute("CLIENT", "LIST").ToString().Replace(
                                                 "id=", "\rid=");

    lazyConnection.Value.Dispose();


    return View();
}
```

30. In the Solution Explorer, right-click Views > Home folder and select Add > View on the contextual menu.

31. In the Add View window, type **RedisCache** for the View Name.

32. Click the Add button.

33. Open the RedisCache.cshtml file.

34. Replace the content of the RedisCache.cshtml file with the content of Listing 4-2.

LISTING 4-2 RedisCache View

```
// C#. ASP.NET.
@{
    ViewBag.Title = "Azure Cache for Redis Test";
}


<h2>@ViewBag.Title.</h2>
<h3>@ViewBag.Message</h3>
<br /><br />
<table border="1" cellpadding="10">
    <tr>
        <th>Command</th>
        <th>Result</th>
    </tr>
    <tr>
        <td>@ViewBag.command1</td>
        <td><pre>@ViewBag.command1Result</pre></td>
    </tr>
```

```
<tr>
    <td>@ViewBag.command2</td>
    <td><pre>@ViewBag.command2Result</pre></td>
</tr>
<tr>
    <td>@ViewBag.command3</td>
    <td><pre>@ViewBag.command3Result</pre></td>
</tr>
<tr>
    <td>@ViewBag.command4</td>
    <td><pre>@ViewBag.command4Result</pre></td>
</tr>
<tr>
    <td>@ViewBag.command5</td>
    <td><pre>@ViewBag.command5Result</pre></td>
</tr>
</table>
```

35. Press F5 to run your project locally.

36. In the web browser running your project, append the */Home/RedisCache* URI to the URL. Your result should look like Figure 4-6.

Command	Result
PING	PONG
GET Message	
SET Message "Hello! The cache is working from ASP.NET!"	True
GET Message	Hello! The cache is working from ASP.NET!
CLIENT LIST	id=9774 addr=127.0.0.1:35187 fd=8 name=PORTAL_CONSOLE age=152 id=9853 addr=83.56.0.194:61343 fd=18 name=DEV-CS age=1 idle=0 id=9854 addr=83.56.0.194:61344 fd=14 name=DEV-CS age=1 idle=1

FIGURE 4-6 Example results

EXAM TIP

You can use Azure Cache for Redis for static content and the most-accessed dynamic data. You can use it for in-memory databases or message queues using a publication/subscription pattern.

Skill 4.2: Instrument solutions to support monitoring and logging

Knowing how your application behaves during regular operation is essential, especially for production environments. You need to get information about the number of users, resource consumption, transactions, and other metrics that can help you to troubleshoot your application if an error happens. Adding custom metrics to your application is also important when creating alerts that warn you when your application is not behaving as expected.

Azure provides features for monitoring the consumption of resources assigned to your application. Also, you can monitor the transactions and any other metrics that you may need, which allows you to fully understand how your application behaves under conditions that are usually difficult to simulate or test. You can also use these metrics for efficiently creating autoscale rules to improve the performance of your application.

This skill covers how to

- Configure instrumentation in an app or service by using Application Insights
- Analyze log data and troubleshoot solutions by using Azure Monitor
- Implement Application Insights Web Test and Alerts
- Implement code that handles transient faults

Configure instrumentation in an app or service by using Application Insights

Microsoft provides you with the ability to monitor your application while it is running by using Application Insights. This tool integrates with your code, allowing you to monitor what is happening inside your code while it is executing in a cloud, on-premises, or hybrid environment. You can also enable Application Insights for applications that are already deployed in Azure without modifying the already deployed code.

By adding a small instrumentation package, you can measure several aspects of your application. These measures, known as telemetry, are automatically sent to the Application Insight component deployed in Azure. Based on the information sent from the telemetry streams from your application to the Azure portal, you can analyze your application's performance and create alerts and dashboards, which help you better understand how your application is behaving. Although Application Insights needs to be deployed in the Azure portal, your application can be executed in Azure, in other public clouds, or in your on-premises infrastructure. When you deploy the Application Insights instrumentation in your application, it monitors the following points:

- **Request rates, response times, and failure rates** You can view which pages your users request more frequently, distributed across time. You may find that your users tend to visit specific pages at the beginning of the day, whereas other pages are more visited at the end of the day. You can also monitor the time that your server takes for delivering the requested page or even if there were failures when delivering the page. You should monitor the failure rates and response times to ensure that your application is performing correctly and your users have a pleasant experience.

- **Dependency rates, response times, and failure rates** If your application depends on external services (such as Azure Storage Accounts), Google or Twitter security services for authenticating your users, or any other external service, you can monitor how these external services are performing and how they are affecting your application.

- **Exceptions** The instrumentation keeps track of the exceptions raised by servers and browsers while your application is executing. You can review the details of the stack trace for each exception via the Azure portal. You can also view statistics about exceptions that arise during your application's execution.

- **Page views and load performance** Measuring the performance of your server's page delivery is only part of the equation. Using Application Insights, you can also get information about the page views and load performance reported from the browser's side.

- **AJAX calls** This measures the time taken by AJAX calls made from your application's web pages. It also measures the failure rates and response time.

- **User and session counts** You can keep track of the number of users who are connected to your application. Just as the same user can initiate multiple sessions, you can track the number of sessions connected to your application. This allows you to clearly measure the threshold of concurrent users supported by your application.

- **Performance counters** You can get information about the performance counters of the server machine (CPU, memory, and network usage) from which your code is executing.

- **Hosts diagnostics** Hosts diagnostics can get information from your application if it is deployed in a Docker or Azure environment.

- **Diagnostic trace logs** Trace log messages can be used to correlate trace events with the requests made to the application by your users.
- **Custom events and metrics** Although the out-of-the-box instrumentation offered by Application Insights offers much information, some metrics are too specific to your application to be generalized and included in the general telemetry. For those cases, you can create custom metrics to monitor your server and client code. This allows you to monitor user actions, such as shopping cart checkouts or game scoring.

Application Insights are not limited to .NET languages. There are instrumentation libraries available for other languages, such as Java, JavaScript, or Node.js. There are also libraries available for other platforms like Android or iOS. You can use the following procedure to add Application Insight instrumentation to your ASP.NET application. To run this example, you need to meet these prerequisites:

- An Azure Subscription.
- Visual Studio 2017/2019. If you don't have Visual Studio, you can download the Community edition for free from *https://visualstudio.microsoft.com/free-developer-offers/*.
- Install the following workloads in Visual Studio:
  - ASP.NET and web development, including the optional components.
  - Azure development.

In this example, you are going to create a new MVC application from a template and then add the Application Insights instrumentation. You can use the same procedure to add instrumentation to any of your existing ASP.NET applications:

1. Open Visual Studio 2019.
2. In the home window in Visual Studio, click the Create A New Project button in the section Get Started on the right side of the window.
3. In the Create A New Project window, in the Search box, type **MVC**.
4. Select the ASP.NET Web Application (.NET Framework) template.
5. Click the Next button in the bottom-right corner of the window.
6. Type a name for your project and solution in the Project Name and Solution Name boxes, respectively.
7. Select the Location where your project will be stored.
8. Click the Create button at the bottom-right corner of the window.
9. On the Create A New ASP.NET Web Application window, select the MVC template.
10. Click the Create button at the bottom-right corner of the window.
11. In the Solution Explorer window, right-click the name of your project.
12. In the contextual menu, shown in Figure 4-7, select Add > Application Insights Telemetry.

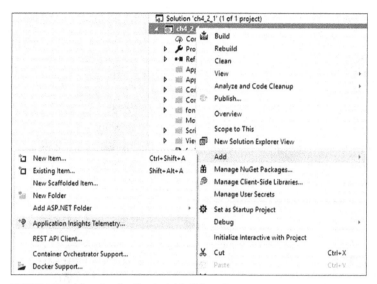

FIGURE 4-7 Adding Application Insights Telemetry

13. On the Application Insights Configuration page, click the Get Started button at the bottom of the page.

14. On the Register Your App With Application Insights page, ensure that the correct Azure Account and Azure Subscription are selected in the drop-down menus.

15. Click the Configure Settings link below the Resource drop-down menu.

16. In the Application Insights Configuration dialog box, select the Resource Group and Location where you want to create the new Application Insight resource.

17. Click the Register button.

18. On the Application Insights Configuration tab, click the Collect Traces From System. Diagnostics button at the bottom of the tab. Enabling this option allows you to send a log message directly to Application Insights.

At this point, Visual Studio starts adding the needed packages and dependencies to your project. Visual Studio also automatically configures the Instrumentation Key, which allows your application to connect to the Application Insights resource created in Azure. Now your project is connected with the instance of the Application Insights deployed in Azure. As soon as you run your project, the Application Insights instrumentation starts sending information to Azure. You can review this information in the Azure portal or your Visual Studio. Use the following steps to access Application Insights from Visual Studio and Azure portal:

1. From the Visual Studio window, in the Solution Explorer window, navigate to your project's name and select Connected Services > Application Insights.

2. Right-click Application Insights.

3. On the contextual menu, click Search Live Telemetry. The Application Insights Search tab appears in Visual Studio.

4. In the Solution Explorer, right-click Application Insights to open the Azure Portal Application Insights from Visual Studio.

5. On the contextual menu, click Open Application Insights Portal.

Apart from the standard metrics that come out of the box with the default Application Insights instrumentation, you can also add your custom events and metrics to your code. Using custom events and metrics, you can analyze and troubleshoot logic and workflows that are specific to your application. The following example shows how to modify the MVC application that you created on the previous example for adding custom events and metrics:

1. Open the project that you created in the previous example.

2. Open the HomeController.cs file.

3. Add the following using statements at the beginning of the file:

```
using Microsoft.ApplicationInsights;
using System.Diagnostics;
```

4. Replace the content of the HomeController class in the HomeController.cs file with the content in Listing 4-3.

LISTING 4-3 HomeController class

```csharp
// C#. ASP.NET.
public class HomeController : Controller
    {
        private TelemetryClient telemetry;
        private double indexLoadCounter;

        public HomeController()
        {
            //Create a TelemetryClient that can be used during the life of the
            // Controller.
            telemetry = new TelemetryClient();

            //Initialize some counters for the custom metrics.
            //This is a fake metric just for demo purposes.
            indexLoadCounter = new Random().Next(1000);
        }

        public ActionResult Index()
        {

            //This example is trivial as ApplicationInsights already registered the
            // load of the page.
            //You can use this example for tracking different events in the
            // application.
            telemetry.TrackEvent("Loading the Index page");
```

```
//Before you can submit a custom metric, you need to use the GetMetric
//method.
telemetry.GetMetric("CountOfIndexPageLoads").TrackValue(indexLoadCounter);


//This trivial example shows how to track exceptions using Application
//Insights.
//You can also send trace message to Application Insights.
try
{
    Trace.TraceInformation("Raising a trivial exception");
    throw new System.Exception(@"Trivial Exception for testing Tracking
    Exception feature in Application Insights");
}
catch (System.Exception ex)
{
    Trace.TraceError("Capturing and managing the trivial exception");
    telemetry.TrackException(ex);
}


//You need to instruct the TelemetryClient to send all in-memory data to
// the ApplicationInsights.
telemetry.Flush();
return View();
}

public ActionResult About()
{
    ViewBag.Message = "Your application description page.";


    //This example is trivial as ApplicationInsights already registers the
    //load of the page.
    //You can use this example for tracking different events in the
    // application.
    telemetry.TrackEvent("Loading the About page");

    return View();
}

public ActionResult Contact()
{
    ViewBag.Message = "Your contact page.";
```

```
//This example is trivial as ApplicationInsights already registers the load
//of the page.
//You can use this example for tracking different events in the
// application.
telemetry.TrackEvent("Loading the Contact page");

        return View();
    }
}
```

5. In the Solution Explorer, open the ApplicationInsights.config file.

6. In the `<Add Type="Microsoft.ApplicationInsights.Extensibility.PerfCounterCollector.PerformanceCollectorModule, Microsoft.AI.PerfCounterCollector">` XML item, add the following child XML item:

```
<EnableIISExpressPerformanceCounters>true</EnableIISExpressPerformanceCounters>
```

> **NOTE CONTROLLERS CONSTRUCTORS**
>
> In the previous example, we used a private property in the constructor for creating and initial-izing a TelemetryClient object. In a real-world application, you should use dependency injec-tion techniques for properly initializing the Controller class. There are several frameworks, like Unity, Autofac, or Ninject, that can help you in implementing the dependency injection pattern in your code.

At this point, you can press F5 and run your project to see how your application is sending information to Application Insights. If you review the Application Insights Search tab, you can see the messages, shown in Figure 4-8, that your application is sending to Application Insights.

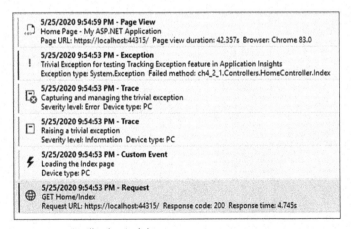

FIGURE 4-8 Application Insights messages

You send messages to Application Insights by using the `TelemetryClass` class. This class provides you with the appropriate methods for sending the different types of messages to Application Insights. You can send custom events by using the `TrackEvent()` method. You use this method for tracking meaningful events to your application, such as when the user creates a new shopping cart in an eCommerce web application or the user wins a game in a mobile app.

If you need to keep track of the value of certain variables or properties in your code, you can use the combination of `GetMetric()` and `TrackValue()` methods. The `GetMetric()` method retrieves a metric from the azure.applicationinsight namespace. If the metric doesn't exist on the namespace, the Application Insights library automatically creates a new one. Once you have a reference to the correct metric, you can use the `TrackValue()` method to add a value to that metric. You can use these custom metrics for setting alerts or autoscale rules. Use the following steps for viewing the custom metrics in the Azure portal:

1. From the Visual Studio window, in the Solution Explorer window, navigate to your project's name and select Connected Services > Application Insights.

2. Right-click Application Insights.

3. In the contextual menu, click Open Application Insights Portal.

4. On the Application Insights blade, click Metrics in the Monitoring section of the navigation menu on the left side of the blade.

5. On the Metrics blade, on the toolbar above the empty graph, on the Metric Namespace drop-down menu, select azure.applicationsight.

6. On the Metric drop-down menu, select CountOfIndexPageLoad. This is the custom metric that you defined in the previous example.

7. On the Aggregation drop-down menu, select Count. The values for your graph will be different but should look similar to Figure 4-9.

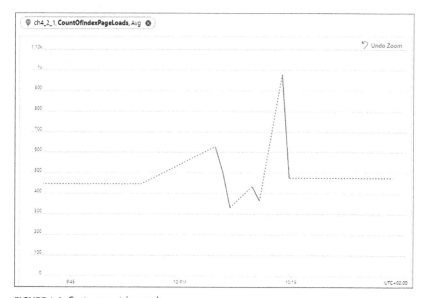

FIGURE 4-9 Custom metric graph

You can also send log messages to Application Insights by using the integration between System.Diagnostics and Application Insights. Any message sent to the diagnostics system using the Trace class appears in Application Insights as a Trace message. In this same line, use the TraceException() method for sending the stack trace and the exception to Application Insights. The advantage of doing this is that you can easily correlate exceptions with the operations that were performing your code when the exception happened.

EXAM TIP

Remember that Application Insights is a solution for monitoring the behavior of an application on different platforms, written in different languages. You can use Application Insights with web applications and native applications or mobile applications written in .NET, Java, JavaScript, or Node.js. There is no requirement to run your application in Azure. You only need to use Azure for deploying the Application Insights resource that you use for analyzing the information sent by your application.

NEED MORE REVIEW? CREATING CUSTOM EVENTS AND METRICS

You can create more complex metrics and events than the one that we reviewed here. For complex operations, you can track all the actions inside an operation for correctly correlating all the messages generated during the execution of the operation. You can learn more about how to create custom events and metrics by reading the article at *https://docs.microsoft.com/ en-us/azure/azure-monitor/app/api-custom-events-metrics*.

Analyze log data and troubleshoot solutions by using Azure Monitor

Azure Monitor is a tool composed of several elements that help you monitor and better understand the behavior of your solutions. Application Insights is a tool for collecting information from your solutions. Once you have the collected information, you can use the Analyze tools for reviewing the data and troubleshooting your application. Depending on the information that you need to analyze, you can use Metric Analytics or Log Analytics.

You can use Metric Analytics for reviewing the standard and custom metrics sent from your application. A metric is a numeric value that is related to some aspect at a particular point in time of your solution. CPU usage, free memory, and the number of requests are all examples of metrics; also, you can create your own custom metrics. Because metrics are lightweight, you can use them to monitor scenarios in near real-time. You analyze metric data by representing the values of the metrics in a time interval using different types of graphs. Use the following steps for reviewing graphs:

1. Open the Azure portal (*https://portal.azure.com*).

2. On the Search Resources, Services, And Docs text box on the top side of the Azure portal, type monitor.

3. Click Monitor in the Services section in the result list.

4. On the Monitor blade, click Metrics on the navigation menu on the left side of the blade.

5. On the Metrics blade, the Select A Scope panel should appear automatically.

6. On the Select A Scope panel, in the scope tree, select the subscription or resource groups that contain the Azure App Service containing the metrics you want to add to the graph.

7. In the Resource Type drop-down menu, below the scope tree, select only the App Services resource type.

8. In the App Service drop-down, select one of your App Services.

9. Click the Apply button at the bottom of the panel.

10. On the Metrics blade, select the Average Response Time metric in the Metric drop-down menu.

11. Click the Add Metric button at the top of the graph. You can add several metrics to the same graph, which means you can analyze different metrics that are related between them.

12. Repeat step 10 for adding the Connections metric. Figure 4-10 shows the metrics added to the graph.

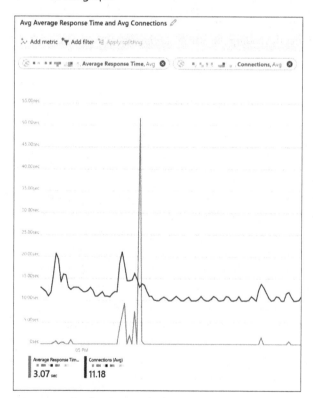

FIGURE 4-10 Configuring metrics for a graph

You use Log Analytics for analyzing the trace, logs, events, exceptions, and any other message sent from your application. Log messages are more complex than metrics because they can contain much more information than a simple numeric value. You can analyze log messages by using queries for retrieving, consolidating, and analyzing the collected data. Log Analytics for Azure Monitor uses a version of the Kusto query language. You can construct your queries to get information from the data stored in Azure Monitor. To do so, complete the following steps:

1. Open the Azure portal (*https://portal.azure.com*).

2. In the Search Resources, Services, And Docs text box at the top of the Azure portal, type **monitor**.

3. Click Monitor in the Services section in the result list.

4. On the Monitor blade, click Logs in the navigation menu on the left side of the blade.

5. On the Logs blade, click the Get Started button.

6. On the Logs blade, the Select A Scope panel should appear automatically.

7. On the Select A Scope panel, in the scope tree, navigate to the resources containing the logs you want to query. Click the check box next to the resource. You can select only resources of the same type. For this example, the resource type should be Application Insights.

8. Click the Apply button at the bottom of the panel.

9. On the Logs blade, type **traces** in the text area.

10. Click the Run button.

11. You can review the result of your query in the section below the query text area.

This simple query returns all the traces error events stored in your Application Insights workspace. You can use more complex queries to get more information about your solution. The available fields for the queries depend on the data loaded in the workspace. The data schema manages these fields. Figure 4-11 shows the schema associated with a workplace that stores data from Application Insights.

Once you get the results from a query, you can easily refine the results of the query by adding where clauses to the query. The easiest way to add new filtering criteria is to expand one of the records in the table view in the results section below the query text area. If you move your mouse over each of the fields in a record, you can see three small dots before the field of the record. If you click the three dots icon, a contextual menu appears for including or excluding the value of the field in the where clause. Based on the example in the previous section, the following query would get all traces sent from the application except those with the message Raising a trivial exception.

```
traces | where message <> "Raising a trivial exception"
```

You can review the results of this query in both table and chart formats. Using the different visualization formats, you can get a different insight into the data. Figure 4-12 shows how the results from the previous query are plotted into a pie chart.

FIGURE 4-11 Workspace schema

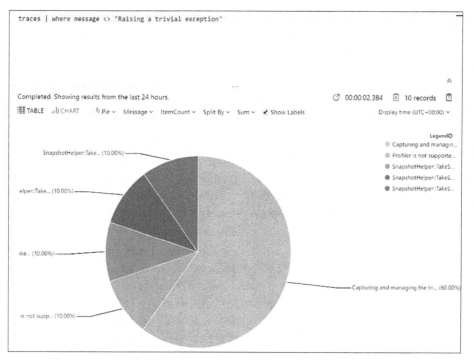

FIGURE 4-12 Rendering query results

EXAM TIP

When you try to query logs from the Azure Monitor, remember that you need to enable the diagnostics logs for the Azure App Services. If you get the message, *We didn't find any logs* when you try to query the logs for your Azure App Service, that could mean that you need to configure the diagnostic settings in your App Service.

Implement Application Insights Web Test and Alerts

As a result of analyzing the data sent from your application to the Azure Monitor using Application Insights, you may find some situations that you need to monitor more carefully. Using Azure Monitor, you can set alerts based on the value of different metrics or logs. For example, you can create an alert to receive a notification when your application generates an HTTP return code 502.

You can also configure Application Insights for monitoring the availability of your web application. You can configure different types of tests for checking the availability of your web application:

- **URL ping test**   This is a simple test for checking whether your application is available by making a request to a single URL for your application.

- **Multi-step web test**   Using Visual Studio Enterprise, you can record the steps that you want to use as the verification for your application. You use this type of test for checking complex scenarios. The process of recording the steps in a web application generates a file with the recorded steps. Using this generated file, you can create a web test in Application Insights; then you upload the recording file.

- **Custom Track Availability Test**   You can create your own availability test in your code using the `TrackAvailability()` method.

When creating a URL ping test, you can check not only the HTTP response code but also the content returned by the server. This way, you can minimize the possibility of false positives. These false positives can happen if the server returns a valid HTTP response code, but the content is different due to configuration errors. Use the following procedure for creating an URL ping test on your Application Insights that checks the availability of your web application:

1. Open the Azure portal (*https://portal.azure.com*).

2. In the Search Resources, Services, And Docs text box at the top of the Azure portal, type **monitor**.

3. Click Monitor in the Services section in the result list.

4. On the Monitor blade, click Applications in the Insights section.

5. On the Applications blade, click the name of the Application Insights resource where you want to configure the alert.

6. On the Applications Insights blade, click Availability in the Investigate section of the navigation menu on the left side of the blade.

7. On the Availability blade, click Add Test at the top left of the blade.

8. On the Create Test blade, shown in Figure 4-13, type a name for the test in the Test Name text box.

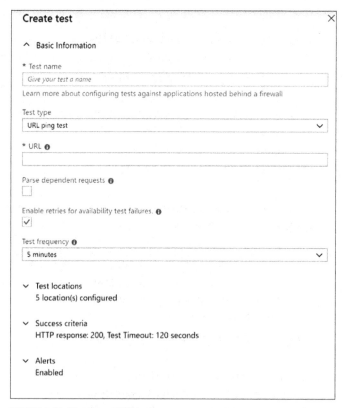

FIGURE 4-13 Creating a URL test

9. Ensure that URL Ping Test is selected in the Test Type drop-down menu.

10. In the URL text box, type the URL of the application you want to test.

11. Expand the Test Location section. Select the locations from which you want to perform the URL ping test.

12. Leave the other options as they are.

13. Click the Create button at the bottom of the panel.

When you configure the URL ping test, you cannot configure the Alert directly during the creation process. You need to finish the creation of the test, and then you can edit the Alert for defining the actions that you want to perform when the alert fires. Use the following procedure for configuring an alert associated with the URL ping test that you configured previously:

1. On the Availability blade, click the ellipsis beside the newly created alert.

2. In the contextual menu, click Open Rules (Alerts) Page.

3. On your alert Rules Management blade, in the Condition section, ensure that there is a default condition with the name *whenever the average failed locations is greater than or equal to 2 count.*

4. On the Action Group section, click the Select Action Group link.

5. On the Configured Actions panel, click the Create Action Group button.

6. On the Select An Action Group To Attach To This Alert Rule panel, click Create Action Group.

7. On the Create Action Group panel, select a resource group to save this action group. Alternatively, you can create a new resource group by clicking the Create New link below the Resource Group drop-down menu.

8. Type a name in the Action Group Name text box. This name needs to be unique in the resource group that you selected in the previous step.

9. Click the Next: Notifications button at the bottom of the panel.

10. In the Notifications section, in the Notification Type drop-down menu, select Email/SMS Message/Push/Voice.

11. On the Email/SMS/Push/Voice panel, select the Email check box.

12. Type an email address in the text box below the Email check box.

13. Click the OK button at the bottom of the panel.

14. Type a name in the Name text box, next to the Notification Type drop-down menu.

15. Click the Next: Actions at the bottom of the panel.

16. Leave the Actions section as is. You can use this section for configuring actions like calling an Azure Function, creating a ticket in an ITSM system, or start an Azure Automation Runbook.

17. Click the Review & Create button.

18. Click the Create button.

19. On your alert Rules Management blade, ensure that the newly created Action Group has been correctly added to the list of Action Groups attached to the alert.

20. Click the Save button on the top-left corner of your alert Rules Management blade.

Now you can test whether the URL ping test is working correctly by temporarily shutting down your testing application. After five minutes, you should receive an email message at the email address you configured in the alert action associated with the URL ping test.

EXAM TIP

Remember that you need a Visual Studio Enterprise license for creating multistep web tests. You use the Visual Studio Enterprise for the definition of the steps that are part of the test, and then you upload the test definition to Azure Application Insights.

NEED MORE REVIEW?   **AZURE MONITOR ALERTS**

Apart from creating alerts when a web test fails, you can also create alerts based on other conditions that depend on the events information stored in the Application Insights. You can review the details about how to create these alerts by reviewing the article at *https://docs. microsoft.com/en-us/azure/azure-monitor/platform/alerts-log*.

Implement code that handles transient faults

Developing applications for the cloud means that your application depends on the resources in the cloud to run your code. As we already reviewed in previous chapters, these resources provide out-of-the-box high availability and fault-tolerant features that make your application more resilient. Azure Cloud Services use redundant hardware and load balancers. Although you are guaranteed not to suffer big breakdowns, there can be situations that can temporarily affect your application, such as performing automatic failovers or load balancing operations. Usually, recovery from that kind of transient situation is as simple as retrying the operation your application was performing. For example, if your application was reading a record from a database and you get a timeout error because of a temporary overload of the database, you can retry the read operation to get the needed information.

Dealing with these transient faults leads you to deal with some interesting challenges. Your application needs to respond to these challenges to ensure that it offers a reliable experience to your users. These challenges are

- **Detect and classify faults**   Not all the faults that may happen during the application execution are transient. Your application needs to identify whether the fault is transient, long-lasting, or a terminal failure. Even the term "long-lasting failure" is dependent on the logic of your application because the amount of time that you consider "long-lasting" depends on the type of operations your application performs. Your application also needs to deal with the different responses that come from different services types. An error occurring while reading data from a storage system is different from an error occurring while writing data.

- **Retry the operation when appropriate**   Once your application determines that it's dealing with a transient fault, the application needs to retry the operation. It also needs to keep track of the number of retries of the faulting operation.

- **Implement an appropriate retry strategy**   Indefinitely retrying the operation could lead to other problems, such as performance degradation or blocking the resources that your application is using. To avoid those performance problems, your application needs to set a retry strategy that defines the number of retries, sets the delay between each retry, and sets the actions that your application should take after a failed attempt. Setting the correct number of retries and the delay between them is a complex task that depends on factors such as the type of resources, the operating conditions, and the application itself.

You can use the following guidelines when implementing a suitable transient fault mechanism in your application:

- **Use existing built-in retry mechanism**   When working with SDKs for specific services, the SDK usually provides a built-in retry mechanism. Before thinking of implementing your retry mechanism, you should review the SDK that you are using to access the services on which your application depends and use the built-in retry mechanism. These built-in retry mechanisms are tailored to the specific features and requirements of the target service. If you still need to implement your retry mechanism for a service—such as a storage service or a service bus—you should carefully review the requirements of each service to ensure that you correctly manage the faulting responses.

- **Determine whether the operation is suitable for retrying**   When an error is raised, it usually indicates the nature of the error. You can use this information to determine whether the error is a transient fault. Once you determine your application is dealing with a transient fault, you need to determine whether retrying the operation can succeed. You should not retry operations that indicate an invalid operation, such as a service that suffered a fatal error or continuing to look for an item after receiving an error indicating the item does not exist in the database. You should implement operation retries if the following conditions are met:

  - You can determine the full effect of the operation.
  - You fully understand the conditions of the retry.
  - You can validate these conditions.

- **Use the appropriate retry count and interval**   Setting the wrong retry count could lead your application to fail or could lock resources that can affect the health of the application. If you set the retry count too low, your application may not have enough time to recover from the transient fault and will fail. If you set the retry count to a value that is too high or too short, you can lock resources that your application is using, such as threads, connections, or memory. This high-resource consumption can affect the health of your application. When choosing the appropriate retry count and interval, you need to consider the type of operation that suffered the transient fault. For example, if the transient fault happens during an operation that is part of user interaction, you should use a short retry interval and count, which avoids having your user wait too long for your application to recover from the transient fault. On the other hand, if the fault happens during an operation that is part of a critical workflow, setting a longer retry count and interval makes sense if restarting the workflow is time-consuming or expensive. Following are some of the most common strategies for choosing the retry interval:

- **Exponential back-off** You use a short time interval for the first retry, and then you exponentially increase the interval time for subsequent retries. For example, you set the initial interval to 3 seconds and then use 9, 27, 81 for the subsequent retries.

- **Incremental intervals** You set a short time interval for the first retry, then you incrementally increase the interval time for the subsequent retries. For example, you set the initial interval to 3 seconds and then use 5, 8, 13, 21 for the subsequent retries.

- **Regular intervals** You use the same time interval for each retry. This strategy is not appropriate in most cases. You should avoid using this strategy when accessing services or resources in Azure. In those cases, you should use the exponential back-off strategy with a circuit breaker pattern.

- **Immediate retry** You retry as soon as the transient fault happens. You should not use this type of retry more than once. The immediate retries are suitable for peak faults, such as network package collisions or spikes in hardware components. If the immediate retry doesn't recover from the transient fault, you should switch to another retry strategy.

- **Randomization** If your application executes several retries in parallel—regardless of the retry strategy—using the same retry values for all the retries can negatively affect your application. In general, you should use random starting retry interval values with any of the previous strategies. This allows you to minimize the probability that two different application threads start the retry mechanism at the same time in the event of a transient fault.

- **Avoid anti-patterns** When implementing your retry mechanism, there are some patterns you should avoid:

  - Avoid implementing duplicated layers of retries. If your operation is made of several requests to several services, you should avoid implementing retries on every stage of the operation.

  - Never implement endless retry mechanisms. If your application never stops retrying in the event of a transient fault, the application can cause resource exhaustion or connection throttling. You should use the circuit breaker pattern or a finite number of retries.

  - Never use immediate retry more than once.

- **Test the retry strategy and implementation** Because of the difficulties when selecting the correct retry count and interval values, you should thoroughly test your retry strategy and implementation. You should pay special attention to heavy load and high-concurrency scenarios. You should test this by injecting transient and nontransient faults into your application.

- **Manage retry policy configuration** When you are implementing your retry mechanism, you should not hardcode the values for the retry count and intervals. Instead, you can define a retry policy that contains the retry count and interval as well as the mechanism that determines whether a fault is transient or nontransient. You should store this retry policy in configuration files so that you can fine-tune the policy. You should also implement this retry policy configuration so that your application stores the values in memory instead of continuously rereading the configuration file. If you are using Azure App Service, you should consider using the service configuration shown in Figure 4-14.

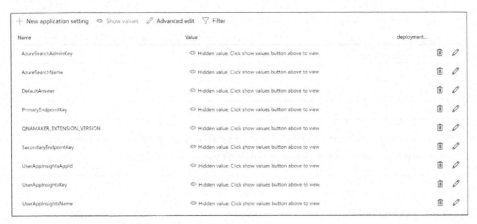

FIGURE 4-14 Azure App Service application settings

- **Log transient and non-transient faults**   You should include a logging mechanism in your application every time a transient or nontransient fault happens. A single transient fault doesn't indicate an error in your application. If the number of transient faults is increasing, this can be an indicator of a more significant potential failure or that you should increase the resources assigned to the faulting service. You should log transient faults as warning messages instead of errors. Using the Error Log Level could lead to triggering false alerts in your monitoring system. You should also consider measuring and logging the overall time taken by your retry mechanism when recovering a faulty operation. This allows you to measure the overall impact of transient faults on user response times, process latency, and efficiency of the application.

NEED MORE REVIEW? **MANAGING TRANSIENT FAULTS**

You can review some general guidelines for implementing a transient fault-handling mechanism by reviewing the following articles:

- *https://docs.microsoft.com/en-us/azure/architecture/best-practices/transient-faults*

- *https://docs.microsoft.com/en-us/aspnet/aspnet/overview/developing-apps-with-windows-azure/building-real-world-cloud-apps-with-windows-azure/transient-fault-handling*

EXAM TIP

Remember to test your retry strategy carefully. Using a wrong retry strategy could lead your application to exhaust the resources needed for executing your code. A wrong retry strategy can potentially lead to infinite loops if you don't use circuit breakers.

Chapter summary

- Your application needs to be able to manage transient faults.
- You need to determine the type of fault before retrying the operation.
- You should not use immediate retry more than once.
- You should use random starting values for the retry periods.
- You should use the built-in SDK mechanism when available.
- You should test your retry count and interval strategy.
- You should log transient and nontransient faults.
- You can improve the performance of your application by adding a cache to your application.
- Azure Cache for Redis allows the caching of dynamic content.
- Using Azure Cache for Redis, you can create in-memory databases to cache the most-used values.
- Azure Cache for Redis allows you to use messaging queue patterns.
- Content Delivery Networks (CDNs) store and distribute static content in servers distributed across the globe.
- CDNs reduce the latency by serving the content from the server nearest to the user.
- You can invalidate the content of the cache by setting a low TTL (Time-To-Live).
- You can invalidate the content of the cache by removing all or part of the content from the cache.
- Application Insights gets information from your application and sends it to Azure.

- You can use Application Insights with different platforms and languages.
- Application Insights is part of the Azure Monitor service.
- Application Insights generates two types of information: metrics and logs.
- Application Insights allows you to create web tests to monitor the availability of your application.
- You can configure alerts and trigger different actions associated with web tests.

Thought experiment

In this thought experiment, demonstrate your skills and knowledge of the topics covered in this chapter. You can find answers to this thought experiment in the next section.

Your company has a Line-of-Business (LOB) application that has been developed by your team. This LOB application is an eCommerce application that has more usage during holiday periods. The LOB application needs to get some information from external systems. You are receiving some complaints about the stability and the performance of the application. Answer the following questions about the troubleshooting and the performance of the application:

1. After reviewing the metrics of your application in the Azure Monitor, you find that you don't have enough detail about the performance of the internal application workflows. What should you do to get information about the internal workflows?

2. After reviewing the metrics of your application in the Azure Monitor, you find that some of the stability issues are due to the external systems. You need to minimize the effect on the user experience. Which strategy should you use?

3. You need to ensure that the purchase process is working correctly. You decide to configure a web test in Application Insights. Which type of test should you configure?

Thought experiment answers

This section contains the solution to the thought experiment. Each answer explains why the answer choice is correct.

1. You should integrate Application Insights instruments with your code. Once you integrate the Application Insights with your code, you can track custom events in your code. You can define operations inside your code to track complex operations compounded of several tasks. This allows you to get more information about the internal workflows executed in the application. Performing Application Insights agent-based monitoring doesn't provide enough information.

2. When you are dealing with the user experience, you should consider implementing a retry strategy consisting of a small number of retries with a short retry interval. Using this kind of strategy allows you to minimize the time that your users need to wait for

your application to recover from a transient fault. You can also consider using an immediate retry as the first retry. If this first retry fails, then you should switch to another retry strategy. There is no one-fits-all strategy, so you need to test your strategy to ensure that you provide the best user experience.

3. The process of a purchase in a web application is a complex testing scenario. In this scenario, you need to use a multistep web test. Using Visual Studio Enterprise, you need to record the steps needed for performing a purchase in your web application. Once you have generated the file with the recorded steps, you can create a web test in Application Insights to monitor the purchase process.

## CHAPTER 5

Connect to and consume Azure services and third-party services

Nowadays, companies use different systems for different tasks that are usually performed by different departments. Although these separate systems work for solving a specific need, they usually act as independent actors in a big scenario. These independent actors manage information about the company that can potentially be duplicated by other independent actors.

When a company realizes that independent actors are managing their data, they usually try to make all the independent actors or systems work together and share information between them. This situation is independent of using cloud services or on-premises services. To make the independent actors work together, you need to make connections between each actor or service that needs to communicate with the other.

You can use different services and techniques to achieve this interconnection. Azure provides some useful services that allow different services to work together without making big changes to the interconnected services.

Skills covered in this chapter:

- Skill 5.1: Develop an App Service Logic App
- Skill 5.2: Implement API Management
- Skill 5.3: Develop event-based solutions
- Skill 5.4: Develop message-based solutions

Skill 5.1: Develop an App Service Logic App

Exchanging information between different applications is a goal for most companies. Sharing the information enriches the internal process and creates more insight into the information itself. By using the App Service Logic App, you can create workflows that interconnect different systems based on conditions and rules and easing the process of sharing information between them. Also, you can take advantage of the Logic Apps features to implement business process workflows.

> **This skill covers how to**
> - Create a Logic App
> - Create a custom connector for Logic Apps
> - Create a custom template for Logic Apps

Create a Logic App

Before you can interconnect two separate services, you need to fully understand which information you need to share between the services. Sometimes the information needs to undergo some transformations before a service can consume it. You could write code for making this interconnection, but this is a time-consuming and error-prone task.

Azure provides the App Service Logic Apps that allows interconnecting two or more services sharing information between them. A business process defines this interconnection between different services. Azure Logic Apps allows you to build complex interconnection scenarios by using some elements that ease the work:

- **Workflows**   Define the source and destination of the information. It connects to different services by using connectors. A workflow defines the steps or actions that the information needs to make to deliver the information from the source to the correct destination. You use a graphical language to visualize, design, build, automate, and deploy a business process.

- **Managed Connectors**   A connector is an object that allows your workflow to access data, services, and systems. Microsoft provides some prebuilt connectors to Microsoft services. These connectors are managed by Microsoft and provide the needed triggers and action objects to work with those services.

- **Triggers**   Triggers are events that fire when certain conditions are met. You use a trigger as the entry or starting point of a workflow. For example, when a new message arrives at your company's purchases mailbox, it can start a workflow that can access information from the subject and body of the message and create a new entry in the ERP system.

- **Actions**   Actions are each of the steps that you configure in your workflow. Actions happen only when the workflow is executed. The workflow starts executing when a new trigger fires.

- **Enterprise Integration Pack**   If you need to perform more advanced integrations, the Enterprise Integration Pack provides you with BizTalk Server capabilities.

You can use Azure Logic Apps for different purposes. The most obvious application for Azure Logic Apps would be implementing business processes. Although there is no direct mapping between Azure Logic Apps actions and Business Process Model Notation (BPMN), you can use Logic Apps for automating some simple business processes or integrate it with Business Process Model (BPM) engines for implementing more complex business processes. You also can use Azure Logic Apps for sending notifications when certain events happen or creating the folder and permission structure in a SharePoint Online document library when a project manager of your company creates a new project.

When you are creating a new Azure Logic App workflow, you need to think about how this workflow is going to start. This is the trigger of your workflow. A trigger can be an event that happened in a service, such as a new file has been uploaded to an Azure Storage Account. A workflow can also start based on a schedule. The schedule that you configure for starting a workflow is the trigger for the workflow. When you set your schedule and the appropriate time arrives, the Azure Logic Apps engine creates a new instance of your workflow. You can configure two different types of schedules:

- **Recurrence**   In this type of trigger, you configure a regular time interval. You can configure a start date and time, and you can also configure the time zone for your schedule. When you configure the time interval, you can choose from seconds to months as the frequency. For example, you can configure a recurrence of executing the workflow every 2 minutes or every 3 weeks. Depending on the interval that you choose, you can select additional details for that interval. For the *Week* interval, you can select on which days the workflow is going to be executed. For the *Day* or *Week* intervals, you can select the hours or minutes for the execution of your workflow. The Recurrence trigger doesn't process the missing recurrences. That is, if a recurrence is missing for whatever reason, the Recurrence trigger doesn't restart the missing recurrence.

- **Sliding Window**   This type of trigger is similar to the Recurrence trigger, except you cannot configure advance scheduling settings, such as specific days in the week or hours or minutes in a day. Another essential difference is that with the Sliding Window trigger, if a recurrence is missing, the Sliding Window trigger goes back and processes the missing recurrence.

Scheduling the execution of your Azure Logic App is not the only way to start your workflow. You can use other triggers for starting the execution of the workflow. In addition to the recurrence triggers that we reviewed previously in this section, you can use two additional types for triggers:

- **Polling**   The trigger queries the configured system or service periodically for new data or if a new event happened. Depending on the specific trigger, you can configure the polling schedule. Once the new data or event happens, the trigger creates a new instance of your workflow, collects the information from the system, and passes the information to the newly created workflow instance.

- **Push**   The trigger listens for new events or data to arrive at the configured system or service. As soon as the new data or event happens, the trigger creates a new instance of your workflow, passing the data to the newly created instance.

Once the workflow starts, it needs to follow some steps for doing the work that it's supposed to do. Each of these steps is an action. An action can be something like getting data from an OData service reading information from a text file stored in an SFTP service, or even transforming the format of a file. There is also another kind of action that is as important as the data gathering or data transformation actions. Setting the value of a variable, loops, conditional or switch statements, or decision branching are other kinds of actions that is critical for defining your workflow. As with any other programming language, these structural actions enable you to control the execution flow of your workflow.

Triggers and actions are packaged together into connectors. You use the connectors for accessing data, events, and actions available from other applications or services. Azure Logic Apps offers thousands of connectors, but all of them fit in one of the following categories:

- **Built-in**   This type of connector contains the fundamental triggers and actions available in Azure Logic Apps. Some of the connectors that fit in this category allow you to schedule the execution of the workflow, call other Azure Logic Apps or App Services, make HTTP and HTTPS calls to endpoints, process messages in batches, or make your Logic App callable from other services.

- **Managed**   These connectors are developed, deployed, and maintained by Microsoft. You use these connectors for accessing cloud services like Office 365, Azure Blob Storage, SharePoint, and many others.

- **On-Premises**   You use this kind of connector when you need your Azure Logic App to work with systems deployed in your on-premises infrastructure. Using these connectors, you can access data from File Systems, Oracle, MySQL, PostgreSQL, Microsoft SQL Server, IBM DB2, IBM Informix, or Teradata databases. For these connectors to work properly, you need to deploy an on-premises data gateway.

- **Integration Account**   Allows you to connect your Azure Logic App with third-party business partners for creating Business-to-Business (B2B) solutions. Integrations Accounts are available only through the Enterprise Integration Pack (EIP) in Azure. You use this kind of connector for transforming the messages between the different B2B systems. You can apply AS2, EDIFACT, X12, or Flat files decoding or encoding, Liquid and XML transformations, or XML validations.

- **ISE** These are the connectors that you need to use when your Azure Logic App needs to run in an Integration Service Environment (ISE). This is a dedicated environment where you execute your Azure Logic Apps. There are special connectors designed for working in an ISE. Those connectors are marked with the label CORE if they are built-in connectors that you can use in an ISE or if they are managed connectors that you can use in an ISE, you will see the ISE label below the name of the connector. When using an ISE you are not limited to ISE connectors; you can also use regular connectors in an Integration Service Environment.

Additionally, to the classification that we reviewed in the previous list, the connectors can be classified as Standard or Enterprise connectors. This classification is essential because it directly affects the costs associated with running your Azure Logic App workflow. When you run a workflow, you are charged when you use the workflow, except when your workflow is running inside an ISE.

When you run your Azure Logic App workflow in the public, multitenant, global environment, you pay only for the actions that your workflow runs. An action is any of the steps that configure your workflow. Triggers, loops, conditional statements, or any of the control actions count for the calculation of the costs of your workflow execution. There are three pricing levels:

- **Basic** This level includes built-in connectors, triggers, and control workflow actions.
- **Standard** This includes the actions defined in managed connectors. Any custom connector that you create also fits into this category.
- **Enterprise** These are specialized connectors for integrating B2B applications with your Azure Logic App. Some examples of enterprise connectors are SAP, IBM 3270, or IBM MQ.

It is also important to note that n-premises connectors can be Standard or Enterprise connectors. In general, when you are calculating the costs of your Azure Logic App, you should review the list of Standard or Enterprise connectors for having an accurate idea of which type of connector you are using in your workflow. You can find a complete list of connectors by reviewing the article at *https://docs.microsoft.com/en-us/connectors/connector-reference/*.

Now that you have a basic understanding of the different parts of an Azure Logic App workflow it is time to create your own workflow. The following procedure shows how to create an Azure Logic App workflow that writes a message in the Microsoft Teams app when a new build completes in Azure DevOps. For this procedure, you need an Azure DevOps account with a configured project that you can build. If you don't have an Azure DevOps account yet, you can create one by following the quick start guide at *https://docs.microsoft.com/en-us/azure/devops/user-guide/sign-up-invite-teammates?view=azure-devops*. You also need a Microsoft Office 365 subscription with access to the Microsoft Teams application. Start by creating and configuring the Azure Logic App:

1. Open the Azure portal (*https://portal.azure.com*).
2. Click the Create A Resource button at the top of the Azure portal.
3. On the New blade, on the Azure Marketplace list at the left side of the blade, click Integration.

4. In the Featured column on the right side of the blade, click Logic App.

5. On the Logic App blade, on the Resource Group drop-down menu, select the resource group where you want to create your Azure Logic App. Alternatively, you can create a new resource group by clicking the Create New link below the resource group drop-down menu.

6. Type a name in the Logic App Name text box.

7. In the Select The Location control, ensure that the Region option is selected.

8. Select a location from the Location drop-down menu.

9. Leave the Log Analytics option set to the Off value.

10. Click the Review + Create button at the bottom of the blade.

11. Click the Create button at the bottom of the blade.

12. In the Microsoft.EmptyWorkflow deployment window, click the Go To Resource button. This button appears once the deployment of your new Azure Logic App finishes successfully.

13. On the Logic Apps blade, in the Logic App Designer, click the Blank Logic App in the Templates section.

14. In the Logic Apps Designer, in the Search Connectors And Triggers text box, type **Azure DevOps**.

15. Click the Azure DevOps icon on the Results panel.

16. On the Triggers tab, select the trigger named When A Build Completes.

17. Click the Sign In button on the Azure DevOps element. At this point, you connect your Azure Subscription with your Azure DevOps account.

18. On the panel for the When A Build Completes trigger, shown in Figure 5-1, select your Organization's name from the Organization Name drop-down menu.

FIGURE 5-1 Configuring an Azure Logic Apps trigger

19. On the Project Name drop-down menu, select the name of the project that you want.

20. Click the New Step button below the trigger panel.

21. On the Choose An Action panel, type **Teams** in the Search Connectors And Actions text box.

22. On the Actions tab, click the Post A Message (V3) action.

23. On the Post A Message (V3) action panel, select a team from the Team drop-down menu.

24. Select General from the Channel drop-down menu.

25. In the Message text area, type **The**.

26. In the Dynamic Content dialog box, shown in Figure 5-2, on the right side of the Message text area, click the See More link. This link shows the list of dynamic attributes that you can add to your message.

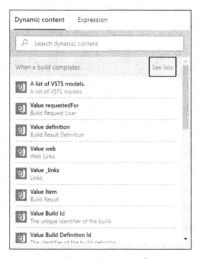

FIGURE 5-2 Dynamic content from a connector trigger

27. Scroll down the list of dynamic attributes and click the Value Build Definition Name dynamic attribute.

28. Type **build finished with status** in the message area next to the dynamic attribute.

29. Click the Value Status dynamic attribute.

30. Click the Save button on the top-left corner of the Azure Logic Apps Designer blade.

31. Click the Run button at the top-left corner of the Azure Logic Apps Designer blade.

At this point, the Azure Logic Apps start listening for the configured trigger in Azure DevOps. When a new build finishes in Azure DevOps, Azure Logic Apps sends a message to the General channel in the configured team in your Microsoft Teams account. Now, you are going to create a pipeline in Azure DevOps for building an example project. Once the build finishes, you are going to receive a new message in the Microsoft Teams channel:

1. Navigate to the following GitHub example repo *https://github.com/MicrosoftDocs/pipelines-dotnet-core* and sign in to your account. If you don't have a GitHub account, you can create a new one for free at *https://github.com/join*.

2. At the top-right corner of the project's page, click the Fork button.

3. Open your Azure DevOps account (*https://dev.azure.com*). If you see the generic Azure DevOps page describing the service instead of your Azure DevOps account, click the Sign In to Azure DevOps link below the Start Free button.

4. In the list of projects in your Azure DevOps account, click the project name that you configured in step 19 of the previous procedure.

5. Click the Pipelines element on the navigation bar on the left side of the project's page.

6. Click the Create Pipeline button.

7. On the New Pipeline window, click GitHub.

8. Sign in to your GitHub account.

9. On the Authorize Azure Pipelines (OAuth) window, click the Authorize Azure Pipelines button at the bottom of the page.

10. In your Azure DevOps account, on the Select A Repository page, click the pipelines-dotnet-core project.

11. In your Azure DevOps account, on the Configure Your Pipeline page, click ASP.NET Core.

12. On the Review Your Pipeline YAML page, review the details for your pipeline.

13. Click the Run button at the top-right corner of the page.

14. Once the pipeline has been created, a page with the details of the execution of your pipeline appears. If everything works correctly, you should see a job with the success status in the list of Jobs in the Job panel.

At this point, the Azure DevOps agent is building the sample project. Once the build finishes, you should receive a new message in your Microsoft Teams channel, as shown in Figure 5-3.

Santiago Fernández Muñoz   19:45
The santifdezmunoz.pipelines-dotnet-core build finished with status completed

FIGURE 5-3 A message in Microsoft Teams from Azure DevOps

NEED MORE REVIEW?   AZURE LOGIC APP PRICING

Calculating the costs associated with an Azure Logic App workflow can be complicated. Each of the iterations in a loop is one or more action executions. The different connector types are charged differently, depending on whether they are Basic, Standard, or Enterprise. A workflow executed in an Integration Service Environment has its own pricing. You can read an article with the details about how Azure calculates how much you have to pay for the execution of your workflow at *https://docs.microsoft.com/en-us/azure/logic-apps/logic-apps-pricing*.

Create a custom connector for Logic Apps

Microsoft provides more than 200 built-in connectors that you can use in your Azure Logic Apps workflow. Despite this number of connectors, there are times when you need some specific features that are not provided by the built-in or managed connectors, or you want to create a connector for your company's application.

You can create custom connectors for Microsoft PowerAutomate (formerly known as Flow), PowerApps, and Azure Logic Apps. Although you cannot share Azure Logic Apps connectors with Microsoft PowerAutomate and PowerApps connectors, the principle for creating custom connectors are the same for the three platforms. A custom connector is basically a wrapper for a REST or SOAP API. This wrapper allows Azure Logic Apps to interact with the API of the application. The application that you want to include in the custom connector can be a public application, like Amazon Web Services, Google Calendar, or the API of your application published to the Internet. Using the on-premises data gateway, you can also connect the custom connector with an on-premises application deployed in your data center. Every custom connector has the following life cycle:

1. **Build your API**   You can wrap any REST or SOAP API in a custom connector. If you are creating your API, you should consider using Azure Functions, Azure Web Apps, or Azure API Apps.

2. **Secure your API**   You need to authenticate the access to your API. If you are implementing your application using Azure Functions, Azure Web Apps, or Azure API Apps, you can enable the Azure Active Directory authentication in the Azure portal for your application. You can also enforce authentication directly on your API's code. You can use any of the following authentication mechanisms:

   - Generic OAuth 2.0

   - OAuth 2.0 for specific services, like Azure Active Directory, Dropbox, GitHub, or SalesForce

   - Basic Authentication

   - API Key

3. **Describe the API and define the custom connector**   You need to provide a description of the different endpoints that your API has. Azure Logic Apps supports two different language-agnostic, machine-readable document formats that you can use for documenting this description: OpenAPI (formerly known as Swagger) or Postman collections. You can create a custom connector from the OpenAPI or Postman collection documentation.

4. **Use the connector in an Azure Logic Apps**   Once you have created the custom connector, you can use it as a regular managed built-in connector in your workflow. You need to create a connection to your API using your custom connector. Then you can use the triggers and actions that you configured in your custom connector.

5. **Share your connector**   Once you have created your custom connector, you can share it with other users in your organization. This step is optional.

6. **Certify your connector**   If you want to share your custom connector with other users outside your organization, you need to send the custom connector to Microsoft. Then Microsoft can review your custom connector to ensure that it works correctly. Once the connector is reviewed and validated, Microsoft certifies it, and you can share it with users outside your organization.

Now that you have reviewed the life cycle of an Azure Logic App Custom Connector, you are going to create a custom connector for connecting with an API. For this example, you are going to create a simple Web API 2 application that simulates a book-managing system. Although this example is quite simple, it covers some key points that you need to consider when creating an Azure Logic App Custom connector. The API that you are going to implement in this example is not appropriate for production environments because it doesn't take into consideration important aspects like performance or security. Use the following steps for creating the API that you are going to use for your custom connector:

1. Open Visual Studio 2019 on your computer.

2. In the start window, click Create A New Project in the Get Started column on the right side of the window.

3. In the Create A New Project window, from the All Languages drop-down menu, select C#.

4. On the Search For Templates text box type **asp.net**.

5. On the result list, click ASP.NET Web Application (.NET Framework).

6. Click the Next button at the bottom right corner of the window.

7. In the Configure Your New Project window, type a Project Name, a Location, and a Solution Name for your project.

8. Click the Create button at the bottom-right corner of the window.

9. In the Create A New ASP.NET Web Application window, select the Web API template on the template list in the middle of the left side of the window.

10. On the right side of the Create A New ASP.NET Web Application window, in the Authentication section, ensure the Authentication is set to No Authentication.

11. Click the Create button on the bottom-right corner of the window.

12. In the Visual Studio window, click Tools > NuGet Package Manager > Manage NuGet Packages For Solution.

13. On the NuGet Package Manager tab, click Browse.

14. Type **swashbuckle** and press Enter.

15. Click the Swashbuckle package.

16. On the right side of the NuGet Manager tab, click the check box next to your project.

17. Click the Install button.

18. In the Preview Changes window, click OK.

19. In the License Acceptance window, click the I Accept button.

20. Repeat steps 13 to 19 and install the TRex NuGet package.

21. On the Solution Explorer window, right-click the Models folder.

22. On the contextual menu, click Add > New Item.

23. In the Add New Item window, select Class from the list of new items.

24. In the name text box at the bottom of the window, type **Book.cs**.

25. Click the Add button at the bottom-right corner of the window.

26. Replace the content of the Book.cs file with the content in Listing 5-1.

LISTING 5-1 *Book.cs*

```
// C# .NET
using System;
using TRex.Metadata;

namespace <replace_with_your_project_name>.Models
{
    public class Book
    {
        public Book()
        {
            this.Id = Guid.NewGuid();
        }

        [Metadata("Callback ID", Visibility = VisibilityType.Internal)]
        public Guid Id { get; }

        [Metadata("Title", "The title of the book")]
        public string Title { set; get; }

        [Metadata("Author", "The author of the book")]
        public string Author { set; get; }
    }
}
```

27. Repeat steps 21 to 25 and create the class **Callback.cs**.

28. Replace the content of the Callback.cs file with the content in Listing 5-2.

LISTING 5-2   *Callback.cs*

```
// C# .NET
using System;
using System.Net.Http;
using System.Net.Http.Headers;
using System.Threading.Tasks;
using TRex.Metadata;
using Newtonsoft.Json.Linq;

namespace <replace_with_your_project_name>.Models
{
    public class Callback
    {
        public Callback()
        {
            this.Id = Guid.NewGuid();
        }
        [Metadata("Callback ID", Visibility = VisibilityType.Internal)]
        public Guid Id { get; }

        [CallbackUrl]
        [Metadata("Callback URL", Visibility = VisibilityType.Internal)]
        public Uri Uri { set; get; }

        public HttpResponseMessage InvokeAsync<TOutput>(TOutput triggerOutput)
        {
            HttpClient httpClient = new HttpClient();

            httpClient.DefaultRequestHeaders.Accept.Clear();
            httpClient.DefaultRequestHeaders.Accept.Add(
            new MediaTypeWithQualityHeaderValue("application/json"));

            return Task.Run(async () => await httpClient.PostAsJsonAsync(Uri,
            JObject.FromObject(triggerOutput))).Result;
        }
    }
}
```

29. On the Solution Explorer window, right-click the name of your project. On the contextual menu, click Add > New Folder.

30. Type **Helpers** as the name of the new folder.

31. Repeat steps 21 to 25 and create two additional classes in the Helpers folder. The two classes should be **BooksSingleton.cs** and **CallbacksSingleton.cs**.

32. Replace the content of file BooksSingleton.cs with the content of Listing 5-3.

LISTING 5-3 *BooksSingleton.cs*

```csharp
// C# .NET
using <replace_with_your_project_name>.Models;
using System;
using System.Collections.Generic;
using System.Linq;

namespace <replace_with_your_project_name>.Helpers
{
    public sealed class BooksSingleton
    {
        private static readonly BooksSingleton m_instance = null;

        private static readonly List<Book> _books;
        public static BooksSingleton Instance
        {
            get
            {
                return m_instance;
            }
        }

        static BooksSingleton()
        {
            m_instance = new BooksSingleton();
            _books = new List<Book>();
        }

        private BooksSingleton()
        {
        }

        public void AddBook(Book book)
        {
            if (book != null)
            {
                _books.Add(book);
            }
        }

        public void ModifyBook(Book book)
        {
            var bookToModify = _books.SingleOrDefault(b => b.Id.Equals(book.Id));
            if (bookToModify != null)
            {
                bookToModify.Author = book.Author;
```

```
                    bookToModify.Title = book.Title;
            }
        }

        public IEnumerable<Book> GetBooks()
        {
            return _books.ToArray();
        }

        public bool DeleteBookById(string id)
        {
            bool deleted = false;
            Guid guidToRemove = Guid.Parse(id);
            var booktToRemove = _books.SingleOrDefault(b => b.Id.Equals(guidToRemove));
            if (booktToRemove != null)
            {
                _books.Remove(booktToRemove);
                deleted = true;
            }

            return deleted;
        }

        public Book GetBookById(string id)
        {
            Guid guid = Guid.Parse(id);
            return _books.SingleOrDefault(b => b.Id.Equals(guid));
        }
    }
}
```

33. Replace the content of the file CallbacksSingleton.cs with the content in Listing 5-4.

LISTING 5-4   *CallbacksSingleton.cs*

```
// C# .NET
using <replace_with_your_project_name>.Models;
using System;
using System.Collections.Generic;
using System.Linq;
using System.Web;

namespace <replace_with_your_project_name>.Helpers
{
```

```csharp
public class CallbacksSingleton
{
    private static readonly CallbacksSingleton m_instance = null;

    private static readonly List<Callback> _callbacks;
    public static CallbacksSingleton Instance
    {
        get
        {
            return m_instance;
        }
    }

    static CallbacksSingleton()
    {
        m_instance = new CallbacksSingleton();
        _callbacks = new List<Callback>();
    }

    private CallbacksSingleton()
    {
    }

    public void AddCallback(Callback callback)
    {
        if (callback != null)
        {
            //avoid duplicates
            Callback callbackToBeAdded = _callbacks.FirstOrDefault(c => Uri.
            Compare(c.Uri, callback.Uri, UriComponents.AbsoluteUri, UriFormat.
            Unescaped, StringComparison.CurrentCultureIgnoreCase) == 0);
            if (callbackToBeAdded == null)
                _callbacks.Add(callback);
        }
    }

    public void ModifyCallback(Callback callback)
    {
        var callbackToModify = _callbacks.SingleOrDefault(b =>
        b.Id.Equals(callback.Id));
        if (callbackToModify != null)
        {

        }
    }
```

```
    public IEnumerable<Callback> GetCallbacks()
    {
        return _callbacks;
    }

    public bool DeleteCallbackById(string id)
    {
        bool deleted = false;
        Guid guidToRemove = Guid.Parse(id);
        var callbackToRemove = _callbacks.SingleOrDefault(b =>
        b.Id.Equals(guidToRemove));
        if (callbackToRemove != null)
        {
            _callbacks.Remove(callbackToRemove);
            deleted = true;
        }

        return deleted;
    }

    public Callback GetCallbackById(string id)
    {
        Guid guid = Guid.Parse(id);
        return _callbacks.SingleOrDefault(b => b.Id.Equals(guid));
    }
    }
}
```

34. On the Solution Explorer window, expand the Controllers folders and remove the ValuesController.cs file.

35. Right-click the Controllers folder and then click Add > Controller.

36. In the Add New Scaffolded Item, select Web API 2 Controller – Empty.

37. Click the Add button on the bottom right corner of the window.

38. In the Add Controller window, type **BooksController** in the Controller Name text box.

39. Click the Add button.

40. Replace the content of the BooksController.cs file with the content of the Listing 5-5.

LISTING 5-5 *BooksController.cs*

```
// C# .NET
using <replace_with_your_project_name>.Models;
using <replace_with_your_project_name>.Helpers;
using Swashbuckle.Swagger.Annotations;
using System;
```

```
using System.Collections.Generic;
using System.Linq;
using System.Net;
using System.Net.Http;
using System.Threading.Tasks;
using System.Web.Http;
using TRex.Metadata;

namespace <replace_with_your_project_name>.Controllers
{
    public class BooksController : ApiController
    {
        private readonly BooksSingleton _books = BooksSingleton.Instance;
        private static readonly CallbacksSingleton _callbacks = CallbacksSingleton.
        Instance;

        // Subscribe to newly created books
        [HttpPost, Route("books/subscribe")]
        [Metadata("New book created", "Fires whenever a new book is added to the
        list.", VisibilityType.Important)]
        [Trigger(TriggerType.Subscription, typeof(Book), "Book")]
        [SwaggerResponseRemoveDefaults]
        [SwaggerResponse(HttpStatusCode.Created, "Subscription created")]
        [SwaggerResponse(HttpStatusCode.BadRequest, "Invalid subscription
        configuration")]
        public IHttpActionResult Subscribe(Callback callback)
        {
            _callbacks.AddCallback(callback);
            return CreatedAtRoute(nameof(Unsubscribe), new { subscriptionId = callback.
            Id }, string.Empty);
        }

        [HttpDelete, Route("books/subscribe/{callbackId}", Name = nameof
        (Unsubscribe))]
        [Metadata("Unsubscribe", Visibility = VisibilityType.Internal)]
        [SwaggerResponse(HttpStatusCode.OK)]
        public IHttpActionResult Unsubscribe(string callbackID)
        {
            _callbacks.DeleteCallbackById(callbackID);
            return Ok();
        }

        [HttpGet, Route("books/subscriptions")]
        [Metadata("Get subscriptions", "Get all the current subscriptions")]
        [SwaggerResponse(HttpStatusCode.OK, "An array of subscriptions",
        typeof(Array))]
```

```csharp
public IEnumerable<Callback> GetCallbacks()
{
    return _callbacks.GetCallbacks();
}


// GET api/books
[HttpGet, Route("books")]
[Metadata("Get books", "Get all the books objects stored in the App")]
[SwaggerResponse(HttpStatusCode.OK, "An array of books", typeof(Array))]
public IEnumerable<Book> Get()
{
    return _books.GetBooks();
}


// GET api/books/5
[HttpGet, Route("books/{id}", Name = "GetBook")]
[Metadata("Get single book", "Get a single book object by its id. You can use
any GUID valid string")]
[SwaggerResponse(HttpStatusCode.OK, "An object represeting a book",
typeof(Book))]
public Book Get(string id)
{
    return _books.GetBookById(id);
}


// POST api/books
[HttpPost, Route("books")]
[Metadata("Add a new book", "Add a new book object to the system. A value
object is compound of a Title and an Author.")]
[SwaggerResponse(HttpStatusCode.Created)]
public IHttpActionResult Post([FromBody] Book book)
{
    _books.AddBook(book);

    foreach(var callback in _callbacks.GetCallbacks())
    {
        callback.InvokeAsync(book);
    }

    return CreatedAtRoute("GetBook", new { id = book.Id }, book);
}

// PUT api/books/5
[HttpPut, Route("books/{id}")]
```

```
    [Metadata("Modify an existing book object", "Modify an existing book. You need
    to provide the new values for the Title or Author of the book. You look for the
    book object using its id")]
    public void Put([FromBody] Book book)
    {
        _books.ModifyBook(book);
    }


    // DELETE api/books/5
    [Metadata("Delete a book object", "Delete a book object by its id.")]
    [HttpDelete, Route("books/{id}")]
    public void Delete(string id)
    {
        _books.DeleteBookById(id);
    }
    }
}
```

41. Open the SwaggerConfig.cs file. You can find this file in the App_Start folder.

42. In the SwaggerConfig.cs file, uncomment the line `c.PrettyPrint();`.

43. Add the line `c.ReleaseTheTRex();` inside the `EnableSwagger` method, just after this line:

```
//c.CustomProvider((defaultProvider) => new CachingSwaggerProvider
(defaultProvider));
```

44. Uncomment this line:

```
c.DocExpansion(DocExpansion.List);
```

45. Add the line using TRex.Metadata at the beginning of the file.

At this point, you can test your API. Use the following steps for testing your API:

1. In your Visual Studio 2019 window, ensure that your API project is open. Then press F5.

2. Once your web application is loaded in your web browser, append the */swagger* URI to the URL in your web browser. The final address should look like similar to *https://localhost:44398/swagger*.

3. On your API list of methods, shown in Figure 5-4, click the *POST /books* link. This expands the options for the *POST /books* endpoint.

4. In the *POST /books* endpoint green area, in the Parameters section, type a JSON object in the value text area. You can find an example of the needed structure in the Data Type column at the end of the same line.

5. Click the Try It Out! button in the bottom-left corner of the endpoint green area.

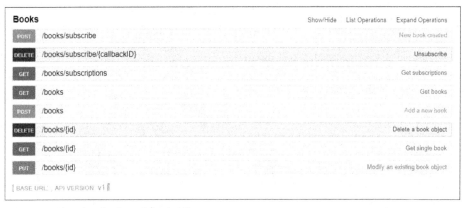

FIGURE 5-4 List of endpoints of a web API

6. In the Response Body section, you should get the JSON representation of your newly created book with a valid ID assigned. You can also check that the book has been created successfully by clicking the Try It Out! button in the *GET /books* endpoint blue area.

Now that you have tested that your web API works correctly, you need to publish to an Azure App Service. An alternative to deploying the web API to an Azure App Service could be using an on-premises data gateway for connecting to the local deployment of our web API. Use the following steps for deploying the web API to an Azure App Service:

1. In your Visual Studio 2019 window, ensure that you have opened the web API.

2. On the right side of the Visual Studio window, in the Solution Explorer window, right-click the project's name.

3. In the contextual menu, click Publish. This opens the Publish window.

4. In the Publish window, make sure that Azure is selected from the list of Targets on the right side of the window.

5. Click Next.

6. Select Azure App Service (Windows) in the Specific Target section.

7. Click Next.

8. On the App Service section, click Create A New Azure App Service at the bottom of the window. If you already have an Azure App Service plan that you want to use for hosting the App Service, you can select it in the tree control in this same window.

9. In the App Service (Windows) window, leave all options as is and click the Create button. Remember to delete the Resource Group and all its associated resources after you finish this example because these resources consume credit from your Azure subscription.

10. On the tree control, expand the newly created resource group and click the newly created Azure App Service.

11. Click the Finish button.

12. Click the Publish button.

13. Once the publishing process has finished, Visual Studio opens your default web browser with the URL of the newly deployed App Service. This URL will have the structure *https://<your_app_service_name>.azurewebsites.net.*

14. Ensure that your API is working correctly by repeating the testing steps previously shown in this section. This time you need to use the URL *https://<your_app_service_name>.azurewebsites.net/swagger.*

At this point, you are ready to create your Azure Logic App Custom Connector. Before proceeding to create your custom connector for your API, let's dig a little bit on the code of the API to understand the Azure Logic App Custom Connector that you are going to create. The API allows you to create, delete, modify, and query a book in the list of books that the application can store. You can also get the complete list of books stored in the API. As previously reviewed in this section, a connector can have a trigger that represents an event that starts the sequence of actions in our workload. In our testing API, the trigger represents the event of adding a new book to the list of books. You can see how we fire the trigger in the following code snippet extracted from the Post method in the *BooksController*:

```
_books.AddBook(book);
foreach (var callback in _callbacks.GetCallbacks())
{
    callback.InvokeAsync(book);
}
```

As you can see in the previous code, after we add a new book to the list of books, we call the InvokeAsync method of the callback object. The reason for doing this is because Azure Logic Apps works with two types of triggers: pull and push triggers. In this example, we decided to use a push trigger. This means that the API notifies the Azure Logic App when the event happens. The way the API can notify the Azure Logic App is by using the webhook pattern. For this reason, we need to provide two additional endpoints to the API, one for allowing the Azure Logic App to subscribe to the API and one for deleting the subscription. In the example, these endpoints are POST /books/subscribe and DELETE /books/subscribe/{callbackID} (you can view these endpoints in Figure 5-3 earlier in this section).

The workflow subscribes to the API when the workflow changes in any way; for example, when you run it for the first time, change the input parameters to the trigger, or renew the credentials for connecting to your API. During the subscription process, your workflow provides the callback URL that your API needs to use for sending back the information needed for the workflow. The unsubscribe process happens automatically when the trigger, the workflow, or the subscription is deleted or disabled.

Swagger provides all this information about which endpoint Azure Logic App should use for subscribing to the events in your API, the structure of the data that uses your API, or the available endpoints for the connector. We could manually create the Swagger document that describes our API, but that would be a time-consuming and error-prone task. To ease the creation and management of the Swagger document that describes the API, we used the packages Swashbuckle (*https://github.com/domaindrivendev/Swashbuckle*) and TRex Metadata Library (*https://github.com/nihaue/TRex*). The Swashbuckle package adds Swagger to the API, providing a Swagger generator and a UI for navigating and testing the API. TRex Metadata Library package extends the capabilities of Swashbuckle, so the Swagger document generated by Swashbuckle is ready to be consumed by the Logic App Designer.

Now that you have a better understanding of the key parts of the API that enable the interaction with Azure Logic Apps, it's time to create a custom connector for your API:

1. In your web browser, download the Swagger definition of your API from *https://<your_app_service_name>.azurewebsites.net/swagger/docs/v1*.

2. In your web browser, right-click the Swagger definition of the API, click Save As in the contextual menu, and save the page to your desktop as a file with the name **swagger.json**. You need this file for a later step.

3. Open the Azure portal (*https://portal.azure.com*).

4. Click Create A Resource button in the top area of the Azure portal.

5. Type *logic apps* in the Search The Marketplace text box.

6. Click Logic Apps Custom Connector in the result list.

7. Click the Create button.

8. On the Create Logic Apps Custom Connector panel, select an existing resource group in the Resource Group drop-down menu where you want to store your custom connector. Alternatively, you can create a new resource group by clicking the Create New link below the Resource Group drop-down menu.

9. Type a name for your custom connector in the Custom Connector Name text box.

10. In the Select The Location control, ensure that the option Region is selected.

11. Select a location in the Location drop-down menu.

12. Click the Review + Create button at the bottom of the panel.

13. Click the Create button.

14. Type the name of your newly created custom connector on the search text box at the top of the Azure portal.

15. Click the name of your Azure Logic App Custom Connector in the results.

16. Click the Edit button on the Custom Connector's Overview blade.

17. On the Edit Logic Apps Custom Connector blade, click the Import button on the How Do You Want To Create Your Connector? panel, which is shown in Figure 5-5.

18. Choose the JSON file that you downloaded in step 2.

19. In the General Information section, review the information in this section. You don't need to make any changes here.

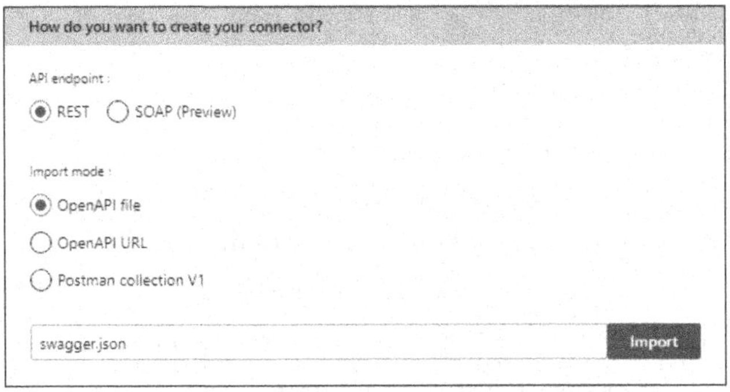

FIGURE 5-5 Importing the OpenAPI definition of a REST API

> **NOTE** **BASE URL**
>
> In this example, the endpoint definition already contains the correct base URL in the endpoint definition. If you change the default Base URL property in the General Information section in your Azure Logic Apps Custom Connector, you will receive a 404 error every time you try to use your custom connector in an Azure Logic Apps workflow.

20. Click the Security link on top of the page. You can also find a Security link at the bottom-left corner of the page. You can use either of these links for navigating to the Security section.

21. Review the options on the Security page. For this custom connector, you aren't using any authentication. Ensure that the option No Authentication is selected.

22. Click the Definition link on top of the page. You can also find a Definition link at the bottom-left corner of the page. You can use either of these links for navigating to the Definition section.

23. Review the settings on the Definition page. On this page, you can find all the endpoints that have been defined in the Swagger JSON file that you imported in step 18. These endpoints translate into Actions or Triggers, depending on the definition in the JSON file. You can also manually add new Actions and Triggers as you need by using this page.

24. Scroll down the page until you see the Triggers section.

25. Click the NewBookCreated trigger. There should be a red circle with an exclamation mark beside the name of the trigger. This icon indicates that there is a problem with the definition of the trigger.

26. On the NewBookCreated trigger definition window, scroll to the end of the Request section. In the Body section inside the Request section, you should see the Callback object with a red circle with an exclamation mark.

27. Click the Callback object.

28. Click Edit on the contextual menu over the Callback object.

29. In the Body section of the callback object, click the Callback URL parameter with the red circle with an exclamation mark icon.

30. Click Edit on the contextual menu over the Callback URL parameter.

31. In the Callback URL parameter definition, in the Is Required? section, select Yes.

32. At the bottom of the Callback URL parameter definition page, in the Validation section, ensure that there is a green icon representing that the definition is okay.

33. Click the Back icon at the top-left corner of the Callback URL parameter definition page.

34. Click the Back icon at the top-left corner of the Callback object definition page.

35. Repeat steps 27 to 34 for the Callback objects with the exclamation mark inside a red circle icon in the References section on the left side of the Definition page.

36. Ensure that there is no exclamation mark inside a red circle icon on the Definition page.

37. Click the Update Connector link at the top-right corner of the Edit Logic Apps Custom Connector blade.

At this point, you have successfully created your Azure Logic Apps Custom Connector. In the following steps, you are going to create a workflow for testing your new custom connector. This workflow uses the trigger defined in your Azure Logic App Custom Connector. It gets the information from the newly created book in the API and puts the information in a Microsoft Teams channel:

1. Open the Azure portal (*https://portal.azure.com*).

2. Click Create A Resource in the top area of the Azure portal.

3. Type **logic app** in the Search The Marketplace text box.

4. Click Logic App in the results list.

5. Click the Create button.

6. On the Logic App panel, select an existing resource group in the resource group drop-down menu, where you want to store your Logic App. Alternatively, you can create a new resource group by clicking the Create New link below the resource group drop-down menu.

7. Type a name for your Logic App in the Logic App Name text box.

8. In the Select The Location control, ensure that the option Region is selected.

9. Select a location in the Location drop-down menu.

10. Click the Review + Create button at the bottom of the panel.

11. Click the Create button.

12. Navigate to the newly created Azure Logic App.

13. On the Logic Apps Designer blade, choose the Blank Logic App template. If you don't get the Logic Apps Designer blade as soon as you open your Azure Logic App, you can click Logic App Designer on the navigation menu on the left side of your Azure Logic App.

14. On the Logic App Designer, click the Custom tab.

15. Click your newly created custom connector.

16. In the Triggers section, click New Book Created. This is a simple trigger that requires no additional parameters.

17. Click the New Step button.

18. Type **Microsoft Teams** in the Search Connectors And Actions text box on the Choose An Action panel.

19. Click the Microsoft Teams icon.

20. Click the Post A Message (V3) (preview) action.

21. Grant access to your Microsoft Teams account.

22. On the Post A Message (V3) (preview) action panel, select an existing team from the Team drop-down menu.

23. Select the General channel in the Add Teams Channel ID drop-down menu.

24. Click inside the Message text box.

25. In the Message text area, type **Title:** followed by a space.

26. In the Dynamic Content dialog box, click the See More link in the New Book Created section.

27. In the New Book Created section, click Title.

28. Write a new line in the Message text area.

29. In the Message text area, type **Author:** followed by a space.

30. Repeat steps 26 and 27 for the Author property. Your Message area should look similar to Figure 5-6.

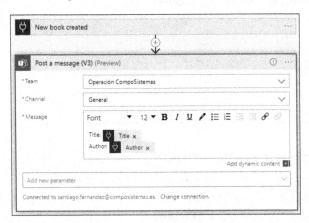

FIGURE 5-6 Send a Message to Microsoft Teams

31. Click the Save button in the top-left corner of the Logic Apps Designer blade.

NEED MORE REVIEW? **VARIABLES**

You can declare and use variables in your workflow. These variables can contain data from your connectors, fixed values, or the result of some operations that you perform inside your workflow. You can learn more about how to use variables in your workflow by reviewing the article *https://docs.microsoft.com/en-us/azure/logic-apps/logic-apps-create-variables-store-values*.

At this point, you should be ready to test your new Azure Logic Apps Custom Connector. For testing this workflow, you can use the same procedure that you used for testing the API earlier in this section. Create a new book in the API. The new book should appear in the Microsoft Teams channel that you configured in the Azure Logic Apps workflow, as shown in Figure 5-7.

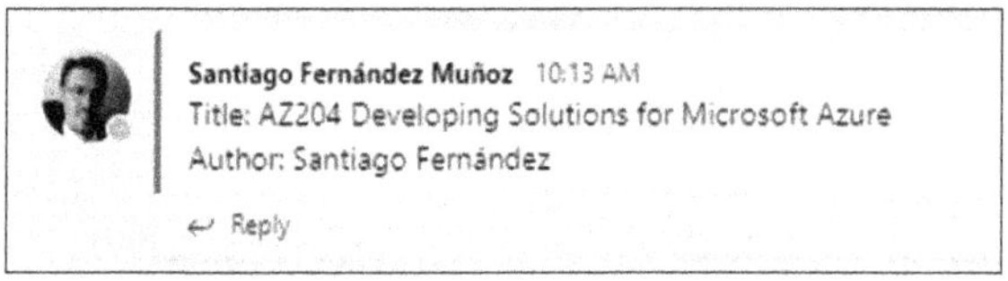
Santiago Fernández Muñoz 10:13 AM
Title: AZ204 Developing Solutions for Microsoft Azure
Author: Santiago Fernández
Reply

FIGURE 5-7 Result of the workflow execution in Microsoft Teams

EXAM TIP

You can create custom connectors for Azure Logic Apps, Microsoft Flow, and Microsoft PowerApps. You cannot reuse a connector created for Azure Logic Apps in Microsoft Flow or PowerApps (or vice versa). You can use the same OpenAPI definition to create a custom connector for these three services.

NEED MORE REVIEW? **CUSTOM CONNECTOR**

You can learn more about custom connectors at *https://docs.microsoft.com/en-us/connectors/custom-connectors/*.

Create a custom template for Logic Apps

Once you have created an Azure Logic App, you can reuse it in other Azure subscriptions or share it with other colleagues. You can create a template from your working Azure Logic App to automate deployment processes. When you create a template, you are converting the definition of your Azure Logic App into an Azure Resource Manager (ARM) template. Using ARM templates enables you to take advantage of the flexibility of the ARM platform by separating the definition of the Azure Logic App from the values used in the logic app. When you deploy a new Azure Logic App from a template, you can provide a parameter file in the same way that you do with other ARM templates. Azure also provides some prebuilt Logic App templates. You can use these templates as a base for creating templates.

You can download an Azure Logic Apps template using several mechanisms:

- **Azure portal**   You can use the Export Template option in the Azure Logic App in the Azure portal for downloading the ARM template.
- **Visual Studio**   You can use the Azure Logic Apps Tools extension for Visual Studio to connect your Azure subscription and download a template from your Azure Logic Apps.
- **PowerShell**   You can use the LogicAppTemplate PowerShell module to download a template from your Azure Logic App.

A Logic App template is a JSON file comprised of three main areas:

- **Logic App resource**   This section contains basic information about the Logic App itself. This information is the location of the resource, the pricing plans, and the workflow definition.
- **Workflow definition**   This section contains the description of the workflow, including the triggers and actions in your workflow. This section also contains how the Logic App runs these triggers and actions.
- **Connections**   This section stores the information about the connectors that you use in the workflow.

Use the following procedure to create a template from your Azure Logic App using Visual Studio:

1. Download the Azure Logic Apps Tool extension for Visual Studio 2019 at *https://aka.ms/ download-azure-logic-apps-tools-visual-studio-2019*.
2. Install the Azure Logic Apps Tool extension.
3. Open Visual Studio 2019.
4. In the Visual Studio 2019 welcome window, click the Continue Without Code link below the Get Started section.
5. In the Visual Studio window, click View > Cloud Explorer.
6. In the Cloud Explorer window, shown in Figure 5-8, click the user icon to open the Account Manager.

FIGURE 5-8 Cloud Explorer window

7. Click the Manage Accounts link.
8. In the All Accounts section, click the Sign In link.

9. Sign in with an account that has privileges to access your Azure subscription.

10. Ensure that your Azure subscription appears in the list of subscriptions in the Cloud Explorer window.

11. Click the Apply button.

12. In the Cloud Explorer tree control, navigate to Your Subscription > Logic Apps.

13. Right-click the Logic App that you want to convert to a template.

14. In the contextual menu shown in Figure 5-9, click Open With Logic App Editor.

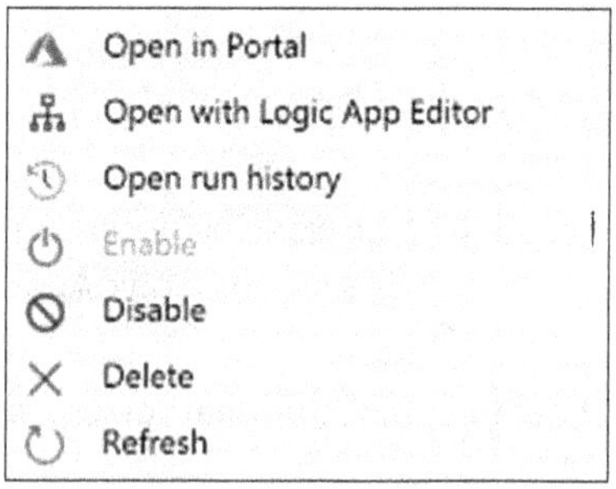

FIGURE 5-9 Logic App tool contextual menu

15. On the Logic App Editor tab, click the Download button.

16. Select a location to which you want to download the JSON file.

At this point, you can edit and customize your template. Once you are done with the modifications to your template, you can create a parameters file for deploying this template.

NEED MORE REVIEW? **LOGIC APP TEMPLATES**

You can learn more by reading the following articles about Logic apps templates:

- **Create Logic App Templates** *https://docs.microsoft.com/en-us/azure/logic-apps/ logic-apps-create-azure-resource-manager-templates*

- **Deploy Logic App Templates** *https://docs.microsoft.com/en-us/azure/logic-apps/ logic-apps-deploy-azure-resource-manager-templates*

Skill 5.2: Implement API Management

Most of the applications and solutions that you can find or develop nowadays offer an API for accessing the features available in the solution. In business environments, it is quite usual that those solutions need to communicate with each other using their respective APIs. Sometimes, you need to expose your solutions to your clients to offer your services. In those situations, you need to ensure that you offer a consistent and secure API. Implementing the necessary mechanism for achieving an enterprise-grade level of security, consistency, and flexibility is not easy. If you also need to publish several of your services under a common API, this task is even harder.

Microsoft provides the Azure API Management (APIM) service. This service allows you to create an enterprise-grade API for your existing back-end services. Using APIM, you can securely publish your back-end applications, providing your customers with a platform protected against DOS attacks or JWT token validations.

> **This skill covers how to**
> - Create an APIM instance
> - Configure authentication for APIs
> - Define policies for APIs

Create an APIM instance

The API Management service allows you to expose a portion (or all) of the APIs offered by your back-end systems. By using the APIM service, you can unify all your back-end APIs in a common interface that you can offer to external users, such as clients or partners, and internal or external developers. In general, the APIM service is a façade of the APIs that you configure in your APIM instance. Thanks to this façade feature, you can customize the front-end API offered by the APIM instance without changing the back-end API.

When exposing your back-end systems, you are not limited to REST API back ends. You can use a back-end service that uses a SOAP API and then publish this SOAP API as a REST API. This means you can update your older back-end systems without needing to modify the code and take advantage of the greater level of integration of the REST APIs.

Use the following procedure to create a new APIM instance:

1. Open the Azure portal (*https://portal.azure.com*).
2. Click Create A Resource at the top of the Azure portal.
3. On the New blade, click Integration in the Azure Marketplace column.
4. Click API Management in the Featured column. If the API Management service doesn't appear in the Featured column, you can use the Search The Marketplace text box and look for the API Management service.
5. On the API Management Service blade, type a name for your new APIM instance.
6. Select a subscription from the Subscription drop-down menu.
7. Select a resource group from the Resource Group drop-down menu. Alternatively, you can create a new one by clicking the Create New link below the drop-down menu.
8. Select a location from the Location drop-down menu.
9. In the Organization Name text box, type the name of your organization. This name appears on the developer's portal and email notifications.

10. In the Administrator Email, type the name of the email account that should receive all notifications from the APIM instance. By default, the value associated with this property is the email address of the logged-in user.

11. In the Pricing Tier, leave the Developer tier selected.

12. Click the Create button at the bottom of the blade. The process of creating the APIM instance takes several minutes. When your new APIM instance is ready, you receive a welcome email at the administrator email address that you configured in step 10.

> **NOTE PRICING TIERS**
>
> The Developer pricing tier is appropriate for testing and development environments, but you should not use it for production because the Developer tier does not offer high-availability features and can be affected by disconnections during the updates of the node. You can review the full offer and the features available on each tier at *https://azure.microsoft.com/en-us/pricing/details/api-management/*.

Once you have created your APIM instance, you can start adding APIs to your instance. In the following procedure, you are going to add two APIs. You are going to take advantage of the API that you created in the section "Create A Custom Connector For Logic Apps" previously in this chapter. For the second API, you are going to create a blank API definition and add only those methods that are appropriate for you.

1. Open the Azure portal (*https://portal.azure.com*).

2. Type the name of your APIM instance in the Search text box at the top of the portal.

3. Click the name your APIM instance in the results list.

4. Click APIs on the navigation menu on your APIM instance blade.

5. On the Add A New API blade, click OpenAPI.

6. On the Create From OpenAPI Specification dialog box, shown in Figure 5-10, in the Open-API Specification text box, type the URL of the Swagger definition of the API that you published in Azure in the section "Create a custom connector for Logic Apps." Remember that the URL should be similar to *https://<your_app_service_name>.azurewebsites.net/swagger/docs/v1*.

7. Ensure that Azure automatically fills the Display Name and Name properties text boxes. This means that Azure was able to import the details of your API successfully.

8. Delete the content of the Display Name text box.

9. Type **Library** in the Display Name text box.

10. Ensure that the Name text box has the value **library**.

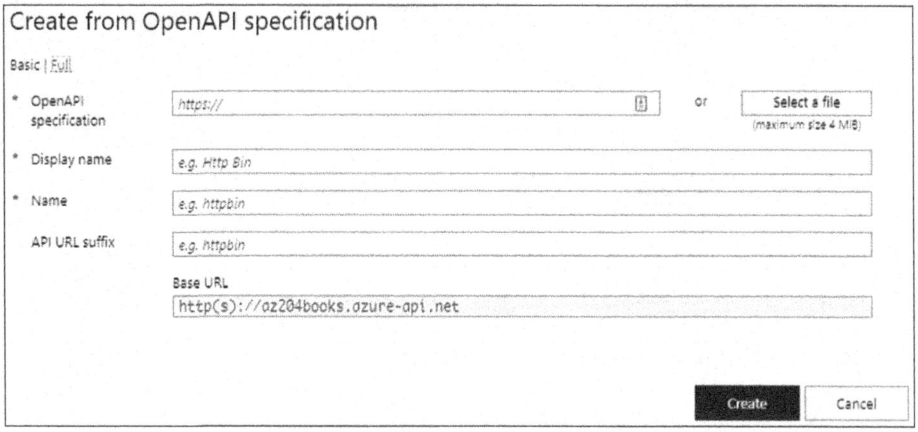

FIGURE 5-10 Adding a back-end API to an APIM instance

11. Type **library** in the API URL Suffix field. If you are going to connect more than one back-end API to the APIM instance, you need to provide a suffix for each API. The APIM instance uses this suffix for differentiating between the different APIs that you connected to the instance.

12. Click the Create button at the bottom of the dialog box.

At this point, you have added your first back-end API to the APIM instance by using the OpenAPI specification of your back-end API. In the following steps, you are going to add a back-end API without using any specification. Creating the front-end endpoints is useful if you need to connect only a few endpoints from your back-end API or if you don't have the OpenAPI or SOAP specification of your API in any format:

1. Click APIs on the navigation menu in your APIM instance blade.

2. On the APIs blade, click Add API.

3. On the Add A New API page, click Blank API.

4. On the Create A Blank API dialog box, type **Fake API** in the Display Name text box.

5. Leave the Name property with the default value.

6. Type **https://fakerestapi.azurewebsites.net** in the Web Service URL text box.

7. Type **fakeapi** in the API URL Suffix text box.

8. Click the Create button.

9. On the Design tab of the API blade with the newly added Fake API selected, click Add Operation.

10. On the Add Operation editor, shown in Figure 5-11, type **GetActivities** in the Display Name text box.

11. In the URL HTTP Method drop-down menu, ensure that the *GET* method is selected.

12. In the URL text box, type **/api/activities**.

13. Click the Save button at the bottom of the editor.

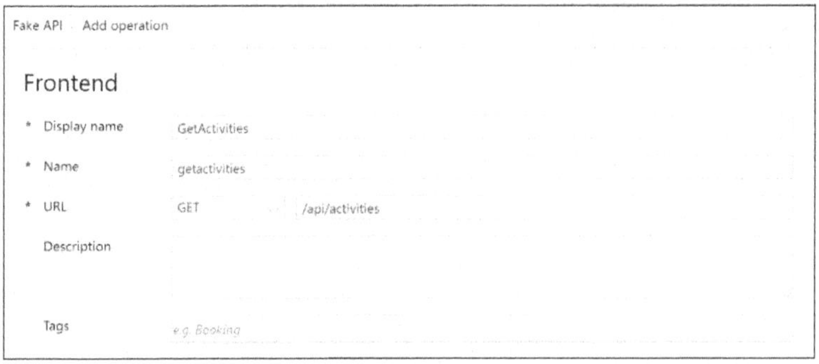

Fake API   Add operation

Frontend

* Display name   GetActivities

* Name   getactivities

* URL   GET   /api/activities

Description

Tags   e.g. Booking

FIGURE 5-11 Adding an API operation to an API in an APIM instance

14. On the API blade, ensure that Fake API is selected.

15. Click the Test tab.

16. Click the GetActivities operation.

17. Click the Send button at the bottom of the GetActivities operation panel. Using this panel, you can test each of the operations that are defined in your API.

At this point, you have two back-end APIs connected to your APIM instance. As you can see in the previous example, you don't need to expose the entire back-end API. By adding the appropriate operations, you can publish only those parts of the back-end API that are useful for you. Once you have created the APIs in your APIM instance, you can grant access to these APIs to your developers by using the Developer portal. You can access the APIM Developer portal by using the URL *https://<your_APIM_name>.developer.azure-api.net/.*

> *NEED MORE REVIEW?* **AZURE API MANAGEMENT DEVELOPER PORTAL**
>
> The Azure API Management developer portal allows you to provide your customers and third parties that want to integrate with your API with a single point of contact for requesting access to your application and providing documentation about your API. You can read more about how to customize the developer experience by reviewing the following article at *https://docs.microsoft.com/en-us/azure/api-management/api-management-howto-developer-portal.*

Bear in mind that you need to associate a product to your API for publishing it. Because you didn't associate your APIs to any product, your APIs won't be available to the external world. You can associate an API to more than one product. By default, Azure provides two products: Starter and Unlimited. These products are associated with the Echo API demo that Azure automatically deploys when you create your API Management instance. Use the following procedure to create a product and associate it with your APIs:

1. Open the Azure portal (*https://portal.azure.com*).

2. Type the name of your APIM instance in the Search text box on the top-middle of the portal.

3. Click the name of your APIM instance in the results list.

4. Click Products on the navigation menu in your APIM instance blade.

5. Click the Add button on the top-left corner of the Products blade.

6. Type a Name in the Display Name text box on the Add Product panel.

7. Leave the value in the ID text box as is.

8. Type a description in the Description text area.

9. Select the Published value in the State switch control. If you don't select this option at this time, you can publish later, or you can publish the Product using its panel.

10. Click the Select API button in the APIs section.

11. On the APIs blade, select Library and Fake APIs by clicking the check box beside the name of the API.

12. Click the Select button at the bottom of the panel.

13. Click the Create button at the bottom of the Add Product panel.

By default, when you create a new product, only members of the Administrators built-in group can access the product. You can configure this by using the Access Control section in the product.

> **NEED MORE REVIEW?**   **REVISIONS AND VERSIONS**
>
> During the lifetime of your API, you may need to make modifications by adding, updating, or removing operations to your API. You can make these modifications without disrupting the usage of your API by using revisions and versions. You can review how to work with revisions and versions in your API by reading the article at *https://azure.microsoft.com/es-es/blog/versions-revisions/.*

Configure authentication for APIs

Once you have imported your back-end APIs, you need to configure the authentication for accessing these APIs. When you configure the security options in the APIM instance, the back-end API delegates the security to the APIM instance. This means that even your API has implemented its own authentication mechanism, it is never used when the API is accessed through the APIM instance.

This ability to hide the authentication of the back-end APIs is useful for unifying all the security using a consistent and unique authentication mechanism. You can manage the authentication options associated with a product or API by using subscriptions. A subscription manages the keys that a developer can use for accessing your API. If an HTTP request made to an API protected by a subscription does not provide a valid subscription key, the request is immediately rejected by the APIM gateway without reaching your back-end API. When you define a subscription, you can use three different scopes for applying it:

- **Product**   The developer can access all the APIs configured in the product assigned to the subscription. Traditionally, the developer could request access to products by using the Developer portal. This is no longer a valid option. You need to provide access to the developer using the Azure portal and configure the appropriate APIM subscription.

- **All APIs**   The developer can access all APIs in your APIM instance using the same subscription key.
- **API**   The developer can access a single API in your APIM instance using a subscription key. There is no need for the API to be part of a product.

If you use the All APIs scope, you don't need to associate the back-end API with an API. The Subscription using this scope allows access directly to all the APIs configured in your API Management instance. You can use the following procedure for creating a subscription and associating it with a program:

1. Open the Azure portal (*https://portal.azure.com*).
2. Type the name of your APIM instance in the Search text box at the top of the portal.
3. Click the name your APIM instance in the results list.
4. Click Subscriptions in the navigation menu in your APIM instance blade.
5. Click the Add Subscription button in the top-left corner of the Subscriptions blade.
6. On the New Subscription panel shown in Figure 5-12, type a Name for the subscription. Beware that this name can only contain letters, numbers, and hyphens.

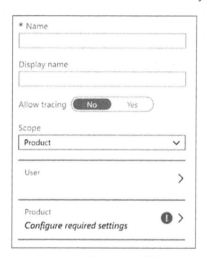

FIGURE 5-12 Creating a new API Management Subscription

7. In the Scope drop-down menu, select the Product value.
8. Click the Product property.
9. In the Products panel, click the name of the product that you created in the previous section.
10. Click the Select button at the bottom of the panel.
11. Click the Save button at the bottom of the panel.

12. On the Subscription blade, click the ellipsis at the end of the row for your newly created subscription.

13. On the contextual menu, click Show/Hide keys. You can use either of these keys to access the APIs configured in the product associated with the Subscription. You need to use the Header Ocp-Apim-Subscription-Key for providing the subscription key in your HTTP requests.

When you are configuring a subscription, you can assign different users to the subscription by using the Users parameters in the New Subscription panel. This is a best practice way of providing different subscription keys to different groups of users.

> *NEED MORE REVIEW?* **OTHER AUTHENTICATION METHODS**
>
> Using subscription and subscription keys is not the only mechanism for protecting access to your APIs. API Management allows you to use OAuth 2.0, client certificates, and IP whitelisting. You can use the following articles to review how to use other authentication mechanisms for protecting your APIs:
>
> - **IP whitelisting** *https://docs.microsoft.com/en-us/azure/api-management/ api-management-access-restriction-policies#RestrictCallerIPs*
>
> - **OAuth 2.0 authentication using Azure AD** *https://docs.microsoft.com/en-us/azure/ api-management/api-management-howto-protect-backend-with-aad*
>
> - **Mutual authentication using client certificates** *https://docs.microsoft.com/en-us/ azure/api-management/api-management-howto-mutual-certificates*

Define policies for APIs

When you publish a back-end API using the API Management service, all the requests made to your APIM instance are forwarded to the correct back-end API, and the response is sent back to the requestor. None of these requests or responses are altered or modified by default, but there could be some situations where you need to modify some requests and/or responses. An example of these modification needs is transforming the format of a response from XML to JSON. Another example could be throttling the number of incoming calls from a particular IP or user.

A policy is a mechanism that you can use to change the default behavior of the APIM gateway. Policies are XML documents that describe a sequence of inbound and outbound steps or statements. Each policy is made of four sections:

- **Inbound** In this section, you can find any statement that applies to requests from the managed API clients.

- **Back End** This section contains the steps that need to be applied to the request that should be sent from the API gateway to the back-end API.

- **Outbound**   This section contains statements or modifications that you need to apply to the response before it's sent to the requestor.

- **On-Error**   In case there is an error on any of the other sections, the engine stops processing the remaining steps on the faulty section and jumps to this section.

When you are configuring or defining a policy, you need to bear in mind that you can apply it different scope levels:

- **Global**   The policy applies to all APIs in your APIM instance. You can configure global policies by using the code editor on the All APIs policy editor in the APIs blade of your APIM instance.

- **Product**   The policy applies to all APIs associated with a product. You can configure product policies on the Policies blade of the product in your API instance.

- **API**   The policy applies to all operations configured in the API. You can configure API-scoped policies by using the code editor in the All Operations option on the Design Tab of the API in your APIM instance.

- **Operation**   The policy applies only to a specific operation in your API. You can configure operation-scoped policies by using the code editor in the specific operation.

Policies are a powerful and very flexible mechanism that allows you to do a lot of useful work, such as applying caching to the HTTP requests, performing monitoring on the request and responses, authenticating with your back-end API using different authentication mechanisms, or even interacting with external services, among others. Use the following procedure to apply some transformations to the Library API that you configured in the "Create an APIM instance" section earlier in this chapter:

1. Open the Azure portal (*https://portal.azure.com*).

2. Type the name of your APIM instance in the Search text box at the top of the portal.

3. Click the name of your APIM instance in the results list.

4. Click APIs on the navigation menu in your APIM instance blade.

5. Click Library API in the APIs blade.

6. Click the *Get Books* operation.

7. Click the Test tab.

8. Click the Send button at the bottom of the tab. This should send a request to the Library API and get results similar to those shown in Figure 5-13. In this procedure, you are going to transform the HTTP headers inside the red rectangles in Figure 5-13. If you don't see any books when you execute this test, create some books using the Swagger application of your API. You can review how to do this by consulting the testing process of the Library API in the "Create a custom connector for Logic Apps" section earlier in this chapter.

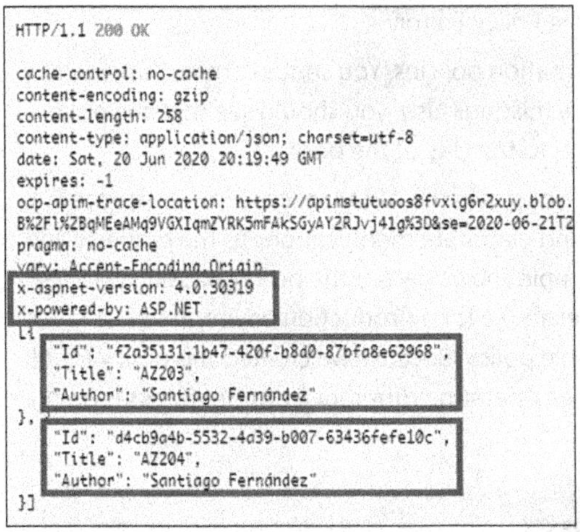

```
HTTP/1.1 200 OK

cache-control: no-cache
content-encoding: gzip
content-length: 258
content-type: application/json; charset=utf-8
date: Sat, 20 Jun 2020 20:19:49 GMT
expires: -1
ocp-apim-trace-location: https://apimstutuoos8fvxig6r2xuy.blob.
B%2F1%2BqMEeAMq9VGXIqmZYRK5mFAkSGyAY2RJvj41g%3D&se=2020-06-21T2
pragma: no-cache
vary: Accent-Encoding,Origin
x-aspnet-version: 4.0.30319
x-powered-by: ASP.NET
[{
    "Id": "f2a35131-1b47-420f-b8d0-87bfa8e62968",
    "Title": "AZ203",
    "Author": "Santiago Fernández"
},
    "Id": "d4cb9a4b-5532-4a39-b007-63436fefe10c",
    "Title": "AZ204",
    "Author": "Santiago Fernández"
}]
```

FIGURE 5-13 Testing an API operation

9. Click the Design tab.

10. Click All Operations in the list of available operations for this API.

11. Click the icon next to Policies in the Outbound Processing section.

12. In the Policy Editor, move the cursor inside the Outbound section, before the base tag, and add a new line by pressing the Enter key.

13. Click the Show Snippets button in the top-right corner of the Policy Editor.

14. In the list of available policies on the right side of the Policy Editor, navigate to Transformation Policies.

15. Click the Set HTTP Header policy twice to insert the policies.

16. Modify the inserted policies with the following content:

```
<set-header name="X-Powered-By" exists-action="delete" />
<set-header name="X-AspNet-Version" exists-action="delete" />
```

17. Add a new line below the inserted policies.

18. Add the following code snippet:

```
<set-body>@{
    var response = context.Response.Body.As<string>();
    var arrayString = "{ \"Library\": " + response + "}";
    JObject books = JObject.Parse(arrayString);
    JArray modifiedBooks = new JArray();
    foreach (JObject book in books["Library"].ToObject<JArray>())
    {
        book.Add("URL", "https://az204books.azure-api.net/library/books/" +
        book["Id"]);
        modifiedBooks.Add(book);
    }
        return (string)modifiedBooks.ToString(Newtonsoft.Json.Formatting.None);
}</set-body>
```

19. Click the Save button at the bottom of the Policy Editor.

20. Repeat steps 6 to 8 to apply the transformation policies. You should notice that headers X-Powered-By and X-AspNet-Version are missing. Also, you should see that all books have an additional property URL pointing to the URL of the book.

As you can see in the previous example, the policies in the API Management service are compelling. You can even use C# code for making elaborate modifications to the requests and responses made to your API. Although this example shows part of the power of using policies with the APIM service, you should not use this example for a production environment, as some critical verifications are missing from this example policy. Because we created this policy for All Operations in the Library API, any call made to an operation different from Get Books is going to fail.

> **NEED MORE REVIEW? MORE ABOUT POLICIES**
>
> There are a lot of useful things that you can do using policies—too many to cover in this section. If you want to learn more about APIM policies, you can review the following articles:
>
> - **Error handling in API Management** *https://docs.microsoft.com/en-us/azure/ api-management/api-management-error-handling-policies*
>
> - **How to Set or Edit Azure API Management Policies** *https://docs.microsoft.com/ en-us/azure/api-management/set-edit-policies*
>
> - **Debug Your APIs Using Request Tracing** *https://docs.microsoft.com/es-es/azure/ api-management/api-management-howto-api-inspector*

Skill 5.3: Develop event-based solutions

One of the main principles of code development is to reuse as much as possible. To make it possible to reuse the code, you need to ensure that the code is as loosely coupled as possible, which reduces the dependencies with other parts of the code or other systems to a minimum.

With this principle in mind, to make loosely coupled systems communicate, you need to use a kind of communication. Event-driven architectures allow communication between separate systems by sharing information through events.

In general, an event is a significant change in the system state that happens in the context of the system. An example of an event could be when a user adds an item to the shopping cart in an e-commerce application, or when an IoT device collects the information from its sensors.

Azure provides different services, like Event Grid, notification hubs, or event hubs, to cover the different needs when implementing Event-Driven architectures.

> **This skill covers how to**
> - Implement solutions that use Azure Event Grid
> - Implement solutions that use Azure Notification Hubs
> - Implement solutions that use Azure Event Hub

Implement solutions that use Azure Event Grid

Azure Event Grid allows you to create an application using serverless architecture by providing a confident platform for managing events. You can use Azure Event Grid for connecting to several types of data sources, like Azure Blob Storage, Azure Subscription, Event Hubs, IoT Hubs, and others; Azure Even Grid also allows you to use different event handlers to manage these events. You can also create your custom events for integrating your application with the Azure Event Grid. Before you can start using the Azure Event Grid in your solution, there are some basic concepts that we should review:

- **Event** This is a change of state in the source (for example, in an Azure Blob Storage or when an event happens when a new blob is added to the Azure Blob Storage).
- **Event source** This is the service or application when the event happens. There is an event source for every event type.
- **Event handler** This is the app or service that reacts to the event.
- **Topics** These are the endpoints where the event source can send the events. You can use topics for grouping several related events.
- **Event subscriptions** When a new event is added to a topic, that event can be processed by one or more event handlers. The event subscription is an endpoint or built-in mechanism to distribute the events between the different event handlers. Also, you can use subscriptions to filter incoming events.

An important consideration that you need to bear in mind is that an event does not contain the full information about the event itself. The event only contains information relevant to the event, such as the source of the event, a time when the event took place, and a unique identifier. For example, when a new blob is added to an Azure Blob Storage Account, the new blob event doesn't contain the blob. Instead, the event contains a reference to the blob in the Azure Blob Storage Account.

When you need to work with events, you configure an event source to send events to a topic. Any system, or event handler, that needs to process those events subscribes to that topic. When new events arise, the event source pushes the event into the topic configured in the Azure Event Grids service. Any event handler subscribed to that topic reads the event and processes it according to its internal programming. There is no need for the event source to have event handlers subscribed to the topic; the event source pushes the event to the topic and forgets it. The following steps show how to create a custom topic. Then you are going to create console applications using C# to send events to the topic and process these events.

1. Open the Azure portal (*https://portal.azure.com*).

2. In the Search Resources, Services, And Docs text box on the top area of the Azure portal, type **event**.

3. Click Event Grid Topic in the results list.

4. On the Event Grid Topics blade, click the Add button in the top-left corner of the blade.

5. On the Create Topic panel, select a subscription in the Subscription drop-down menu.

6. Select a resource group in the Resource Group drop-down menu. Alternatively, you can create a new resource group by clicking the Create New link below the drop-down menu.

7. In the Name text box, type a name for the Event Grid Topic.

8. Select a location in the Location drop-down menu.

9. Click the Review + Create button at the bottom of the panel.

10. Click the Create button.

When the Azure Resource Manager finishes creating your new Event Grid Topic, you can subscribe to the topic for processing the events. Also, you can send your custom events to this topic. Use the following steps to publish custom events to your newly created Event Grid Topic:

1. Open Visual Studio 2019.

2. On the start window, click Create A New Project.

3. On the Create A New Project window, select the template Console App (.NET Core).

4. Click the Next button at the bottom-right corner of the window.

5. Type a Project Name.

6. Select a location for your solution.

7. Click the Create button.

8. Click Tools > NuGet Package Manager > Manage NuGet Packages For Solution.

9. On the NuGet – Solution tab, click Browse.

10. In the Search text box, type **Microsoft.Azure.EventGrid**.

11. Click Microsoft.Azure.EventGrid in the results list.

12. On the right side of the NuGet – Solution tab, click the check box next to the name of your project.

13. Click the Install button.

14. On the Preview Changes window, click the OK button.

15. In the License Acceptance window, click the I Accept button.

16. Repeat steps 10 to 15 and install the Microsoft.Extensions.Configuration.Json NuGet Package.

17. In the Solution Explorer window, right-click your project's name.

18. On the contextual menu, click Add > New Item.

19. On the Add New Item, type **json** in the Search text box.

20. Click the JSON File template.

21. Type **appsettings.json** in the Name text box.

22. Click the Add button at the bottom-right corner of the window.

23. On the Solution Explorer window, click the appsettings.json file.

24. On the properties window, set the Copy To Output Directory setting to Copy Always.

25. Open the appsettings.json file and replace the content of the file with the content of Listing 5-6. You can get the access key from the Access Key blade in your Event Grid Topic.

LISTING 5-6 appsettings.json file

```
{
    "EventGridAccessKey": "<Your_EventGridTopic_Access_Key>",
    "EventGridTopicEndpoint": "https://<Your_EventGrid_Topic>.<region_name>-1.eventgrid.
                            azure.net/api/events"
}
```

26. On the Solution Explorer window, right-click your project's name.

27. On the contextual menu, click Add > New Item.

28. In the Add New Item window, select Class from the list of new items.

29. In the name text box at the bottom of the window, type **NewItemCreatedEvent.cs.**

30. Click the Add button at the bottom-right corner of the window.

31. Replace the content of the NewItemCreatedEvent.cs file with the content of Listing 5-7.

LISTING 5-7 NewItemCreatedEvent.cs

```
// C# .NET
using Newtonsoft.Json;

namespace <your_project_name>
{
    class NewItemCreatedEvent
    {
        [JsonProperty(PropertyName = "name")]
        public string itemName;
    }
}
```

32. Open the Program.cs file.

33. Add the following using statements:

```
using Microsoft.Azure.EventGrid;
using Microsoft.Azure.EventGrid.Models;
using Microsoft.Extensions.Configuration;
using System.Collections.Generic;
```

34. Replace the content of the Main method with the content in Listing 5-8.

LISTING 5-8   Program.cs Main method

```
// C# .NET
IConfigurationBuilder builder = new ConfigurationBuilder().AddJsonFile("appsettings.
json");
IConfigurationRoot configuration = builder.Build();

string topicEndpoint = configuration["EventGridTopicEndpoint"];
string apiKey = configuration["EventGridAccessKey"];

string topicHostname = new Uri(topicEndpoint).Host;
TopicCredentials topicCredentials = new TopicCredentials(apiKey);
EventGridClient client = new EventGridClient(topicCredentials);

List<EventGridEvent> events = new List<EventGridEvent>();
events.Add(new EventGridEvent()
{
    Id = Guid.NewGuid().ToString(),
    EventType = "MyCompany.Items.NewItemCreated",
    Data = new NewItemCreatedEvent()
    {
        itemName = "Item 1"
    },
    EventTime = DateTime.Now,
    Subject = "Store A",
    DataVersion = "3.7"
});

client.PublishEventsAsync(topicHostname, events).GetAwaiter().GetResult();
Console.WriteLine("Events published to the Event Grid Topic");
Console.ReadLine();
```

At this point, your console application publishes events to the Event Grid topic that you previously created. Press F5 to run your console application to ensure that everything compiles and works correctly; you will not be able to see the published message yet. Use the following steps to create a subscriber Azure Function that connects to the Event Grid Topic and processes these events:

1. Open Visual Studio 2019.

2. In the start window, click Create A New Project.

3. On the Create A New Project window, click the template Azure Functions.

4. Click Next.

5. Type a Project Name.

6. Select a location for your project.

7. Click Create.

8. On the Create A New Azure Functions Application window, click the Event Grid Trigger.

9. In the Storage Account drop-down menu on the right side of the window, click Browse.

10. In the Azure Storage window, select an Azure Storage Account from your subscription for using with the Azure Function. Alternatively, you can create a new Azure Storage Account by clicking the Create A Storage Account link at the bottom of the window.

11. Click the Add button.

12. Click Create.

13. Create a new empty C# class called `NewItemCreatedEventData`.

14. Replace the content of the `NewItemCreatedEventData.cs` file with the content of Listing 5-9.

LISTING 5-9   NewItemCreatedEvent.cs

```
// C# .NET
using Newtonsoft.Json;

namespace <your_project_name>
{
    class NewItemCreatedEvent
    {
        [JsonProperty(PropertyName = "name")]
        public string itemName;
    }
}
```

15. Replace the content of Function1.cs with the content in Listing 5-10.

LISTING 5-10   *Function1.cs*

```
// C# .NET
using Microsoft.Azure.WebJobs;
using Microsoft.Azure.EventGrid.Models;
using Microsoft.Azure.WebJobs.Extensions.EventGrid;
using Microsoft.Extensions.Logging;
```

```
using Newtonsoft.Json.Linq;

namespace <your_project_name>
{
    public static class Function1
    {
        [FunctionName("EventGridTrigger")]
        public static void Run([EventGridTrigger]EventGridEvent eventGridEvent,
        ILogger log)
        {
            log.LogInformation("C# Event Grid trriger handling EventGrid Events.");

            log.LogInformation($"New event received: {eventGridEvent.Data}");


            if (eventGridEvent.Data is StorageBlobCreatedEventData)
            {
                var eventData = (StorageBlobCreatedEventData)eventGridEvent.Data;
                log.LogInformation($"Got BlobCreated event data, blob URI {eventData.
                Url}");
            }
            else if (eventGridEvent.EventType.Equals("MyCompany.Items.NewItemCreated"))
            {
                NewItemCreatedEventData eventData = ((JObject)eventGridEvent.Data).
                ToObject< NewItemCreatedEventData >();
                log.LogInformation($"New Item Custom Event, Name {eventData.
                itemName}");
            }
        }
    }
}
```

16. Publish the Azure Function to your Azure Subscription. Use the procedure at the following URL to publish an Azure Function to Azure: *https://docs.microsoft.com/en-us/azure/azure-functions/functions-develop-vs#publish-to-azure*.

17. Open your Event Grid Topic in the Azure portal.

18. On your Event Grid Topic Overview blade, click the Event Subscription button.

19. On the Create Event Subscription blade, shown in Figure 5-14, type a Name for the subscription.

20. In the Endpoint Type drop-down menu, select Azure Function.

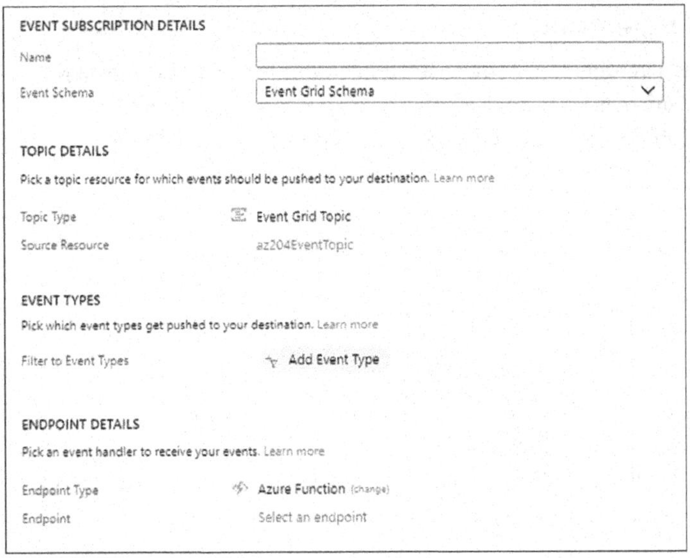

FIGURE 5-14 Creating a subscription using a WebHook endpoint

21. Click the Select An Endpoint link below the Azure Function endpoint type.

22. On the Select Azure Function panel, in the Function App drop-down menu, select the Azure Function that you published previously in this section.

23. Leave the Slot drop-down menu with the Production value.

24. Ensure that your Azure Function's name appears in the Function drop-down menu.

25. Click the Confirm Selection button.

26. Click the Create button.

At this point, you should be able to publish and process events using the Event Grid Topic that you created previously. Use the following steps to ensure that everything works correctly:

1. Open the publisher console application in Visual Studio 2019.

2. Run the console application to publish an event to the topic.

3. Open the Azure portal and navigate to your Azure Function.

4. In the Azure Functions blade, click Monitor in the tree control.

5. In the Monitor blade, click the Configure button for configuring the Application Insights integration. You need this integration for being able to capture invocation logs.

6. On the Application Insights blade, leave the Create New Resource option selected. Alternatively, you can use an existing Application Insights instance by using the option Select Existing Resource.

7. Click the OK button.

8. You should be able to see a list of invocations when the function has been called because a new event arrived at the Event Grid Topic.

9. Click one of the successful invocations; you will get a result similar to Figure 5-15.

> ***NOTE* AZURE FUNCTION MONITORING**
>
> **You need to have Application Insight integration enabled to be able to see the log messages generated from the Azure Function. Review the article about how to monitor Azure Functions using Application Insights at *https://docs.microsoft.com/en-us/azure/azure-functions/functions-monitoring*.**

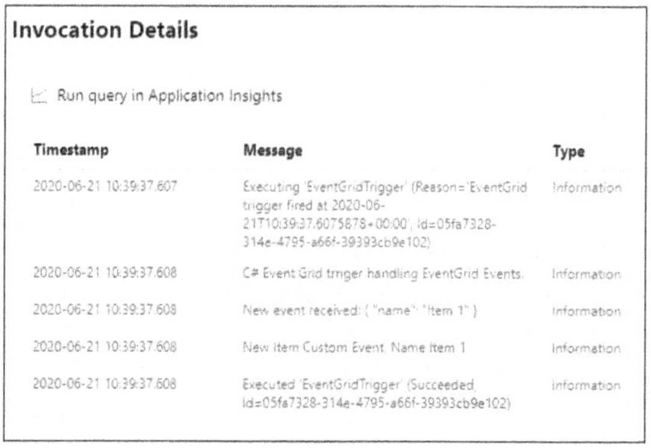

Invocation Details

Run query in Application Insights

Timestamp	Message	Type
2020-06-21 10:39:37.607	Executing 'EventGridTrigger' (Reason='EventGrid trigger fired at 2020-06-21T10:39:37.6075878+00:00', Id=05fa7328-314e-4795-a66f-39393cb9e102)	Information
2020-06-21 10:39:37.608	C# Event Grid trriger handling EventGrid Events.	Information
2020-06-21 10:39:37.608	New event received: { "name": "Item 1" }	Information
2020-06-21 10:39:37.608	New Item Custom Event, Name Item 1	Information
2020-06-21 10:39:37.608	Executed 'EventGridTrigger' (Succeeded, Id=05fa7328-314e-4795-a66f-39393cb9e102)	Information

FIGURE 5-15 Log messages from a successful event processing

The Azure Function that we used in this example can manage not only custom events but also events from an Azure Storage Account. As an exercise, you can create a new subscription that listens only to Azure Storage Account events and uses the Azure Function that you published previously in this section to manage the events produced by the Azure Storage Account.

Another important consideration that you need to deal with when you add a handler to an Azure Event Grid subscription is the handler validation. Depending on the type of handler that you use, this validation process is performed automatically by the SDK, or you need to implement it manually. When you use an HTTP endpoint as an event handler, you need to deal with the subscription verification. This verification process consists of a verification code sent by the Event Grid service to the webhook endpoint. Your application needs to reply to the Event Grid service by using the same verification code. You can find a detailed example of how to perform this verification by reviewing the code available at *https://github.com/Azure-Samples/azure-event-grid-viewer*.

> ***NEED MORE REVIEW?* DEAD LETTER AND RETRY POLICIES**
>
> **When you work with event-driven architectures, there can be situations when the event cannot deliver to the event handler. In those situations, it's appropriate to set a retry strategy to try to recover the event before it expires. You can learn more about these retry policies and dead letter management at *https://docs.microsoft.com/en-us/azure/event-grid/manage-event-delivery*.**

Implement solutions that use Azure Notification Hubs

Developing applications that can be accessed using mobile devices can be challenging because you usually need to allow access to your application from different mobile platforms. The challenge becomes even bigger because different mobile platforms use different notification systems to send events. You need to deal with the Apple Push Notification Service (APNS), Google Firebase Cloud Messaging (FCM), or Windows Notification Service (WNS), and these are just the leading mobile platforms on the market. There are many other mobile platforms that you can use for pushing notifications to your mobile app.

The Azure Notification Hubs provide an abstraction layer that you can use for connecting to different push notification mobile platforms. Thanks to this abstraction, you can send the notification message to the Notification Hub, which manages the message and delivers it to the appropriate platform. You can also define and use cross-platform templates. Using these templates, you ensure that your solution sends consistent messages independently of the mobile platform that you are using.

When you develop a mobile app, there is a high probability that you need to send information to your users when they are not using the app. In doing so, you use the well-known push notifications. This asynchronous communication mechanism allows you to interact with your users when they are offline. For making this interaction happens, some key players are part of this asynchronous communication:

- **The mobile app client**   This is your actual mobile app, which runs on your user's device. The user must register with the Platform Notification System (PNS) to receive notifications. This generates a PNS handler that is stored in the mobile app back end for sending notifications.

- **The mobile app back end**   This is the back end for your app client, and it stores the PNS handler that the client received from the PNS. Using this handler, your back-end service can send push notifications to all registered users.

- **A Platform Notification System (PNS)**   These platforms deliver the actual notification to the user's device. PNSes are platform-dependent, and each vendor has its own PNS. Apple has the Apple Push Notification Service, Google uses the Firebase Cloud Messaging, and Microsoft uses the Windows Notification Service.

Even if your mobile app is targeted to a single platform, implementing push notifications requires a good amount of effort. This is because some Platform Notification Systems only focus on delivering the notification to the user's device but don't deal with requirements like targeted notifications or broadcasting notifications. Another requirement for most PNSes is that device tokens need to be refreshed every time you release a new version of your app. This operation requires that your back end deals with a large amount of traffic and database updates simply to keep device tokes updated. If you need to support different mobile platforms, these tasks become even more complicated.

Microsoft provides you with the Azure Notification Hub. This service provides cross-platform push notification to your mobile app back end, allowing you to abstract from the details of managing each Platform Notification System to provide a consistent API for interacting with the Notification Hub. When you need to add push notifications to your mobile app, you integrate the Notification Hub service with your back-end service hosted on the Mobile App Service. Figure 5-16 shows the workflow for sending push notifications to users using the Notification Hub.

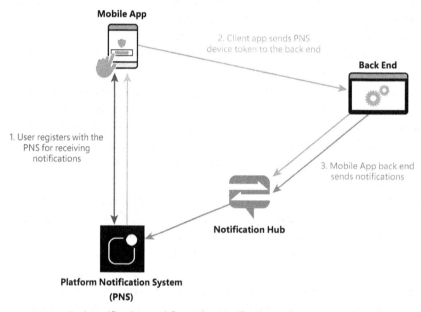

FIGURE 5-16 Push notification workflow using Notification Hub

---

NOTE **NOTIFICATION HUB INTEGRATION**

Microsoft also provides an SDK for easing the direct integration between your native (iOS, Android, or Windows) or cross-platform (Xamarin or Cordoba) code and Azure Notification Hub, without using your back end. The drawback of this approach is that the Mobile Apps Client SDK removes all tags that you can associate with the device for security purposes. If you need these tags for performing segmented notifications, you should register your users' devices using the back end.

The interaction between your back-end Mobile App and Notification Hub is performed using the Mobile App SDK for ASP.NET or Node.js web applications. Before your back-end application can send push notifications, you need to connect your App Service with your Notification Hub. Use the following procedure to make this connection:

1. Sign in to the Azure portal (*http://portal.azure.com*).
2. At the top of the portal, click Create A Resource.
3. On the New blade, in the Search the Marketplace text box, type **notification**.
4. Click Notification Hub in the result list.
5. On the Notification Hub blade, click the Create button.
6. On the Create Notification Hub blade, select your subscription in the Subscription drop-down menu.
7. Select your resource group in the Resource Group drop-down menu. Alternatively, you can create a new resource group by clicking the Create New link.
8. Type a namespace in the Notification Hub Namespace text box. A namespace is a group of one or more hubs.
9. Type a name in the Notification Hub text box.
10. Select the location of the notification hub in the Location drop-down menu.
11. Leave the pricing tier as Free.
12. Click the Create button at the bottom of the blade.
13. Once the Notification Hub has been created, type the name of your new Notification Hub in the Search Resources, Services, And Docs text box at the top of the Azure portal.
14. At this point, you can configure the integration of the Notification Hub with each Platform Notification System that you want to use for sending notifications.

Now that you have your Notification Hub ready, you can register your PNS with your Notification Hub and send notifications to your mobile app. This step requires that you have a developer account associated with the PNS that you want to use. The following procedure shows how to create an application in the Firebase console:

1. Open the Firebase console (*https://console.firebase.google.com*).
2. Click the Add Project button.
3. Type a name for your project.
4. Click the Continue button.
5. On the Google Analytics page, disable the Google Analytics For This Project.
6. Click the Create Project button.
7. Once your project is ready, click the Continue button. This forwards you to your project's main page.
8. On your project's main page, click the Android icon below the title Get Started By Adding Firebase To Your App.
9. On the Add Firebase To Your Android App, type a package name. You need this package name in the next example.

10. Click the Register App button.

11. Click the Download google-services.json button. You need this file later in this section.

12. Click the Next button.

13. Click the Next button again.

14. Click the Continue To Console button.

15. In the Console window, click the cog icon next to the Project Overview on the navigation panel on the left side of the console.

16. On the contextual menu, click Project Settings.

17. Click the Cloud Messaging tab.

18. In the Project Credentials section, copy the token associated with the Server Key. You need this in a later step.

19. Navigate to the Azure portal (*https://portal.azure.com*).

20. Type the name of your Notification Hub in the Search Resources, Services, And Docs text box at the top of the Azure portal.

21. Click the Google (GCM/FCM) option in the Settings section on the navigation menu on the left side of your Notification Hub blade.

22. Paste the Server Key that you copied on step 18 in the API Key text box.

23. Click the Save button.

At this point, you have configured your Notification Hub for sending notifications to your Android application by using Firebase. For the sake of brevity, I omit how to program a mobile application for getting notifications from the Notification Hub. You can find examples of how to perform this notification management for each platform by reviewing the following articles:

- **iOS** *https://docs.microsoft.com/en-us/azure/notification-hubs/ios-sdk-204*
- **Android** *https://docs.microsoft.com/en-us/azure/notification-hubs/ notification-hubs-android-push-notification-google-fcm-get-started*
- **Windows Universal** *https://docs.microsoft.com/en-us/azure/notification-hubs/ notification-hubs-windows-store-dotnet-get-started-wns-push-notification*

When you need to add push notification support to your solution, you should think of the notification hub as a part of a bigger architecture. An example of this could be a solution that needs to connect your line-of-business applications with a mobile application. In such a scenario, a possible architecture could be to use Event Grid topics. The line-of-business applications would be the publishers of events to the appropriate topic, and then you can deploy one or more Azure Apps Services that are subscribed to these topics. When one of the line-of-business applications publishes an event in the Event Grid topic, your Azure App Service, which is acting as an event handler, can process the event and send a notification to your mobile users by using the Azure Notification Hub. Figure 5-17 shows a schema of this architecture. As you can see in that figure, the key component of the architecture is the Event Grid service and the implementation of an event-driven architecture.

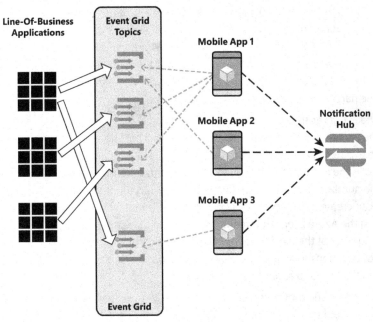

FIGURE 5-17 Diagram of event-driven architecture, including notification hubs

NEED MORE REVIEW?   **SAMPLE ARCHITECTURE IMPLEMENTATION**

You can review a sample architecture implementation using Service Bus messages instead of Event Grid by reading the article at *https://docs.microsoft.com/en-us/azure/notification-hubs/ notification-hubs-enterprise-push-notification-architecture*.

Implement solutions that use Azure Event Hub

Azure Event Grid is an excellent service for implementing event-driven solutions, but it is only one piece of a more complex pipeline. Although Event Grid is appropriate for working with event-driven, reactive programming, It is not the best solution when you need to ingest millions of events per second with low latency.

Azure Event Hub is a more suitable solution when you require a service that can receive and process millions of events per second and provide low-latency event processing. Azure Event Hub is the front door of a big data pipeline that processes millions of events. Once the Azure Event Hub receives the data, it can deliver the event to Azure Event Grid, store the information in an Azure Blob Storage Account, or store the data in an Azure Data Lake Storage.

When you work with event hubs, you send events to the hub. The entity that sends events to the event hub is known as an event publisher. An event publisher can send events to the event hub by using any of these protocols: AMQP 1.0, Kafka 1.0 (or later), or HTTPS.

You can publish events to the event hub by sending a single event or grouping several events in a batch operation. Independently if you publish a single event or a batch of them, you are limited to a maximum size of 1 MB of data per publication. When Azure Event Hub stores an event, it distributes the different events in different partitions based on the partition key provided as one of the data of the event. Using this pattern, Azure Event Hub ensures that all events sharing the same partition key are delivered in order to the same partition.

A partition stores the events as they arrive at the partition. This way, the newer events are added to the end of the partition. You cannot delete events from a partition. Instead, you need to wait for the event to expire to be removed from the partition. As each partition is independent of other partitions in the event hub, the growth rates are different from partition to partition. You can define the number of partitions that your event hub contains during the creation of the event hub. You can create between 2 and 32 partitions, although you can extend the limit of 32 by contacting the Azure Event Hub team. Bear in mind that once you create the event hub and set the number of the partitions, you cannot change this number later. When planning the number of partitions to assign to the event hub, consider the maximum number of parallels downstream that need to connect to the event hub.

You can connect event receiver applications to an event hub by using consumer groups. A consumer group is equivalent to a downstream in a stream processing architecture. Using consumer groups, you can have different event receivers or consumers, accessing different views (state, position, or offset) of the partitions in the event hub. Event consumers connect to the event hub by using the AMQP protocol that sends the event to the client as soon as new data is available.

The following procedure shows how to create an Azure Event Hub:

1. Open the Azure portal (*https://portal.azure.com*).
2. Expand the navigation menu by clicking the icon with three parallels lines on the top-left corner of the Azure portal.
3. Click All Services on the navigation menu.
4. In the Search All text box, type **event**.
5. Click Event Hubs in the results list.
6. On the Event Hubs blade, click the Add button at the top-left corner of the blade.
7. On the Create Namespace panel, ensure that the correct subscription is selected in the Subscription drop-down menu.
8. Select a resource group from the Resource Group drop-down menu. Alternatively, you can create a new resource group by clicking the Create New link below the drop-down menu.
9. Type a name for the Event Hub namespace.
10. Select a location in the Location drop-down menu.
11. Select the Basic tier in the Pricing Tier drop-down menu.
12. Leave the Throughput Units as 1.

13. Click the Review + Create button at the bottom of the panel.

14. Click the Create button.

15. Navigate to your newly created Event Hub namespace.

16. On the Overview blade in the Event Hub namespace blade, click the Event Hub button.

17. On the Create Event Hub panel, type a Name for the Event Hub.

18. Leave the Partition Count at 2. Remember that you cannot change this value once the event hub is created.

19. Click the Create button.

20. Click Shared Access Policies in the navigation menu on the left side of the Event Hub namespace.

21. Click the `RootManageSharedAccessKey`.

22. Copy the Connection String-Primary Key value. You need this value for step 9 in the next procedure.

Once you have created your event hub's namespace and your hub, you can start sending and consuming events from the hub. Use the following procedure to create two console applications, one for sending events and another for receiving events:

1. Open Visual Studio 2019.

2. On the Welcome screen, click Create A New Project.

3. Select the Console App (.NET Core) template.

4. Click the Next button.

5. Type a Project Name.

6. Select a location for the project.

7. Click the Create button.

8. Install the Microsoft.Azure.EventHubs NuGet package.

9. Replace the content of the Program.cs file with the content of Listing 5-11. You received the Event Hub Namespace connection string in the last step of the previous procedure.

LISTING 5-11 Function1.cs

```
// C# .NET
using System;
using System.Text;
using System.Threading.Tasks;
using Microsoft.Azure.EventHubs;

namespace <your_project_name>
{
    class Program
    {
        private static EventHubClient eventHubClient;
```

```
private const string EventHubConnectionString = "<Your_event_hub_
namespace_connection_string>";
private const string EventHubName = "<your_event_hub_name>";
private const int numMessagesToSend = 100;

static void Main(string[] args)
{
    var connectionStringBuilder = new EventHubsConnectionStringBuilder(
    EventHubConnectionString)
    {
        EntityPath = EventHubName
    };

    eventHubClient = EventHubClient.CreateFromConnectionString(
    connectionStringBuilder.ToString());

    for (var i = 0; i < numMessagesToSend; i++)
    {
        try
        {
            var message = $"Message {i}";
            Console.WriteLine($"Sending message: {message}");
            eventHubClient.SendAsync(new EventData(Encoding.UTF8.
            GetBytes(message)));
        }
        catch (Exception exception)
        {
            Console.WriteLine($"{DateTime.Now} > Exception: {exception.
            Message}");
        }

        Task.Delay(10);
    }

    Console.WriteLine($"{numMessagesToSend} messages sent.");

    eventHubClient.CloseAsync();

    Console.WriteLine("Press ENTER to exit.");
    Console.ReadLine();
    }
  }
}
```

At this point, you can press F5 and run the console application. This application console
sends 100 messages to the event hub that you configured in the EventHubName constant. In the

next procedure, you are going to create another application console for implementing an Event Processor Host. The Event Processor Host is an agent that helps you receive events from the event hub. The Event Processor automatically manages the persistent checkpoints and parallel event reception. The Event Processor Host requires an Azure Storage Account to process the persistent checkpoints.

> **NOTE EXAMPLE REQUIREMENTS**
>
> You need to create an Azure Blob Storage container to run this example. You can review how to create a blob container and how to get the access key by reading the following articles:
>
> - **Create a container** *https://docs.microsoft.com/en-us/azure/storage/blobs/storage-quickstart-blobs-portal#create-a-container*
>
> - **Get access keys** *https://docs.microsoft.com/en-us/azure/storage/common/storage-account-manage#access-keys*

Follow these steps to create the console application that implements the Event Processor Host:

1. Open Visual Studio 2019.
2. On the Welcome screen, click Create A New Project.
3. Select the Console App (.NET Core) template.
4. Click the Next button.
5. Type a Project Name.
6. Select a location for the project.
7. Click the Create button.
8. Install the following NuGet packages:
   - Microsoft.Azure.EventHubs
   - Microsoft.Azure.EventHubs.Processor
9. Create a new empty C# class and name it **SimpleEventProcessor**. In later steps, this class implements the IEventProcessor interface that contains the signature of the methods needed for the Event Processor.
10. Replace the content of the SimpleEventProcessor.cs file with the content of Listing 5-12.

LISTING 5-12 SimpleEventProcessor.cs

```
// C# .NET
using Microsoft.Azure.EventHubs;
using Microsoft.Azure.EventHubs.Processor;
using System;
using System.Collections.Generic;
using System.Text;
```

```csharp
using System.Threading.Tasks;

namespace <your_project_name>
{
    public class SimpleEventProcessor : IEventProcessor
    {
        public Task CloseAsync(PartitionContext context, CloseReason reason)
        {
            Console.WriteLine($"Processor Shutting Down. Partition
            '{context.PartitionId}', Reason: '{reason}'.");
            return Task.CompletedTask;
        }

        public Task OpenAsync(PartitionContext context)
        {
            Console.WriteLine($"SimpleEventProcessor initialized. Partition: '{context.
            PartitionId}'");
            return Task.CompletedTask;
        }

        public Task ProcessErrorAsync(PartitionContext context, Exception error)
        {
            Console.WriteLine($"Error on Partition: {context.PartitionId}, Error:
            {error.Message}");
            return Task.CompletedTask;
        }

        public Task ProcessEventsAsync(PartitionContext context, IEnumerable
        <EventData> messages)
        {
            foreach (var eventData in messages)
            {
                var data = Encoding.UTF8.GetString(eventData.Body.Array, eventData.
                Body.Offset, eventData.Body.Count);
                Console.WriteLine($"Message received. Partition: '{context.
                PartitionId}', Data: '{data}'");
            }

            return context.CheckpointAsync();
        }
    }
}
```

11. Replace the content of the Program.cs file with the content of the Listing 5-13.

LISTING 5-13 Program.cs

```csharp
// C# .NET
using Microsoft.Azure.EventHubs;
using Microsoft.Azure.EventHubs.Processor;
using System;

namespace <your_project_name>
{
    class Program
    {
        private const string EventHubConnectionString =
                        "<your_event_hub_namespace_connection_string>";
        private const string EventHubName = "<your_event_hub_name>";
        private const string StorageContainerName = "<your_container_name>";
        private const string StorageAccountName = "<your_storage_account_name>";
        private const string StorageAccountKey = "<your_storage_account_access_key>";
        private static readonly string StorageConnectionString = string.Format(
                            $"DefaultEndpointsProtocol=https;
                            AccountName={StorageAccountName};
                            AccountKey={StorageAccountKey}");

        static void Main(string[] args)
        {
            Console.WriteLine("Registering EventProcessor...");

            var eventProcessorHost = new EventProcessorHost(
                EventHubName,
                PartitionReceiver.DefaultConsumerGroupName,
                EventHubConnectionString,
                StorageConnectionString,
                StorageContainerName);

            // Registers the Event Processor Host and starts receiving messages
            eventProcessorHost.RegisterEventProcessorAsync<SimpleEventProcessor>();

            Console.WriteLine("Receiving. Press ENTER to stop worker.");
            Console.ReadLine();

            // Disposes of the Event Processor Host
            eventProcessorHost.UnregisterEventProcessorAsync();
        }
    }
}
```

Now you can press F5 and run your console application. The console application registers itself as an Event Processor and starts waiting for events not processed in the event hub. Because the default expiration time for the events in the event hub is one day, you should receive all the messages sent by your publishing console application in the previous example. If you run your event publisher console application without stopping the event processor console application, you should be able to see the messages in the event processor console almost in real time as they are sent to the event hub by the event publishing console. This simple example also shows how the event hub distributes the events across the different partitions.

EXAM TIP

The Azure Event Hub is a service appropriate for processing huge amounts of events with low latency. You should consider the event hub as the starting point in an event processing pipeline. You can use the event hub as the event source of the Event Grid service.

NEED MORE REVIEW? EVENT HUBS CONCEPTS

The Azure Event Hub service is designed to work with big data pipelines where you need to process millions of events per second. In those scenarios, making a bad decision when planning the deployment of an event hub can have a big effect on the performance. You can learn more about the event hub service by reading the article at *https://docs.microsoft.com/en-in/azure/event-hubs/event-hubs-features*.

Skill 5.4: Develop message-based solutions

In the previous skill, we reviewed how to use event-driven services in which a publisher pushes a lightweight notification or event to the events management system and forgets about how the event is handled or if it is even processed.

In this section, we are going to review how to develop message-based solutions using Azure services. In general terms, a message is raw data produced by a service with the goal of being stored or processed elsewhere. This means that the publisher of the messages has an expectation of some other system or subscriber process the message. Because of this expectation, the subscriber needs to notify the publisher about the status of the message.

This skill covers how to
- Implement solutions that use Azure Service Bus
- Implement solutions that use Azure Queue Storage queues

Implement solutions that use Azure Service Bus

Azure Service Bus is an enterprise-level integration message broker that allows different applications to communicate with each other in a reliable way. A message is a raw data that an application sends asynchronously to the broker to be processed by another application connected to the broker. The message can contain JSON, XML, or text information.

There are some concepts that you need to review before starting to work with the Azure Service Bus:

- **Namespace**   Is a container for all the components of the messaging. A single namespace can contain multiple queues and topics. You can use namespaces as application containers associating a single solution to a single namespace. The different components of your solution connect to the topics and queues in the namespace.
- **Queue**   A queue is the container of messages. The queue stores the message until the receiving application retrieves and processes the message. The message queue works as a FIFO (First-In, First-Out) stack. As a new message arrives at the queue, the Service Bus service assigns a timestamp to the message. Once the message is processed, the message is held in redundant storage. Queues are appropriate for point-to-point communication scenarios in which a single application needs to communicate with another single application.
- **Topic**   You use topics for sending and receiving messages. The difference between queues and topics is that topics can have several applications receiving messages used in publish/subscribe scenarios. A topic can have multiple subscriptions in which each subscription in a topic receives a copy of the message sent to the topic.

Use the following procedure to create an Azure Service Bus namespace; then, you can create a topic in the namespace. We are going to use that topic to create two console applications to send and receive the messages from the topic:

1. Open the Azure portal (*https://portal.azure.com*).
2. Click Create A Resource at the top of the portal.
3. Click Integration in the Azure Marketplace column.
4. Click Service Bus in the Featured column.
5. On the Create Namespace panel, ensure that the correct subscription is selected in the Subscription drop-down menu.
6. Select a resource group in the Resource Group drop-down menu. Alternatively, you can create a new resource group by clicking the Create New link below the drop-down menu control.
7. Type a name for the Service Bus in the Namespace Name text box.
8. Select a location in the Location drop-down menu.
9. Select the Standard tier in the Pricing Tier drop-down menu. You cannot create topics in the Basic pricing tier; you need to use at least the Standard tier.
10. Click the Review + Create button at the bottom of the panel.

11. Click the Create button.

12. Go to the resource once the Azure Resource Manager finishes the deployment of your new Service Bus Namespace.

13. On the Overview blade in the Service Bus Namespace, click the Topic button.

14. On the Create Topic panel, shown in Figure 5-18, type a Name for the topic.

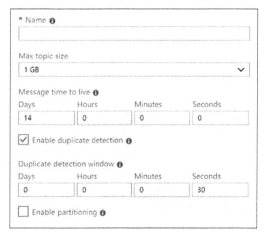

FIGURE 5-18 Creating a new topic

15. Leave the Max Topic Size and Message Time To Live parameters as they are.

16. Check Enable Duplicate Detection. This option ensures that the topic doesn't store duplicated messages during the configured detection window.

17. Click the Create button.

18. Click Shared Access Policies on the navigation menu on the left side of the Service Bus Namespace.

19. Click the RootManageSharedAccessKey policy.

20. Copy the Primary Connection String. You are going to use the connection string later in this section.

21. Click Topics in the navigation menu on the left side of the Service Bus Namespace.

22. Click your topic.

23. On the Overview blade on the Service Bus Topic, click the Subscription button.

24. On the Create Subscription panel, shown in Figure 5-19, type a name for the subscription.

25. Type **10** in the Max Delivery Count text box. This is the number of retries for delivering a message before moving the message to the Dead Letter Queue.

26. Leave the other properties as they are.

27. Click the Create button at the bottom of the panel.

Create subscription
Service Bus

SUBSCRIPTION SETTINGS

Name * ⓘ

Max delivery count * ⓘ

Auto-delete after idle for ⓘ

Days	Hours	Minutes	Seconds
14	0	0	0

☐ Never auto-delete

☐ Forward messages to queue/topic ⓘ

MESSAGE SESSIONS

Service bus sessions allow ordered handling of unbounded sequences of related messages. With sessions enabled a subscription can guarantee first-in-first-out delivery of messages. Learn more.

☐ Enable sessions

MESSAGE TIME TO LIVE AND DEAD-LETTERING

Message time to live (default) ⓘ

Days	Hours	Minutes	Seconds
14	0	0	0

☐ Move expired messages to the dead-letter subqueue

☐ Move messages that cause filter evaluation exceptions to the dead-letter subqueue

FIGURE 5-19 Creating a new subscription

Now you are going to create two console applications. One console application is going to publish messages to the Service Bus Topic; the other console application is going to subscribe to the Service Bus Topic, process the message, and update the processed message. Use the following procedure to create the console application that publishes messages to the Service Bus Topic:

1. Open Visual Studio 2019.

2. On the Welcome screen, click Create A New Project.

3. Select the Console App (.NET Core) template.

4. Click Next.

5. Type a Project Name.

6. Select a location for the project.

7. Click Create.

8. Install the Microsoft.Azure.ServiceBus NuGet package

9. Replace the content of the Program.cs file with the content of Listing 5-14. Remember that you copied the connection string needed for this code in step 20 of the previous example.

LISTING 5-14   Program.cs

```csharp
// C# .NET
using Microsoft.Azure.ServiceBus;
using System;
using System.Text;

namespace <your_project_name>
{
    class Program
    {
        const string ServiceBusConnectionString =
                    "<your_service_bus_connection_string>";
        const string TopicName = "<your_topic_name>";
        const int numberOfMessagesToSend = 100;

        static ITopicClient topicClient;

        static void Main(string[] args)
        {
            topicClient = new TopicClient(ServiceBusConnectionString, TopicName);

            Console.WriteLine("Press ENTER key to exit after sending all the
                            messages.");
            Console.WriteLine();

            // Send messages.
            try
            {
                for (var i = 0; i < numberOfMessagesToSend; i++)
                {
                    // Create a new message to send to the topic.
                    string messageBody = $"Message {i} {DateTime.Now}";
                    var message = new Message(Encoding.UTF8.GetBytes(messageBody));

                    // Write the body of the message to the console.
                    Console.WriteLine($"Sending message: {messageBody}");

                    // Send the message to the topic.
                    topicClient.SendAsync(message);
                }
            }
            catch (Exception exception)
            {
                Console.WriteLine($"{DateTime.Now} :: Exception: {exception.Message}");
            }
```

```
        Console.ReadKey();

        topicClient.CloseAsync();
    }
  }
}
```

You can now press F5 and publish messages to the topic. Once you publish the messages, you should be able to see an increase in the Message Count column in the Overview blade of your Service Bus Topic. The next steps show how to create the second console application that subscribes to the topic and processes the messages in the topic:

1. Open Visual Studio 2019.

2. On the Start window, click Create A New Project.

3. Select the Console App (.NET Core) template.

4. Click Next.

5. Type a Project Name.

6. Select a location for the project.

7. Click Create.

8. Install the Microsoft.Azure.ServiceBus NuGet package.

9. Replace the content of the Program.cs file with the content of Listing 5-15.

LISTING 5-15 Program.cs

```
// C# .NET
using Microsoft.Azure.ServiceBus;
using System;
using System.Text;
using System.Threading;
using System.Threading.Tasks;

namespace <your_project_name>
{
    class Program
    {
        const string ServiceBusConnectionString = "<your_service_bus_
        connection_string>";
        const string TopicName = "<your_topic_name>";
        const string SubscriptionName = "<your_subscription_name>";
        static ISubscriptionClient subscriptionClient;

        static void Main(string[] args)
        {
```

```
    subscriptionClient = new SubscriptionClient(ServiceBusConnectionString,
                        TopicName, SubscriptionName);

    Console.WriteLine("Press ENTER key to exit after receiving all the
                        messages.");

    // Configure the message handler options in terms of exception handling,
    // number of concurrent messages to deliver, etc.
    var messageHandlerOptions = new MessageHandlerOptions(
                        ExceptionReceivedHandler)
    {
        // Maximum number of concurrent calls to the callback
        // ProcessMessagesAsync(), set to 1 for simplicity.
        // Set it according to how many messages the application wants to
        // process in parallel.
        MaxConcurrentCalls = 1,

        // Indicates whether the message pump should automatically complete
        // the messages after returning from user callback.
        // False below indicates the user callback handles the complete
        // operation as in ProcessMessagesAsync().
        AutoComplete = false
    };

    // Register the function that processes messages.
    subscriptionClient.RegisterMessageHandler(ProcessMessagesAsync,
    messageHandlerOptions);

    Console.ReadKey();

    subscriptionClient.CloseAsync();
}

static async Task ProcessMessagesAsync(Message message, CancellationToken
token)
{
    // Process the message.
    Console.WriteLine($"Received message: SequenceNumber:{message.
    SystemProperties.SequenceNumber} Body:{Encoding.UTF8.GetString(message.
    Body)}");

    // Complete the message so that it is not received again.
    // This can be done only if the subscriptionClient is created in
    // ReceiveMode.PeekLock mode (which is the default).
    await subscriptionClient.CompleteAsync(message.SystemProperties.LockToken);
```

```
            // Note: Use the cancellationToken passed as necessary to determine if the
            // subscriptionClient has already been closed.
            // If subscriptionClient has already been closed, you can choose to not
            // call CompleteAsync() or AbandonAsync() etc.
            // to avoid unnecessary exceptions.
        }

        // Use this handler to examine the exceptions received on the message pump.
        static Task ExceptionReceivedHandler(ExceptionReceivedEventArgs
        exceptionReceivedEventArgs)
        {
            Console.WriteLine($"Message handler encountered an exception
            {exceptionReceivedEventArgs.Exception}.");
            var context = exceptionReceivedEventArgs.ExceptionReceivedContext;
            Console.WriteLine("Exception context for troubleshooting:");
            Console.WriteLine($"- Endpoint: {context.Endpoint}");
            Console.WriteLine($"- Entity Path: {context.EntityPath}");
            Console.WriteLine($"- Executing Action: {context.Action}");
            return Task.CompletedTask;
        }
    }
}
```

You can now press F5 and run the console application. As the console application processes the messages in the topic, you can see that the count of the messages in the subscription is decreasing.

> **NEED MORE REVIEW?** **SERVICE BUS ADVANCED FEATURES**
>
> You can learn more about Service Bus in the following articles:
>
> - **Queues, Topics, and Subscriptions** *https://docs.microsoft.com/en-us/azure/ service-bus-messaging/service-bus-queues-topics-subscriptions*
>
> - **Service Bus Performance Improvements** *https://docs.microsoft.com/en-us/azure/ service-bus-messaging/service-bus-performance-improvements*
>
> - **Topic Filters and Actions** *https://docs.microsoft.com/en-us/azure/service-bus- messaging/topic-filters*

Implement solutions that use Azure Queue Storage queues

Azure Queue Storage is the first service that Microsoft released for managing message queues. Although Azure Service Bus and Azure Queue Storage share some features, such as providing message queue services, Azure Queue Storage is more appropriate when your application needs to store more than 80 GB of messages in a queue. Another important feature of the

Azure Queue Storage service that you need to consider is although the queues in the service work as a FIFO (First-In, First-Out) stack, the order of the message is not guaranteed.

> **NOTE   AZURE QUEUE STORAGE VS. AZURE SERVICE BUS**
>
> You can review a complete list of differences between these two queuing services at *https://docs.microsoft.com/en-us/azure/service-bus-messaging/service-bus-azure-and-service-bus-queues-compared-contrasted*.

The maximum size of a single message that you can send to an Azure Queue is 64KB, although the total size of the queue can grow to over 80GB. You can only access an Azure Queue using the REST API or using the .NET Azure Storage SDK. Here are the steps for creating an Azure Queue Storage Account and a queue for sending and receiving messages:

1. Open the Azure portal (*https://portal.azure.com*).
2. Click Create A Resource at the top of the portal.
3. Click Storage in the Azure Marketplace column.
4. Click Storage Account – Blob, File, Table, Queue in the Featured column.
5. On the Create Storage Account blade, select a subscription in the Subscription drop-down menu.
6. Select a resource group in the Resource Group drop-down menu.
7. Type a Storage Account Name.
8. Select a location in the Location drop-down menu.
9. Select Locally-Redundant Storage in the Replication drop-down menu.
10. Leave the other properties as is.
11. Click the Review + Create button.
12. Click the Create button.
13. Click the Go To Resource button once the deployment finishes.
14. Click Access Keys on the navigation menu in the Azure Storage account blade.
15. Copy the Connection String from the key1 section. You need this value later in this section.

At this point, you can create queues in your Azure Storage account by using the Azure portal. You can also add messages to the queue using the Azure portal. This approach is useful for development or testing purposes, but it is not suitable for applications. Use the following steps to create a console application that creates a new queue in your Azure Storage Account. The application also sends and reads messages from the queue:

1. On the Welcome screen, click Create A New Project.
2. Select the Console App (.NET Core) template.
3. Click Next.

4. Type a Project Name.

5. Select a location for the project.

6. Click Create.

7. Install the following NuGet packages:

   - Azure.Storage.Common

   - Azure.Storage.Queue

8. Replace the content of the Program.cs file with the content of Listing 5-16.

LISTING 5-16   Program.cs

```csharp
// C# .NET
using Azure.Storage.Queues;
using Azure.Storage.Queues.Models;
using System;

namespace <your_project_name>
{
    class Program
    {
        private const string connectionString = "<your_storage_account_
        connection_string>";
        private const string queueName = "az204queue";
        private const int maxNumOfMessages = 10;
        static void Main(string[] args)
        {
            QueueClient queueClient = new QueueClient(connectionString, queueName);

            //Create the queue
            queueClient.CreateIfNotExists();

            //Sending messages to the queue.
            for (int i = 0; i < maxNumOfMessages; i++)
            {
                queueClient.SendMessageAsync($"Message {i} {DateTime.Now}");
            }

            //Getting the length of the queue
            QueueProperties queueProperties = queueClient.GetProperties();
            int? cachedMessageCount = queueProperties.ApproximateMessagesCount;

            //Reading messages from the queue without removing the message
            Console.WriteLine("Reading message from the queue without removing them
            from the queue");
            PeekedMessage[] peekedMessages = queueClient.PeekMessages((int)
            cachedMessageCount);
```

```
        foreach (PeekedMessage peekedMessage in peekedMessages)
        {
            Console.WriteLine($"Message read from the queue: {peekedMessage.
                            MessageText}");

            //Getting the length of the queue
            queueProperties = queueClient.GetProperties();
            int? queueLenght = queueProperties.ApproximateMessagesCount;
            Console.WriteLine($"Current lenght of the queue {queueLenght}");
        }

        //Reading messages removing it from the queue
        Console.WriteLine("Reading message from the queue removing");
        QueueMessage[] messages = queueClient.ReceiveMessages((int)
                                        cachedMessageCount);
        foreach (QueueMessage message in messages)
        {
            Console.WriteLine($"Message read from the queue: {message.
                            MessageText}");
            //You need to process the message in less than 30 seconds.
            queueClient.DeleteMessage(message.MessageId,message.PopReceipt);

            //Getting the length of the queue
            queueProperties = queueClient.GetProperties();
            int? queueLenght = queueProperties.ApproximateMessagesCount;
            Console.WriteLine($"Current lenght of the queue {queueLenght}");
        }
    }
  }
}
```

Press F5 to execute the console application that sends and reads messages from the queue. You can see how the messages are added to the queue by using the Azure portal and navigating to your Azure Storage account > Queues > az204queue. You should see a queue similar to one shown in Figure 5-20.

ID	MESSAGE TEXT	INSERTION TIME	EXPIRATION TIME	DEQUEUE COUNT	SIZE
350ba362-a307-40ce-b4b3-bd960069e298	Message 8 22/06/2020 0:28:47	22/6/2020 0:28:47	29/6/2020 0:28:47	0	28 B
ea3fd335-2009-4fcf-8210-dd3adf2a3e82	Message 4 22/06/2020 0:28:47	22/6/2020 0:28:48	29/6/2020 0:28:48	0	28 B
61291a8f-a1fc-420d-a670-7d46451dd18e	Message 0 22/06/2020 0:32:34	22/6/2020 0:32:34	29/6/2020 0:32:34	0	28 B
8496df6d-4e04-45a8-890d-af84519b6379	Message 4 22/06/2020 0:32:34	22/6/2020 0:32:35	29/6/2020 0:32:35	0	28 B
2bf7169b-2905-4535-a74a-ebdbb456329f	Message 8 22/06/2020 0:32:34	22/6/2020 0:32:35	29/6/2020 0:32:35	0	28 B
e2922180-d74c-48d3-8e82-b7b3ddc7f956	Message 3 22/06/2020 0:32:34	22/6/2020 0:32:35	29/6/2020 0:32:35	0	28 B
37a0d855-bc45-4b28-aab4-60f930f18ac2	Message 1 22/06/2020 0:32:34	22/6/2020 0:32:35	29/6/2020 0:32:35	0	28 B
4cf62756-fbae-4b76-8864-eb0e5c49edce	Message 2 22/06/2020 0:32:34	22/6/2020 0:32:35	29/6/2020 0:32:35	0	28 B
43a53fa6-ac1a-4cf0-b380-44c105300c51	Message 6 22/06/2020 0:32:34	22/6/2020 0:32:35	29/6/2020 0:32:35	0	28 B
558cde99-475e-4296-a379-bfa1ad7f184b	Message 7 22/06/2020 0:32:34	22/6/2020 0:32:35	29/6/2020 0:32:35	0	28 B
781bd7bf-e5b4-462b-9bc1-406055b9c065	Message 5 22/06/2020 0:32:34	22/6/2020 0:32:35	29/6/2020 0:32:35	0	28 B
8c7a0f2c-5ddb-44f2-8294-801b35348b4c	Message 9 22/06/2020 0:32:34	22/6/2020 0:32:35	29/6/2020 0:32:35	0	28 B

FIGURE 5-20 Creating a new subscription

Chapter summary

- Azure App Service Logic Apps allows you to interconnect different services without needing to create specific code for the interconnection.
- Logic App Workflows define the steps needed to exchange information between applications.
- Microsoft provides connectors for getting and sending information to and from differ-ent services.
- Triggers are events fired on the source systems.
- Actions are each of the steps performed in a workflow.
- Azure Logic Apps provides a graphical editor that eases the process of creating workflows.
- You can create your custom connectors for connecting your application with Azure Logic Apps.
- A Custom Connector is a wrapper for a REST or SOAP API.
- You can create custom connectors for Azure Logic Apps, Microsoft Flow, and Microsoft PowerApps.
- You cannot reuse custom connectors created for Microsoft Flow or Microsoft Power-Apps with Azure Logic Apps.
- You can export your Logic Apps as Azure Resource Manager templates.
- You can edit and modify the Logic Apps templates in Visual Studio.
- The API Management service allows you to publish your back-end REST or SOAP APIs using a common and secure front end.
- You need to create subscriptions in the APIM service for authenticating the access to the API.
- You need to create a product for publishing a back-end API.
- You can publish only some operations of your back-end APIs.
- APIM Policies allow you to modify the behavior of the APIM gateway.
- An event is a change in the state of an entity.

- In an event-driven architecture, the publisher doesn't have the expectation that the event is processed or stored by a subscriber.
- Azure Event Grid is a service for implementing event-driven architectures.
- An Event Grid Topic is an endpoint where a publisher service can send events.
- Subscribers are services that read events from an Event Grid Topic.
- You can configure several types of services as event sources or event subscribers in Azure Event Grid.
- You can create custom events for sending them to the Event Grid.
- You can subscribe to your custom application with an Event Grid Topic by using WebHooks.
- The Azure Notification Hub is a service that unifies the push notifications on mobile platforms.
- You can connect the push notification services from the different manufacturers to the Azure Notification Hub.
- The Azure Event Hub is the entry point for Big Data event pipelines.
- Azure Event Hub is specialized in ingesting millions of events per second with low latency.
- You can use Azure Event Hub as an event source for the Event Grid service.
- You can use AMQP, Kafka, and HTTPS for connecting to Azure Event Hub.
- In a message-driven architecture, the publisher application has the expectation that the message is processed or stored by the subscriber.
- The subscriber needs to change the state once the message is processed.
- A message is raw data sent by a publisher that needs to be processed by a subscriber.
- Azure Service Bus and Azure Queue message are message broker services.

Thought experiment

In this thought experiment, demonstrate your skills and knowledge of the topics covered in this chapter. You can find answers to this thought experiment in the next section.

Your organization has several Line-Of-Business (LOB) applications deployed on Azure and on-premises environments. The information managed by some of these LOB applications overlaps between applications. All your LOB applications allow you to use SOAP or REST API for connecting to the applications.

Your organization needs to implement some business processes that require sharing information between the LOB applications. Answer the following questions about connecting Azure services and third-party applications:

1. You need to implement a business process that requires that an application deployed in Azure share information with an application deployed in your company's on-premises datacenter. How can you implement this business process?

2. Your company needs to share some information managed by one of the LOB applications with a partner. The LOB application uses a SOAP API for accessing the data. You need to ensure that the partner is authenticated before accessing the information. Your partner needs to get the information from your application in JSON format, so you also need to ensure that the information provided by your application is published using a REST API. Which service should you use?

3. One of the LOB applications of your company is becoming obsolete. Your company decides to develop a new web application for replacing the legacy LOB application. You are designing the architecture for the new web application. You need to implement a decoupled architecture that needs to process millions of events per second. Which service should you use?

Thought experiment answers

This section contains the solution to the thought experiment. Each answer explains why the answer choice is correct.

1. You should use Azure Logic Apps for implementing the business process. Azure Logic Apps allows you to create workflows that can be used to implement your business process. You can connect Azure Logic Apps with your on-premises LOB applications by using the on-premises data gateway. You also need to create custom connectors for Azure Logic Apps being able to work with your LOB applications.

2. You should use the API Management service. This service allows you to share your backed APIs with partners and external developers securely. Using the APIM policies, you can also convert the XML message provided by the SOAP API to JSON documents needed for REST APIs. You can use Azure AD, mutual certificate authentication, or API keys for authenticating access to the API.

3. You should use Azure Event Hub. This service is specially designed to ingest millions of events per second. Once the service has ingested the events, you forward the event to other services like Azure Storage, Azure Data Lake, or Azure Event Grid. The critical point here for choosing Azure Event Hub instead of Event Grid is the number of events that need to be ingested. Another clue for choosing Event Hub instead of Azure Queue Storage or Azure Service Bus is you need to process events instead of messages. Azure Queue or Azure Service Bus are services aimed to use in message-driven architectures.

Index

SYMBOLS

A

T

Plug into learning at

MicrosoftPressStore.com

The Microsoft Press Store by Pearson offers:

- Free U.S. shipping

- Buy an eBook, get three formats – Includes PDF, EPUB, and MOBI to use with your computer, tablet, and mobile devices

- Print & eBook Best Value Packs

- eBook Deal of the Week – Save up to 50% on featured title

- Newsletter – Be the first to hear about new releases, announcements, special offers, and more

- Register your book – Find companion files, errata, and product updates, plus receive a special coupon* to save on your next purchase

 Pearson